Newtown & Mach... RAILWAY

Railffordd
Y Drefnewydd a Machynlleth

At Dirfeddianwyr, Ffarmwyr, Masnachwyr, Celfyddydwyr, a phob Dosbarth o breswylwyr Siroedd Maldwyn, Aberteifi a Meirionydd.

GYDWLADWYR,

Y gwyn gyffredin yn eich mysg er ys cryn amser bellach ydyw,—

"A ydym ni byth i gael Reilffordd? A ydym ni i gael ein bythol gau yn ein glynoedd heb ddim i'n cario o honynt ond yr hen Stage Coach? Na dim i gludo ein cynyrch i farchnadoedd poblog. Lloegr ond yr hen Stage Waggon? Pa hyd y rhaid i'n gwartheg a'n defaid oddiar fil o fynyddoedd orfod araf ymlusgo i'r farchnadfa drwy y llwch a'r tes neu y llaid a'r gwlawogydd? Pa hyd eto y caiff y fath hen drefn golledfawr ein digaloni a'n drygu pan y mae trefn well i'w chael?"

Wel! Dyma i chwi o'r diwedd atebiad i'ch cwynion. Y maent wedi cynhyrfu amryw o'r Boneddwyr mwyaf eu dylanwad yn y wlad i roddi eu hysgwydd wrth yr olwyn i gael Railffordd drwy eich cymydogaethau; ac y maent wedi tanysgrifio yn eu mysg eu hunain filoedd lawer er rhag-drysori yn y Bank of England y "Deposits" gofynedig yn ol Deddf y Railffyrdd; ac y mae y Bill yn awr yn barod i gael ei benderfynu yn Eisteddiad dyfodol y Senedd.

Y mae y mater yn awr yn eich llaw chwi. Y mae yn gorphwys arnoch *chwi* i brofi a ydych yn foddlon i oedi yr adeg bwysig yma heibio, a bod am hatter can mlynedd eto ar ol parthau eraill y deyrnas; neu ynte a ydych am gydweithio yn egniol er cario eich Bill drwy y Senedd yn ddiwrthwynebiad ac ar unwaith?

Y mae llaweroedd o honoch heb ddyfod ymlaen hyd yma i gynorthwyo yn y gorchwyl, dan yr ofn y bydd iddo fethu fel y cynhygion blaenorol. Ond na ddigaloner chwi felly. Y mae cychwynwyr y cynllun presenol yn benderfynol i'w ddwyn i ben os cant eich cydweithrediad chwi. Rhaid i chwi gofio nad yw Railffyrdd ddim yn disgyn o'r cymylau wrth i bobl swrth-gwyno fod eu heisiau. Rhaid *gweithredu* heblaw cwyno. Ni bu erioed fwy o angen Railffordd nag sydd drwy eich cylchoedd chwi; a rhaid i chwi eich hunain gydymroi i gynorthwyo ei gwneuthuriad. Cofiwch er eich calondid fod yspryd y gwaith wedi disgyn ar ganoedd, a'i fod yn gweithio yn iawn ar hyd ac ar led y wlad. Yn awr yw yr adeg am dani. Na oddefwch i'r agerdd wanychu a darfod o ddiffyg tanwydd. Os goddefwch i'r tan ddiffodd y tro hwn, ni welwch byth y fath gyfle i'w ail-enyn.

Am hyny, Gyfeillion a Chydwladwyr, codwch ati a chydymegniwch. Gall pob un o honoch gymeryd rhyw gyfran yn y gorchwyl; ac ond i bob un wneud ei ran, yn ol ei sefyllfa, daw y gwaith i ben yn rhwydd ac yn gyflym. Ffurfier Pwyllgorau ym mhob tref a phentref i dderbyn enwau am *Shares*: a gellwch dderbyn fy ngair i y bydd y Shares hyny ymhen deuddeg mis *ar godiad* yn y farchnad.

Yr wyf unwaith eto yn taer ddeisyf arnoch i beidio colli yr adeg auraidd yma i fynu cyfleusdra o'r fath werth i chwi eich hunain ac i'ch gwlad.

Ydwyf yr eiddoch yn ffyddlawn,

A SHAREHOLDER.

Ionawr, 1857.

NLW

RAILWAY THROUGH TALERDDIG

A fine but completely anonymous station group at Machynlleth c. 1890: not even the little Sharp Stewart 2-4-0 is identifiable, although some of the assembled gathering bear an occasional resemblance to present-day Maglonians. The Refreshment Rooms were administered by Messrs Spiers & Pond, advertisements for 'Old Bushmills Whisky' abound and there is an intriguing reference in another poster to events 'Thirty Years Ago'! The footbridge had yet to be constructed.

John Thomas Coll. NLW

Railway Through Talerddig

The Story of the Newtown & Machynlleth and associated railways in the Dyfi valley

Gwyn Briwnant-Jones

First Impression—1990

© Gwyn Briwnant-Jones

ISBN 0 86383 662 3

All rights reserved. No part of this book may be reproduced, stored in a retrieval system, or transmitted in any form or by any means, electronic, electrostatic, magnetic tape, mechanical, photocopying, recording or otherwise, without permission in writing from the Publishers, Gomer Press, Llandysul, Dyfed.

Printed by J. D. Lewis and Sons Ltd., Gomer Press, Llandysul, Dyfed

Contents

	Page
Foreword by Lord Davies of Llandinam	vii
Acknowledgements	viii
Introduction	ix
Chapter 1: The Dyfi Valley Before the Railway	1
Chapter 2: The Formation of the Newtown & Machynlleth Railway	5
Chapter 3: Preparations for Construction	19
Chapter 4: Grand Opening	50
Chapter 5: Railways Related to the Newtown & Machynlleth Railway	66
Chapter 6: Some Early Developments . . .	93
Chapter 7: Locomotives & Rolling Stock	102
Chapter 8: All Change	133
Appendix I	137
Appendix II	138
Appendix III	139
Bibliography	141
Index	142

Foreword

The years which distance us from the Industrial Revolution have brought greater tolerance and understanding of the achievements of the past and, more recently, our interest in industrial archaeology has increased dramatically to become one of the cultural phenomena of our time.

The history of our railways, particularly, represents one of the most celebrated facets of industrial archaeology and the vast amount of interest in the topic is reflected in bookshops and libraries by entire sections devoted to Rail Transport. In addition to ever-increasing lists of new titles, our appetite for more and greater detail, especially of the earlier periods, appears as voracious as ever. The publication of *Railway through Talerddig* exemplifies this trend, for although the history of the Cambrian Railways has been faithfully recorded and most of the major facts are already familiar, the search continues for equally intriguing aspects which either evaded the attention of previous researchers or had no place in the broader histories.

Gwyn Briwnant-Jones, a native of Machynlleth, was confident there was more to the story of the coming of the railway than had hitherto been published and although he was initially concerned that sufficient information of the early period would have survived to make this publication possible, he appears to have gleaned more than was originally anticipated. Significant gaps in our knowledge still persist, however, for opportunities have undoubtedly been missed in the past to safeguard and secure our industrial heritage, which was grossly undervalued until recent times. Certain plans may have been irretrievably lost unless, perhaps, they dwell uncatalogued in some archive system. Not one of the original drawings of the line is known to exist and it is also remarkable that no photograph of the Opening Day ceremony of 1863 appears to have survived.

The formation of the Newtown & Machynlleth Railway was the venture which provided David Davies, my great great grandfather, with his most challenging contract, to that time. As he carved the route through Talerddig, towards the Dyfi Valley and Machynlleth, the view was held by some that the task would prove too great for him without the help of Thomas Savin his former partner, but, as he later pointed out, what could well have been the rock of his destruction emerged as the rock of his salvation. Talerddig provided a sound foundation for his subsequent ambitions and he progressed to even greater accomplishments.

I have again derived much pleasure from the realisation that so much was achieved during the building of the Montgomeryshire lines by the men of the county. They planned and constructed the railways themselves; they made the fullest use of their own resources and called upon the minimum of outside help. It was truly a team effort and I am proud of my family's contribution to the construction of the railways of Mid-Wales.

This volume's timely appearance marks not only the centenaries of both David Davies and David Howell, the Secretary of the Newtown & Machynlleth Company, but also the 125th Anniversary of the amalgamation of the Aberystwyth & Welsh Coast Railway with the original Cambrian Railways. *Railway through Talerddig*, therefore, provides a fitting tribute to all who contributed to those early ventures or maintained and worked the lines in the ensuing years.

LORD DAVIES OF LLANDINAM   *March 1990*

Acknowledgements

I am greatly indebted to many people for support and assistance during compilation of this book, particularly Lord Davies, whose Foreword links past with present in such a unique way.

The idea of an account of the railway at Machynlleth, although formed initially many years ago, might still be dormant but for the prompting of Dr Stuart Owen-Jones, Keeper of the Welsh Industrial & Maritime Museum, Cardiff. His encouragement and interest have been greatly appreciated, as has the assistance unfailingly offered by the Museum staff, particularly Dr Bill Jones, Dr David Jenkins and Gordon Hayward.

The sources of photographs and diagrams are credited where appropriate, but amongst many who rendered assistance in other ways, I would like to acknowledge:

Michael Scott Archer, Michael Back, John Beaumont, British Rail, particularly Alex Murray, Public Affairs Manager, London Midland Region, Birmingham, and Mike Walters at Chester, Ray Bowen, Mrs Wm. Breese, Albert Caffrey, Miss Maud Caffrey, A.J. Clayton, Ron Cowell, R.A. Cooke, T.P. Dalton, D.W. Davies, Ken Davies, Henry Evans, Murray Evans, Len Evans, the late Mrs E. Evans, Mrs H. Field, E.D. Hughes, H.R. Hughes, the late O. B. James, Mrs Dilys Jones, R.D. Jehu, Emrys Jones, Elwyn V. Jones, Derek Wynne Jones of the Central Registry of Air Photography for Wales, Peter Kay, Roger Kidner, Lord Londonderry, M.M. Lloyd, Huw Lewis, Glyn Lewis, Machynlleth Community Council, C.W. Mottram, Harold Morgan, R. Morgan of Powys County Council, the late David Vaughan Owen, Dr. John Owen of Ceredigion Museum, John H. Parsons, Neville Pritchard, J. P. Richards, the late Maurice Richards, Gwyn Roderick, and Ralph Tutton.

I must also acknowledge the steadfast help provided throughout by the staff of the National Library of Wales at Aberystwyth; the County Record Offices of Gwynedd, Clwyd, and Dyfed, together with the County Libraries of Powys and Salop; between them they safeguard so many priceless local records. All were courteous and efficient, but none more so than the staff of the Public Record Office who were always helpful and fully supported my attempts to make the best possible use of my limited time at Kew.

I am particularly indebted to W.B. Jones, Machynlleth, for reading the manuscript and making many valuable suggestions and to Dr Dyfed Elis-Gruffydd and Gwasg Gomer. Special thanks must also be extended to Ifor Higgon; it has always been a pleasure to share Ifor's affection for things Cambrian and his generosity with time and information has been endless, whilst his excellent photographs comprise the single most comprehensive record of steam in the Central Wales Division during GW and early WR days.

My final thanks are reserved for my wife Gwyneth, whose support and encouragement have made the project possible.

Gwyn Briwnant-Jones,
Llangollen
February 1990

Introduction

The history of the Cambrian Railways is well recorded but no detailed account has hitherto been published of the development of any of its constituent companies.

The Newtown & Machynlleth Railway (N & M), the third of the Montgomeryshire railways to be built and one of the original quartet which later formed the Cambrian, served as an important link line which opened up the beautiful Cambrian coastline to thousands from the north, the midlands and south Wales. In the reverse direction, it benefited those Welshmen who found employment in the cities, or sought new markets for local products. Over the years the main role and form of the line have changed, inevitably, but it is now the only Montgomeryshire line to retain its original mileage. Although the freight services have almost disappeared, the line has survived through difficult times and its contribution to the social life of mid Wales and the coast is as vital today as ever. Thankfully, this fact is recognised by the public bodies in the region; their support and the resultant increase in public patronage can ensure that the line will prosper in the years to come and restore our confidence in the fervent prediction of 1863 that,

> The railway will continue to be worked doubtless to the end of time. The whistle of the engine will be heard in our valleys long after we have been forgotten.
>
> —David Howell,
> Secretary, Newtown & Machynlleth Railway Co.

Information and photographs of developments during this century are plentiful but a major

Matrix (1) and imprint (r) of the Common Seal of the Newtown & Machynlleth Railway Company. The Seal bears two shields of arms: sinister, 3 heraldic eagles of Owain Gwynedd; dexter, lion rampant of Montgomery. Above, a harp; below, a rose, leek, thistle and shamrock, symbolising the United Kingdom. *WIMM*

concern at the outset of the task was that sufficient early material had survived to make the project feasible; happily, research and compilation have proved both rewarding and enlightening, although the content was finally dictated less by choice than by material available. The reiteration of some familiar aspects of the story is unavoidable but less significant details, perhaps equally well-known, are frequently omitted in an attempt to concentrate upon information which has not previously, or recently, been published.

The National Library of Wales, Aberystwyth, The Public Record Office, Kew, and the files of the local press, particularly the Oswestry and the Shrewsbury papers, have proved to be the major sources of information on the Newtown & Machynlleth Railway.

The National Library holds some of the Account Books of David Davies of Llandinam, the noted Montgomeryshire railway contractor and later founder of the Ocean Coal Company. Largely the work of a clerk, David Evans, the accounts are hand-written and not always easily deciphered; they appear at first glance to be somewhat colourless and repetitive, yet they chronicle the names of David Davies's key-workers and record progress at the sites of greatest activity. They also detail in fascinating fashion the minutiae of railway construction, from the simple purchase of nails or replacement pick-handles to payments for blasting powder, medical attention or a complete locomotive. The National Library is also the depository for a collection of letters addressed by David Howell, the Secretary of the N&M, to Laurence Ruck, one of the original Committee of Management. This invaluable correspondence is quoted liberally in the initial chapters and the source, in an effort to avoid constant repetition, is only acknowledged here; other sources are credited where appropriate. The Public Record Office in Kew is the custodian of the Minute books of the Board of Directors of the Newtown & Machynlleth Railway, as well as the Cambrian Railways: these also proved to be a valuable source of information.

David Howell 1816-1890

D. Davies, 1818-1890   *NLW*

In the absence of any diaries relating specifically to the construction of the railway, we are extremely fortunate to be able to refer to old newspaper files, particularly those of the *Oswestry & Border Counties Advertiser*. Collectively, they form a priceless store of eye-witness accounts, although they were not written with historians particularly in mind and certain topographic or operational details which might well fascinate us today were, regrettably, allowed to pass unrecorded. Another void in our knowledge of the very early days emanates from the almost total absence of plans or maps. It is all the more frustrating to realise that they were, in fact, produced in quantity, for Engineers' and Directors' Reports constantly refer to such drawings. Apart from the Deposited Plans & Sections of 1856, which furnish few details, no authentic track-plan has yet been traced which pre-dates 1895. Even the First Edition Ordnance Survey Maps of the 1887 period, valuable as they are, are decidedly suspect in essential details so it is to be hoped that a few of the original drawings and plans may yet emerge from some dusty corner of a half-forgotten archive. Although nominally outside the area of the N&M, reference is made to the development of the Aberystwyth & Welsh Coast Railway (A&WCR) within the Aberdyfi, Machynlleth and Ynyslas triangle. As the N&M had always nurtured ambitions in that direction and also formed an end-on junction with the Welsh Coast Railway at Machynlleth, a short synopsis of some of the physical and practical arrangements represents a logical progression.

Each researcher is limited, to a greater or lesser degree, by time, finance and knowledge; the optimum moment to draw the line between the gathering of information and the compilation of the text is not always easily recognised and there is a strong temptation to continue the search for greater knowledge at the expense of publication. What follows, therefore, can be no more than a personal sketch which, although the culmination of a life-long ambition, has been researched and written within a comparatively brief period. Many facts herein were unknown to the writer when the venture commenced and a personal regret is that the task had not been started many years earlier, before the Oswestry Works and records had been dispersed or destroyed.

Partly for this reason, certain aspects of the story remain obscure but it is hoped, nonetheless, that this attempt to shed more light on the development of railways in the Dyfi valley may encourage an abler hand to trace those elements which have been neglected because of the limitations outlined.

The spelling of Welsh place-names is based on the standard book of reference, *A Gazeteer of Welsh place-names,* University of Wales Press. Quotations, original documents or other references within a railway context frequently follow the form used during the construction and initial operation of the railways.

Dolgellau	—	Dolgelly
Dyfi	—	Dovey
Porthmadog	—	Portmadoc

are amongst the more prominent examples.

ABBREVIATIONS USED IN THE TEXT

AO:	Aberystwyth Observer.
A&WCR:	Aberystwyth & Welsh Coast Railway.
B&M:	Brecon & Merthyr Tydfil Junction Railway.
CCA:	Clwyd County Archives.
CM&RDT:	Corris, Machynlleth & River Dovey Tramroad.
CMA&TR:	Corris, Machynlleth, Aberdovey & Towyn Railway.
CN:	Cambrian News.
DCA:	Dyfed County Archives.
ESJ:	Eddowes's Shrewsbury Journal.
GCA:	Gwynedd County Archives.
GWR:	Great Western Railway.
GWS:	Great Western Society, Didcot.
LDMP:	Llandinam Papers, National Library of Wales.
L&N:	Llanidloes & Newtown Railway.
LGRP:	Locomotive & General Railway Photographs.
LNWR:	London North Western Railway.
LPCo:	Locomotive Publishing Company.
MA&TR:	Machynlleth, Aberystwyth & Towyn Railway.
MCT:	Montgomeryshire County Times.
ME:	Montgomeryshire Express.
MH:	Merionethshire Herald.
MRSJ:	Monmouthshire Railway Society Journal.
M&M:	Manchester & Milford Railway.
NLW:	National Library of Wales, Aberystwyth.
N&M:	Newtown & Machynlleth Railway.
N&WE:	Newtown & Welshpool Express.
OA:	Oswestry & Border Counties Advertiser.
O&N:	Oswestry & Newtown Railway.
PRO:	Public Record Office, Kew.
P&TR:	Pembroke & Tenby Railway.
RAIL:	PRO file & number.
RCTS:	Railway Correspondence & Travel Society.
ROD:	Railway Operating Department.
SC:	Shrewsbury Chronicle.
SM.Lib:SK:	Science Museum Library, South Kensington.
S&MT:	Shropshire & Montgomeryshire Times.
WIMM:	Welsh Industrial & Maritime Museum, Cardiff.

GWR SHED CODES

BAN	BANBURY
CNYD	CROES NEWYDD
LDR	LANDORE
MCH	MACHYNLLETH
OXY	OXLEY
SRD	STAFFORD ROAD

Chapter 1
The Dyfi Valley Before the Railway

Until the coming of the railway, communications in mid Wales depended largely upon rough tracks and inadequate roads. Wheeled traffic was minimal and where wagons or carriages did exist, their use was restricted mainly to local journeys; progress was inevitably slow and tedious. Most traffic went afoot and the drovers, the prime example, were also the means of conveying parcels or letters in addition to the animals; they rapidly established tracks which offered the shortest distance between two points although this frequently necessitated covering difficult, remote routes over high ground. The early turnpike roads generally followed the easier valley routes and brought some initial improvement, but they were often ill-maintained and burdened with tolls.

In such circumstances, it was not surprising that coastal shipping thrived and a river with navigable tidal reaches, such as the Dyfi, offered considerable advantages for trade. The Dyfi's tidal waters extend from Aberdyfi and Ynyslas to a point just west of Machynlleth, some seven miles inland. Consequently, the town's favourable location at the junction of several roads and the lowest bridging point on the river helped to establish it as a commercial centre, serving a hinterland encompassing southern Merionethshire and western Montgomeryshire. Lime, to improve the poor agricultural quality of the upland regions, or machinery and other products of the early industrial revolution were some of the main imports during the first decades of the nineteenth century whilst wool, flannel, slate, lead ore and other minerals constituted the major exports.

The highest navigable point on the river was near Derwenlas, a hamlet which grew around the coastal trade, some two miles west of Machynlleth. Here, nestling in a sheltered bend of the river and at the nearby Morben Wharves, the 'flats' and sloops discharged their cargoes and re-loaded with the products of the region, which frequently needed trans-shipment at Aberdyfi if bound for foreign parts. Shipbuilding, which also took place here, survived no more than a decade after the coming of the railway in 1862/3, although an impressive brig was launched in April, 1865. Possibly the *Rowland Evans*, this was reported 'of 400 tons burthen',[1] and classed A1 at Lloyds for 12 years. It was built by master builder John Jones for John Evans, *Y Morben*, the owner of several vessels and the nearby wharf. Jones also built a barque for John Evans, in 1867,[2] which in all probability was the last vessel of any size and importance to be constructed at Morben, although at least one smaller vessel, the schooner *Catherine*, (76 tons), was constructed as late as 1869.[3]

A few small craft still plied the river even after the construction of the Glandovey railway bridge, in 1867, but the era of sail gradually drew to a close; the new mode of transport was not to be denied.

The enemy ashore[4]

Railways had been projected through central Wales from as early as 1837. At that time the aim was to capture the lucrative Irish traffic and Wales was merely the difficult terrain which had to be traversed *en route*. Several schemes were prepared including one by C.B. Vignoles for a line from Shrewsbury to a remote natural harbour at Porth Dinllaen in north Caernarfonshire. Two years later, in 1839, I.K. Brunel prepared a scheme of his own to reach Porth Dinllaen. Whereas Vignoles chose a route through Llan-

Contemporary evidence of the flourishing shipping trade at Derwenlas c. 1812   *GBJ Collection*

gollen, Bala, Barmouth and Porthmadog, Brunel boldly planned a broad-gauge line (Worcester & Porthdinlleyn Railway), from Worcester via Ludlow and Montgomery to Newtown; here it was to follow an interesting course through the mountains to Talerddig and Dinas Mawddwy, before emerging above the Mawddach and pursuing a more predictable route through Barmouth and along the coast to Porth Dinllaen. Had this line been built, there is little doubt that it would have influenced the development of mid Wales during the latter part of the nineteenth century, much as the M4 corridor has affected south Wales in more recent times.

Neither scheme was adopted, for by 1844 two easier routes along the coast had been promoted for the Irish traffic; through Holyhead in the north and Fishguard in the south.

The central regions of Wales remained without a railway but there was no shortage of schemes, for the thirty years from 1837 to 1867 were decades of frantic railway activity, although no map of the area suggests that the region was ever in the grip of the famous 'railway mania' which beset other parts of the country during this period. A few examples only are quoted here: one bore the grandiose title of The Great North & South Wales and Worcester Railway (1845).[5] Projected from Carmarthen to Porth Dinllaen, it was routed from Aberystwyth via Tre'rddol to Machynlleth where a junction was intended for the Newtown, Ludlow and Worcester line. In the same year, the original Manchester & Milford Railway scheme hoped to utilise the West Wales port for the import and export of Lancashire's raw materials and goods, and would also have crossed

At Pickle Herring Upper Wharf, Southwark

F. M. BERESFORD, Wharfinger

Shaw, Printer, 41 Tooley Street, and 180, Tottenham Court Ro.d.

Now Loading for
ABERYSTWITH,
Aberdovey, Machynlleth,

Carmarthen
AND ALL PLACES ADJACENT
The BLANCHE, JOHN EVANS, Master.
A CONSTANT TRADER, TAKES IN GOODS

The last day of loading 22 Sept/46

All Goods received on board the above Vessel are to be regularly suffered by the shipper before taken on board.

Goods for the above mentioned and adjacent places are not received at this Wharf, but on the conditions following: to say, that the Wharfinger will not be accountable, or engage to forward them by any particular vessel named in the receipt given, or for any loss that may be incurred in shipping in bye vessels of whatever description, loss by fire, high tides, vermin, leakage, or wastage, act of God, the Queen's enemies, or loss occasioned by imperfect directions, marks, or packing; neither will any advice be given of the shipment of Goods which may have been left out of former vessels; neither will any description of merchandize by water be received by or for any vessels lying at this Wharf without being subject to the usual charge of Wharfage—The Receipts given to be in force only twelve months.

The Master or Wharfinger to be spoken with on the said Wharf, or on the Irish Walk in Change hours.

Please to be particular in ordering the Goods for the above Vessel at Pickle Herring Wharf.

INSURANCES EFFECTED ON SHIP OR CARGO,

| Mark | Wharfage and Sufferance | s. | d. | Received. |

Pickle Herring Wharf Bill NLW

mid Wales, but as Liverpool was much more convenient the plan had little validity although it was revived later, during the 1850s and 1860s.

Part of the route surveyed for Brunel's line, between Tremadoc and Dinas Mawddwy, featured in another scheme of the mid-1840s, to connect Bangor and Pembroke. The Great Welch Junction Railway,[6] as it was called, would also have served Porth Dinllaen, by a branch from Tremadoc. From Dinas Mawddwy the route went east to Pool, then south to Newtown before heading south-east to Ludlow, where it was still a long way from Pembroke and pointing in the wrong direction: there is little wonder that it was never built. Such was the fate of other schemes also, for they were generally ill-conceived both in financial and practical terms.

Possibly, Montgomeryshire's most likely opportunity of obtaining an early railway arose with an 1852 scheme which bore the county's name. The Montgomeryshire Railways would have begun at Shrewsbury and passed through Minsterley, Montgomery, Newtown, Llanidloes and Llangurig to Aberystwyth. When the LNWR took an interest in the scheme it was modified to embrace Welshpool and Machynlleth,[7] at the expense of Montgomery and Llanidloes. Incensed at being by-passed in this manner, the people of Llanidloes took matters into their own hands rather than rely on outside help and resolved to finance and construct their own railway, to connect at Newtown with the projected Shrewsbury line. There was a slight delay whilst their Bill passed through the House of Lords but this difficulty was overcome and the first of Montgomeryshire's railways came into being with the incorporation of the Llanidloes & Newtown Railway (L&N), in 1853. Ironically, the two schemes to build railways into Newtown from the east, the Shrewsbury & Chester's Newtown Extension line and the Montgomeryshire Railways' modified plans, both failed to pass through the Commons and the L&N was thus created, quite inadvertently, in grand isolation.

Within two years, it became apparent that such a state of affairs was only temporary, for the formation of the Oswestry & Newtown Railway (O&N), in 1855, forged a link with the border counties lines while a railway to the Welsh coast appeared more feasible than at any previous time. The most direct route from the Severn to the coast at Aberystwyth lay across the mountains of Plynlimon but the easier course lay to the north, along the valleys of the Carno, Twymyn and Dyfi. This route was already seen by the people of the Machynlleth district as representing their own opportunity to join the railway network. They also had realised that help did not come readily from without; if they were to have a railway at all, it would only be by their own endeavours.

The people of the Dyfi valley were fortunate to find the inspiration and leadership for such a venture within their own ranks and an energetic and resourceful contractor within their own county. Powerfully led by Machynlleth solicitor, David Howell (1816-1890), they succeeded in gaining Royal Assent for the Newtown & Machynlleth Railway on 27 July 1857. The line, through 'expensive' country, was successfully constructed for a modest £9000 per mile by the redoubtable David Davies, Llandinam, (1818-1890). It opened officially for passenger traffic on 3 January 1863 and formed one of the constituent companies of the Cambrian Railways on 25 July 1864.

Condensed thus into a brief paragraph the task would appear to have been straight-forward and without undue difficulty but such simplicity belies the political, financial and practical problems

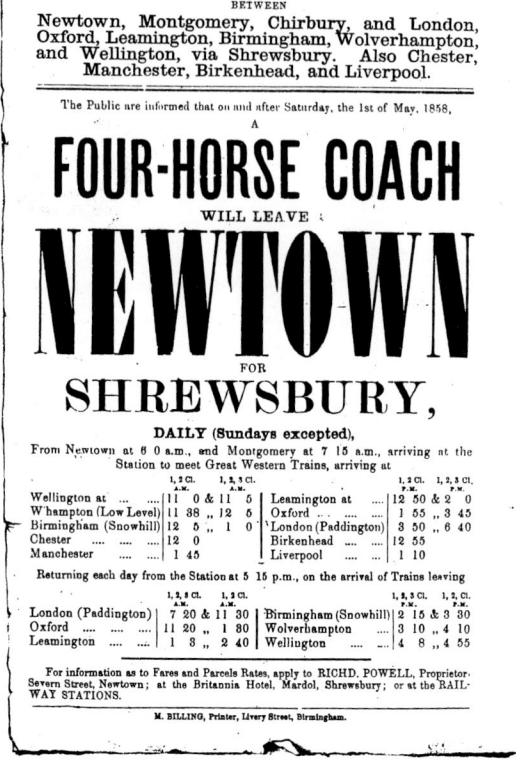

The mid Wales connection, 1858   *NLW*

which faced Howell and Davies. This is the triumphant story of their endeavour to establish the railway at Machynlleth.

Chapter 1: Notes & References

[1] *S&MT*: 4.4.1865 and Morgan D.W. (1948) *Brief Glory, The story of a quest.* Brython Press. Morgan gives the tonnage for *Rowland Evans* as 208 tons and the year of construction as 1864.

[2] Morgan D.W. A tonnage of 258 tons is given for the barque Mary Evans.

[3] ibid.

[4] ibid. p.187.

[5] Plans & Sections; Great North & South Wales and Worcester Railway, National Library of Wales, Aberystwyth.

[6] Plans & Sections; Great Welch Junction Railway, NLW.

[7] Christiansen R. & Miller R.W. 1967, *The Cambrian Railways, Vol.I* p.20. David & Charles, Newton Abbot.

Chapter 2

The Formation of the Newtown & Machynlleth Railway

The first moves to establish a railway to connect the Dyfi valley with the greater railway network were made around November 1856, by Morgan & Howell, the Machynlleth solicitors and Benjamin Piercy, the Trefeglwys engineer. Subsequent events reveal that Morgan became a secondary figure whereas Piercy and Howell, personal friends even before the venture, played key roles in the realisation of their dream. Piercy had experience of railway construction with Henry Robertson on the Shrewsbury & Chester Railway in 1848 and afterwards, on his own account, on the Bangor & Caernarvon Railway (1852): Howell was a shrewd professional as much inspired by a desire to improve the lot of his fellow country-men as the fulfilment of any personal ambition.

Even though the eventual success of the project must be attributed to the co-operation and dedication of a team of key figures, Howell emerges as the scheme's main protagonist and constant source of inspiration. The seventh of twelve children, he was born and raised at Bontdolgadfan, Llanbrynmair, the locality also of the Rev. Samuel Roberts (S.R.), philosopher and earlier advocate of railways for Montgomeryshire. Howell moved the few miles to Machynlleth in 1840, where he became articled to Hugh Davies and was taken into partnership by 1845. His brother, Abraham, moved to Welshpool and became the solicitor of the Oswestry & Newtown Railway. That the Newtown & Machynlleth Railway Bill made comparatively rapid progress through Parliament is directly attributable to the sagacity and zeal of the tenacious David Howell, and it is entirely to his credit that the scheme remained on course through difficult times.

Whilst he may have been the venture's principal architect, Howell could not, however, have achieved success single-handed. Without the constant and invaluable support of David Davies of Llandinam, all of Howell's endeavours could have been in vain. In a public tribute to David Davies, Howell later said;

> In Mr Davies we had throughout a tower of strength. He bore up amidst difficulties which would have filled most men with dismay. No disaster could affect his indomitable spirit. He was ever ready with fresh resources.[1]

Howell also enjoyed the co-operation of influential and industrious members on the Board, particularly The Right Honorable The Earl Vane, *Y Plas*, Machynlleth, John Foulkes Esq., Aberdyfi, Capt. Robert Davies Pryce Esq., *Cyfronydd*, Laurence Ruck Esq., *Pantlludw*, and Capt. Charles Thomas Thruston R.N. *Pennal Towers*. During the early stages, Robert Davies Jones Esq., of *Trefri*, John Carnac Morris Esq., F.R.S. *Fronfelen*, David Pritchard Esq., *Ceniarth*, and William Watkin Edward Wynne Esq., M.P. *Peniarth*, were also involved in the venture but, for various reasons, did not remain with the project and had withdrawn by the time the Company was incorporated in 1857. Sir Watkin Williams Wynn, Bart., *Wynnstay*, was later persuaded to join the Board and played a vital role, and the final addition to the Board, Charles Wynn Esq., M.P. for Montgomeryshire, was elected in 1862; 'though too late to join in their labours . . . not too late to join in their triumphs.'[2]

The new venture was launched on 20 December 1856, when a Public Meeting was held, at 12 noon, at the old Town Hall, Machynlleth. Howell informed Laurence Ruck by letter, the previous Saturday, that;

> The preliminary requirements of the Standing Orders have been complied with, and the promoters

NEWTOWN and MACHYNLLETH RAILWAY COMPANY,

CAPITAL £150,000 DIVIDED INTO SHARES OF £10 EACH.

DEPOSIT £1 per Share.

LETTER OF ALLOTMENT.

No. of Shares _100_

Deposit £ _100 - 0 - 0_

Machynlleth, _2 January_ 185_7_.

Sir,

The Provisional Directors have allotted you _100_ Shares in this undertaking, and will thank you to pay the Deposit into one of the undermentioned Banks, to their credit on or before Friday the 9th day of January, 1857,

I am, Sir,

Your obedient Servant,

D Howell

To _Lawrence Ruck Esq_

Banks to either of which the deposits are to be paid:—

The National Provincial Branch Banks at Machynlleth, Newtown, Aberystwith and Dolgelly. _or elsewhere_

BANKERS' RECEIPT.

Received the _9th_ day of _January_, 185_7_, from the above-named _Lawrence Ruck Esq_ on account of the Provisional Directors of the Newtown and Machynlleth Railway Company, the sum of _One hundred_ pounds, being the Deposit of One Pound per Share on the above-mentioned number of Shares in that undertaking.

£_100 - 0 - 0_

For _the National Provincial Bank of England_ _[signature]_ _manager_ will be in a position to go to Parliament next session if the Capital can be made up in time.

Much careful planning, including the initial survey, had obviously been undertaken before the venture was announced publicly and with the undertaking powerfully supported by Earl Vane and the other influential parties, success must have seemed assured from the outset. David Howell, on the other hand, was well aware of the many pitfalls which lay ahead and saw no grounds for complacency. He emphasised that;

> There is no place of equal extent or importance in England [!] which can suffer more for want of a railway, or that would be more benefitted by one than our district. Our only chance of obtaining one is by relying on our local resources and our own exertions. It is hoped that all classes and persons residing in or connected with the neighbourhood will now give their fair share of assistance. If the support is not general it can be of no avail, and the scheme will have to be withdrawn. Such a prospect of success as now exists is not likely to occur again for many years if the present movement fails.

Early in January, 1857, both Welsh and English posters appeared in the district extolling the virtues of a railway and calling for general support, stressing in a commendably realistic manner that 'railroads will not drop down from heaven.'

A series of public meetings was quickly organised and the issue of the *Wrexham & Denbighshire Weekly Advertiser* for 3 January 1857, reported such a gathering at Dolgellau, in support of the Newtown & Machynlleth undertaking. Mr W.W.E. Wynne M.P. *Peniarth*, was in the Chair and David Howell was happy to state that £30,000 had already been subscribed. Benjamin Piercy, also in attendance to explain the scheme, dismissed the idea of a line to Dolgellau from Ruabon, via

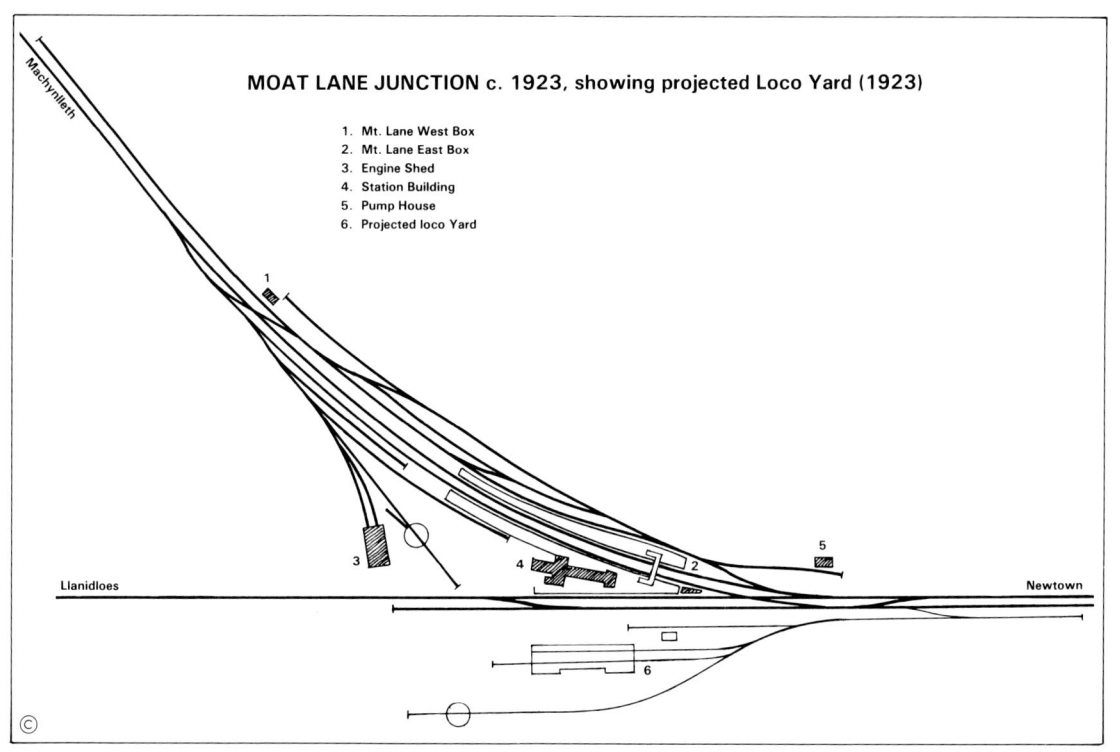

MOAT LANE JUNCTION c. 1923, showing projected Loco Yard (1923)

1. Mt. Lane West Box
2. Mt. Lane East Box
3. Engine Shed
4. Station Building
5. Pump House
6. Projected loco Yard

Llangollen, when he 'forcibly pointed out the difficulty of carrying out such a scheme...and strongly urged the inhabitants of Dolgellau to give up a myth for a certainty and to support this project which would place the town within 16 miles of a railway station'.

Now that Dolgellau is once more without rail access, it would be interesting to learn how frequently passengers today travel the sixteen miles to Machynlleth to catch a train.

Further meetings in the locality served to stimulate interest and generate enthusiasm. The response in the valley of the Dyfi and along the route to Caersws was predictable and encouraging, as was the reaction of the people of Merioneth. This was acknowledged at what the *Shrewsbury Chronicle* termed a 'very influential and numerously attended meeting of gentlemen interested in the promotion of the Newtown & Machynlleth Railway',[3] when it was stated that 'the inhabitants of Dolgelley and the neighbourhood are particularly anxious for the line'[4] but the response from Cardiganshire, on the other hand, was decidedly cool. The hardworking Capt. Thruston, who had visited Aberystwyth for a period of ten days to assess public reaction, expressed considerable disappointment. Referring to a meeting he conducted at the town with his colleague T. O. Morgan Esq., he reported,

> I am sorry to say that although we did our best, neither the persuasion of the learned gentleman nor my own, had the smallest effect. We offered to give explanations to any question they might choose to put to us, but there was not a single response, not a man answered. But if the men did not answer, by George, the women did, for two or three ladies, heading a deputation of lodging-house keepers, came forward and stated energetically to the meeting, 'We are already half ruined; not one third of the visitors now come to the place; our lodgings are not let, and our trade diminished in value; unless you support this project, or someone that will bring a railroad to Aberystwyth, we shall be totally ruined.'[5]

Amongst the reasons for the disappointing Cardiganshire response was the plea, 'we are too poor',[6] and the expectancy of a 'grand trunk line',[7] the second Manchester & Milford scheme. Intended to link Llanidloes with Pencader, this generated much speculation and optimism regarding a branch also to Aberystwyth. A more realistic reason for the reluctance of the Cardiganshire folk to offer financial support at this time was 'that they intended to reserve their capital until the road was brought to Machynlleth'.[8]

In 1855, many Aberystwyth people had invested in the Oswestry & Newtown Railway. Two years hence this had yet to be started so perhaps their caution may be appreciated. Not all were of the same persuasion, however, and there were those who 'felt rather sorry that Aberystwith was not at once included in the bill'.[9] Financial support from North Cardiganshire did eventually improve but was never a major factor in the Machynlleth line's success for much of Cardiganshire's capital was, understandably perhaps, reserved for railway ventures nearer home.

The first meeting of the provisional Directors took place at the Wynnstay Arms Hotel, Machynlleth, on Saturday, 27 December 1856, just one week, and Christmas, after the inaugural public meeting at the Town Hall. Those in attendance were R.D.Jones Esq., who took the Chair, Capt. C.T.Thruston, John Foulkes Esq, Laurence Ruck Esq, and David Pritchard Esq. Also in attendance were David Howell and Benjamin Piercy. At the Directors' third meeting it was resolved that the newly drawn prospectus was to be advertised once in two London daily papers, together with *The Railway Times, The Mining Journal, The Midland Counties Herald* and the *Manchester Guardian*, and several times in the two Shrewsbury papers and the *Caernarvon Herald*. The minutes also record that 'the special thanks of the meeting are offered to Capt. Thruston for the able Prospectus he has drawn.'[10]

Capt C. T. Thruston RN was one of the staunchest supporters of the undertaking from the outset. He took the Chair at the inaugural public meeting at the Town Hall and although his health was failing he played an active role in promoting

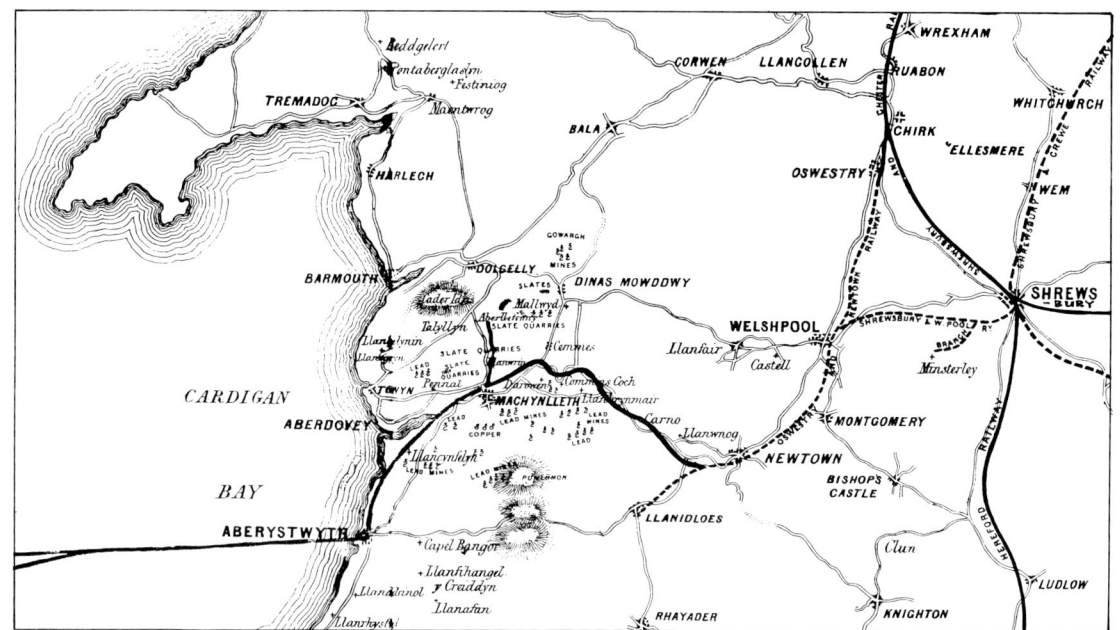

The Newtown & Machynlleth Prospectus map of 1856, revealing early ambitions toward the coast
WIMM

the project. In the ensuing months he presided at further meetings and proved a most able deputy for Earl Vane, the Chairman of the new venture, who was not available at that time. Capt. Thruston also supported Howell in London during the difficult period before the safe passage of the Bill through Parliament. Howell himself paid tribute to Thruston's invaluable services;

> ...I shall ever retain a grateful recollection of his determination to remain in London, as he did at personal inconvenience, during the summer until the Act passed. His words when I called upon him to congratulate him on the safety of the Bill have still a melancholy interest. He said, 'It is a great undertaking, and you will probably live to see it accomplished, but I can scarcely hope to have that satisfaction'.[11]

Capt. C.T. Thruston RN died on 24 July, 1858, seven months before construction commenced at Caersws.

Most of the Directors worked tirelessly for the cause. Capt. R.D. Pryce, for example, crossed on the Aberdyfi ferry during a severe storm to conduct a meeting at Aberystwyth. On reaching the Cardiganshire side he had to wade up to his middle in water for some distance and then, in his wet clothes, walk the nine miles to Aberystwyth. Indeed, during those early days the more committed Directors were kept fully occupied attending various meetings and attracting new subscribers. Several members habitually spent time in London and throughout this period they were joined by David Howell who travelled extensively between his practice at Machynlleth, various local meetings and his London base at 25, Gutter Lane, Cheapside. In a letter headed simply, 'Shrewsbury, 12 January 1857,' Howell wrote,

> Mr R.D.Jones...will no doubt go up to London with me this evening by express train. Mr Pritchard and Mr J.Jones of the Bank will...travel by the Mail from Machynlleth today and meet us to close everything to-morrow morning.

The Mail, of course, was horse-drawn and the 'everything' referred to is explained in a brief letter which followed from Gutter Lane, dated 13 January 1857, which informed Ruck;

> that the deposit of £11,250 has been this day duly paid into the Bank of England in compliance with the Standing Orders.

Further evidence of Howell's drive and commitment are revealed in another letter from London, dated 22 January 1857, in which he expresses a wish to form a committee in the Carno district, and arrange meetings there and at Llanbrynmair 'for Monday and Tuesday, which Mr Piercy and myself will attend' . . . also . . . 'It would be desirable to have a meeting of Directors in the course of next week. . . .'

On the surface at least, matters appeared to progress well during the spring, but such impressions proved deceptive for doubts began to form in the minds of some of the Directors. Aware of this hesitancy and dissatisfaction by one or two of the members, Howell wrote an optimistic but illuminating letter to Earl Vane on 8 May which arrived in time for the Committee of Management Meeting later that same day; a meeting in which one of the Directors made the dramatic proposal that the Bill be abandoned. Due to Howell's timely injection of confidence, this move found no support and it was resolved to proceed in Parliament to obtain the Act. David Howell fully appreciated that it was vital at that time to display confidence in the venture, particularly as not all the required capital had been subscribed. Those who felt that their investment was at risk would place the whole scheme in jeopardy if they sought to withdraw their support; if all remained committed to the project, Howell was confident that the balance of the capital would quickly be found. In his letter to Earl Vane he focussed on the financial security required before proceeding with the Bill through Parliament;

> . . . The Engineers now report that we may rely on the cost of the Works not exceeding £125,000. On paying or securing the payment of £75,000 of the Capital, the deposit would be repaid and the borrowing powers would come into operation by means of which £50,000 more would probably be easily made available, making together the entire £125,000. Shares have already been taken or promised to be taken exceeding £45,000 thus leaving £30,000 only to be further provided. Practically therefore, the simple question is whether within 5 years, being the time proposed to be limited for the completion of the railway (or say 7 years as allowed in the case of the Llanidloes Railway), a further sum of £30,000 may be reasonably expected to be obtained? I shall not contemplate the necessity of seeking for pecuniary assistance from contractors, nor of reducing our expenditure by means of avoiding tunnelling and cuttings and adopting unfavourable curves and gradients—It is both self-evident and borne out by the experience of neighbouring Companies that the contribution towards capital usually rendered by contractors having no interest in common with the district, is and necessarily must be worse than delusion. Nor should I be prepared to entertain the possibility of being driven for want of funds to accept an inferior railway, destined as ours is to become such an important trunk line. Though it is needless to observe that either of the contingencies supposed would be preferable to having no railway at all . . . Hitherto, members of the Board have had pardonable misgivings as to our ever being able to obtain the necessary funds. This has necessarily had a highly prejudicial effect on our past canvass. The position of the Promoters has been one of great delicacy and difficulty. It was necessary to show confidence in order to inspire it in others and at the same time to let it be unmistakenly understood that success depended upon general co-operation. The decision of today, if it should be as anticipated, to proceed without further hesitation of any kind will remove one great obstacle in the way of getting the remaining capital subscribed . . . There is a large portion of the district remaining almost wholly uncanvassed and there are numerous parties who have as yet done nothing but who ought and I believe would render assistance on being properly applied to . . . I feel sanguine that the greater portion of the additional £30,000 might, with proper exertions, be obtained in the course of the present summer to say nothing of 5 to 7 years. I see no reason if the Board shall decide on going on, why preparations should not be at once made for letting the contracts in anticipation of the Act being

obtained, nor why the works should not be actually commenced early in the autumn . . . It is right also to take a calm and dispassionate view of the probable consequences of withdrawing from the undertaking at the present moment. There is probably a conviction in the mind of everyone . . . that the present is the only chance of obtaining a railway into the neighbourhood during the present age. It would be unreasonable to calculate at any future time upon such circumstances, among which may be enumerated the general and influential and probably unprecedented local support already promised and the absence of rival schemes and opposing interests . . . I believe it to be wholly beyond the range of probability that an equal amount of energy could be brought to bear in aid of any future attempt to bring a Railway into the District. Speaking for myself as regards the humble part I have taken I feel certain I could not command either the resolution or strength to try such a thing again. I am sure that this must also be the feeling of all those patriotic men who have so worthily devoted their best talents and exertions on the present occasion . . . I believe that there is scarcely a person in the country, whether a shareholder or not and whether rich or poor, that would not deplore the failure of the present scheme as a national and personal calamity.'

Although an immediate crisis had been averted, the months of May and June, 1857, proved a most difficult time; securing the essential £30,000 still appeared an unsurmountable obstacle in the minds of some of the Directors. Foremost amongst those who questioned the validity of the whole project was W.W.E.Wynne Esq. of *Peniarth,* the M.P. for Merioneth, who was supported and prompted by his solicitor W. Jones, of *Glandwr* near Dolgellau.

In a letter to David Howell from Crosby Square, London, dated 28 May 1857, Jones wrote, in a clear hand but somewhat devoid of punctuation,

I am bound in candour . . . to declare to you that I have such strong misgivings on the subject as to compel me in the discharge of my duty towards Mr Wynne to say that I do not like his position and cannot recommend him to permit the Bill to proceed further unless in the meantime he is relieved from the £9000 Subscription temporarily submitted to as well as from his liability under the joint promissory note on which the deposit was raised. To the extent of £1000 Mr Wynne heartily subscribed but beyond this he does not for well known prudential reasons feel himself justified in going on . . .

This unwelcome set-back caused others to doubt the undertaking, for not only was W.W.E. Wynne withdrawing a substantial amount of capital from the scheme but also his name as a Director. This was an important consideration for other Merionethshire subscribers and a factor which must have influenced David Pritchard Esq, who also decided to withdraw his support at this time. (Evidently, this experience did not affect them adversely for both men were later associated with the Welsh Coast Railway and both became Directors of the Cambrian Railways, Wynne having the added distinction of designing the original version of that Company's Common Seal.)

It was fortuitous that David Howell had been in London since 9 May, for he was well placed to deal with this latest crisis. By 1 June, written notice of W.W.E.Wynne's resignation had reached him and he was also aware of the withdrawl of David Pritchard's support. In a letter to Laurence Ruck, that day, he declared:

Mr Davies, the Contractor of the Llanidloes Railway, will subscribe for £10,000 or £15,000 which will enable us to get rid of the difficulty as to Mr Wynne.

David Davies, who had worked on the Llanidloes and other lines in north and mid Wales, mostly in partnership with Thomas Savin, had shown an interest in the Machynlleth development from the outset. Although no formal contract then existed, Davies and Savin were obviously the men in mind to construct the new line. Davies's financial lifeline was therefore both opportune for the venture and prudent on his own part for, unknown to Howell at the time, a third member of the provisional Directors was contemplating withdrawl from the scheme; without Davies's timely aid the problem could have been unsurmountable.

The expectation that Earl Vane would take up Mr Pritchard's shares led Howell to believe that the crisis had been averted, for the remaining members of the Board seemed 'all in the same boat and . . . unanimous for proceeding for the Act'. Howell's joy was shortlived, however, for on the 3 June, Laurence Ruck declared his own misgivings when he wrote to Howell expressing his dissatisfaction and withdrawing support.

Howell and Charles Thruston, both in London to support the Bill through Parliament, were most concerned at this latest development although, in separate letters to Laurence Ruck, neither expressed any surprise.

Howell's response on 5 June records that;

> the events of the past few days, at one time, produced much the same effect upon me—I however now feel much more sanguine, and am induced to hope you will be able to take a more favourable view of matters. Lord Vane and Sir Watkin will meet on Monday morning, and I am pretty confident the result will be that the one will take to Mr Pritchard's extra shares and the other to Mr W.W.E. Wynne's, and be it remembered that Mr Wynne and Mr Pritchard continue their original subscriptions.

Despite conveying an impression of confidence to subscribers and the public at large, there is no doubt that Howell was under considerable pressure at this time. In the same letter he confides to Ruck that,

> The non-payment by several of the Shareholders of their Deposits is entitled to no weight—The answer is simply that they have not been asked to pay. The Subscribers who have not paid are as bona fide as those who have—My exertions in regard to the Deposits and in getting more shares taken have been quite paralysed by the sort of ordeal I have had lately to go through—people in subscribing do so on the faith that we are going on, and it would be wrong to ask for more Subscriptions whilst we ourselves are so undecided. Those who (like Mr Wm. Jones of Crosby Square), entertain misgivings as to our subscribers paying in full, lose sight of the difference between our *bona fide* undertaking and the bubble schemes of former years. If it had not been for the withdrawl of Mr Pritchard and Mr Wynne and the consequent anxiety and trouble to which I have been put, I should 'ere this have gone a great way towards making up the £30,000 we were short of—I believe it might still be managed without much trouble . . . Our difficulties have been serious and numerous but our prospects are, at the present moment, better than ever—we have very nearly got thro' all the difficulty and expence [sic] of obtaining an Act.

Thruston also wrote a short note of encouragement to Ruck which opened;

> I have seen your letter of withdrawl addressed to David Howell. I am not surprised at it—but still regret it—If I had listened to the warnings of Mr W. Wynne's legal adviser, I should have done the same—he hates the whole scheme and perhaps not being employed in the legal part of it may have strengthened his dislike.

On 6 June, Howell wrote again to Ruck, endeavouring to restore his confidence in the venture by placing the recent events in perspective and generally sounding an optimistic note:

> . . . All we have lost is W.W.E. Wynne's assistance as a Director which as you know was *nil*—He never attended a meeting—I believe the other Montgomeryshire Companies are now in an excellent position—which will be a great encouragement to us . . . I have no doubt whatever you will be sorry to reflect hereafter that you have been the cause of upsetting our undertaking at a moment when its success (not withstanding the discouragement caused by other parties whose conduct cannot be defended) was certain. I sincerely hope that you will reconsider your decision—do not let the scheme fail without cool and mature deliberation. Let the Directors (including yourself) be unanimous if possible . . . If we withdraw, let it be on grounds that will clearly exonerate us from blame in our own minds—in the minds of each other and in the opinion of the Country.

This encouragement appeared to have the desired effect upon Ruck for he withdrew his resignation and remained to see the Bill through Parliament. The Minutes of Proceedings of the Board of Directors record his attendance at the first meetings of the new Board, but he did not remain with the venture long afterwards; the reason for his withdrawal is not recorded. Also obscure is the reason for the expectation, at this time, that Sir Watkin would take up Mr W.W.E. Wynne's shares, in preference to Mr David Davies.

David Howell wrote a second letter on 6 June, this time to Earl Vane, asking;

> to be informed of the determination you and Sir Watkin may come to with reference to the extra shares of Mr David Pritchard and Mr W.W.E. Wynne.

His Lordship was also informed that Laurence Ruck had 'become desponding' and that it would be as well to ascertain how far the other Directors were prepared to subscribe towards making up the proposed £30,000. John Foulkes had already intimated that he was prepared to follow, as far as he possibly could, the wealthier Directors in adding to the number of shares already named.

Earl Vane's response was prompt so that by the 8th inst., Howell was able to report that His Lordship was fully prepared to take up Mr Pritchard's shares, and proceed with the Act, provided Sir Watkin took up Mr Wynne's shares and became a member of the Board. This arrangement met with the full approval of Mr Upton, Earl Vane's Solicitor, who then supported this course of action although he had previously entertained considerable doubt regarding Earl Vane's commitment.

It now seemed that success or failure, the culmination of several months of strenuous lobbying and hard work, hinged on the willingness of Earl Vane and Sir Watkin to share the financial burden created by the resignations. Whilst Earl Vane had declared his intention clearly, Sir Watkin's response was not known and could not be taken for granted. They were expected to meet for discussion in London initially but, by the time Earl Vane arrived, Sir Watkin had already left for Ascot. Howell was then hopeful that they would meet there either on Wednesday or Thursday, (10/11 June) and that Earl Vane would be able to persuade Sir Watkin to carry Mr Wynne's shares and become a member of the Board.

Perhaps Ascot was inappropriate for consideration of such a vital issue but, for whatever reason, Sir Watkin elected to decline the invitation: without his support, and with time running out it looked yet again as though the venture was destined to fail ignominiously. When Earl Vane informed David Howell of this disastrous news on the evening of Saturday, June 13th, it appeared that the only course of action then remaining was to call a meeting of the shareholders and dissolve the scheme. There was no time to introduce any form of counter measure for the date for the next reading of the Bill (Thursday, the 18th inst.) was already the result of two previous postponements. Suddenly, all the promoters' hopes and aspirations seemed to evaporate as easily as did the steam in which they had placed their faith.

Yet, even with this colossal eleventh-hour setback, David Howell was reluctant to admit defeat but felt that one final attempt had still to be made. Later, he recalled;

> In this crisis, I felt that one last chance alone remained of saving the Bill, and that was to enlist, if at all possible, the powerful help of Sir Hugh Williams[12]. I sat down to write him a full explanation of matters.[13]

That letter, however, was not completed, for Howell was persuaded by a young clergyman friend of the importance of seeking a personal interview immediately with Sir Hugh rather than trust a letter which might not be read until the Monday, when it would be too late. This timely advice was accepted and David Howell and his young adviser proceeded at once to Spring Gardens where the pair were fortunate to meet Sir Hugh at the door, on his way out for the evening. They were invited into the house and allowed to present their case: Sir Hugh held little hope of success but promised to do what he could.

Later, addressing Earl Vane in a meeting at Machynlleth, in 1863, Howell related:

On my calling, by appointment, at Sir Watkin's home in St. James's Square, on the Monday morning, I found that Sir Hugh had not been idle and that your Lordship was at that moment closetted with Sir Watkin and that there was every prospect of your coming to an understanding. I joined in the discussion and the result of our deliberation led to the Bill's passing at once through Committee . . . .[14]

It must have been a much relieved David Howell who wrote a short note to Ruck on 18 June, stating that the Newtown & Machynlleth Railway Bill had just passed Committee and would be reported to the House of Commons that evening. He had already indicated in an earlier letter (15th inst.) that Sir Watkin had consented to become a member of the Board, and be appointed Vice-Chairman, but 'with an understanding that he is to be at liberty not to attend meetings.' Sir Watkin was also to see Mr W.W.E. Wynne in an endeavour to induce him to retain his liabilities and seat on the Board.

Mr Wynne did not, in fact, remain on the Board, despite Sir Watkin's expectations, but matters finally appeared to be resolved. Having seen the Bill through Committee in the House of Lords late on the evening of 14 July, Howell was confident that the remaining stages were mere formalities; he wasted no further time but proceeded at once to seek new subscribers!

After a brief delay caused by the returning of the Bill to the Commons for a slight amendment, Royal Assent was granted on Monday evening, 27 July, 1857. The Newtown & Machynlleth Railway was incorporated and about to become a reality.

Disappointment and delay

With the undertaking's first and most vital objective achieved in just over six months and with the majority of shareholders unaware of the problems which had beset the Board, expectations ran high for an early and successful completion of the scheme.

The first meeting of the Board of Directors took place on 6 August when John Foulkes and

Howell's partner, Edward Morgan, was responsible for informing the local directors of the success of the scheme in Parliament.   *NLW*

Laurence Ruck met at *Pantlludw*, near Machynlleth. Despite the low attendance, Messers Foulkes and Ruck formed a quorum and resolved to invite Sir Watkin to act as Chairman of the Directors until the first general meeting of the Company, to be held on Saturday 22 August 'at 11 in the forenoon', at the Town Hall. They also resolved that David Howell be formally appointed as Secretary, and that 'the sketch produced at the present meeting be, and the same is hereby approved of, for the Common Seal of the Company.'[15]

At the first meeting of the newly formed Cambrian Board, on 13 August 1864, it was resolved: 'That the seals of the several dissolved Companies now amalgamated be destroyed, with the exception of that belonging to the late Newtown & Machynlleth Company, which is given to Earl Vane'. (RAIL 92/1)
WIMM

Howell's earlier suggestion (8 May) for 'at once' letting the contracts in anticipation of the Act being obtained and the works actually commencing in the autumn, had not been acted upon for a variety of reasons and long delays ensued. The slow purchase of land was presented as one reason, although this was eventually accomplished most favourably and the delay was fully justified when David Howell discovered a means of avoiding the use of ready money for the purchase of land! This was achieved by converting the payment for almost the entire line into a rent charge. As Howell recalled;

> We got the whole land for a line of 23 miles at a cost, in ready money, of no more than £5000—a result probably unprecedented in the history of railways.[16]

This scheme made the optimum use of limited financial resources

> ... and when this fund was exhausted, Mr Davies brought his own resources to our help and he enabled us to reach our borrowing powers, which placed £50,000 more at our disposal. The monetary arrangements, although apparently complicated, were well considered. They involved no real risk, but it required large confidence on all hands to carry them into effect. I felt that a great responsibility rested upon me to see that all parties were kept harmless.[17]

Other reasons for the apparent stagnation of the project were the absence from Wales of the Chairman and Vice-Chairman and the lamented death of Capt. Thruston, recognised by the Board as one of the venture's most zealous and able supporters. Furthermore, whilst the neighbouring lines remained unfinished, there seemed less reason for urgency on the part of the N&M who felt they still had nearly two years for the purchase of land and four years for the completion of the railway.

No tangible progress was made until a meeting of the Directors on 23 November, 1858, saw the appointment of the brothers Benjamin and Robert Piercy as the Company's engineers. Their renumeration, including all incidental charges and expenses, was decided at £5000 up to the opening of the railway for public traffic through to Machynlleth; this sum was also to include the bills of Mr Cubitt and the Messrs. Piercy previous to the passing of the N&M Railway Act. Other than lending his name as Engineer-in-Chief, Mr Cubitt does not appear to have played any significant role in the work. The contract for the construction of the line was now let formally to Messrs. Davies & Savin who were to furnish all the materials and complete the line for the sum of £130,000, of which £102,000 was to be paid in cash, £23,000 in paid up shares and £5000 on loan.[18] [NB. The sum of £133,000 is quoted three times in the Llandinam Account Books]

15

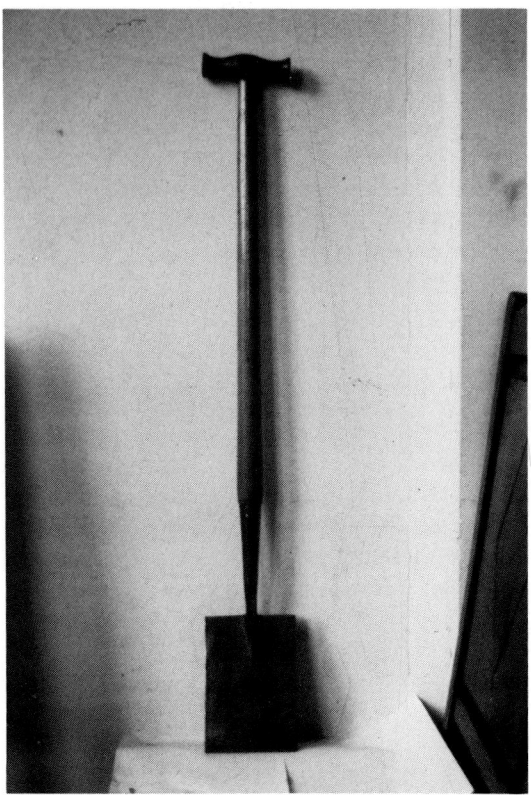

The small spade used by Countess Vane for the Ceremony of Cutting the first sod, at Machynlleth, on 27 November 1858.

tunnel into a cutting but this eventually proved a most profitable move for the contractor. Because of the strata and some high quality stone at Talerddig, it was soon realised that the material for the construction of bridges and permanent stations was readily to hand and the decision to open a cutting may well have been reached when the initial excavations revealed this factor.

The final resolution of this productive Board Meeting decreed that,

> The first Sod of the Railway shall be cut at Machynlleth terminus on the 27th of November and that the Rt. Hon. The Countess Vane be requested to perform the ceremony.[20]

After so much apparent inactivity during the previous months, events now moved quickly. Even the preparations for the ceremony were arranged so speedily that Countess Vane had to

Thomas Savin, 1826-1889

WIMM

The Board now sought to make up for lost time and with a view to hastening the proceedings they resolved that the contractors be allowed to commence the works as soon as the neccessary land had been obtained. Construction was to commence between the site of the junction with the Llanidloes & Newtown near Caersws, 'and the tunnel at Talerddig, it being intended to open that portion of the railway for public traffic on or before the first day of January, 1860.'[19]

It is worth noting that at this time, (Nov. 1858), it was still the intention to drive a tunnel through the summit at Talerddig. No reference has yet emerged relating to the decision to open the

Moat Lane Junction, 1956, looking west towards Machynlleth. The Ivatt 2-6-0 in the centre distance stands outside the small shed, whilst on the extreme right, a mid Wales train has conveniently set back onto the outer face of the island platform.

Mowat Collection

use an ordinary iron spade for the purpose because there was insufficient time for the contractor to acquire a more ornate implement normally supplied on such occasions. The *Advertiser* furnishes a full account of this colourful event which was featured also in *The Story of the Cambrian*.[21]

Chapter 2: Notes & References

[1] OA 25.6.1863
[2] OA 7.1.1863
[3] SC 6.3.1857
[4] ibid.
[5] ibid.
[6] ibid.
[7] ibid.
[8] ibid.
[9] ibid.
[10] RAIL 517/1. p.4.
[11] OA 24.6.1863.
[12] Of Bodelwyddan Castle, Sir Watkin's brother-in-law.
[13] OA 24.6.1863.
[14] ibid.
[15] RAIL 517/1. p.10.
[16] OA 24.6.1863.
[17] ibid.
[18] RAIL 517/1. p.32.
[19] ibid.
[20] ibid.
[21] Gasquoine C.P. (1922) *The Story of the Cambrian*, Woodall, Minshall, Thomas & Co., Oswestry, pp. 55-57.

A rare view of Talerddig during the opening of the Cutting in 1861-2, showing clearly the strata which yielded so much building stone. An entry in the Llandinam Account Books, dated 21 May 1861 reads: 'Paid photographic man's expenses . . . 4/-'.
BR/WIMM

Chapter 3
Preparations for Construction

During 1858-59, Messrs Davies & Savin worked simultaneously on several sizeable contracts. Even by present-day standards, we must marvel at the scale and flexibility of their organisation, and the efficiency of their workforce.

David Davies commenced construction of the Llanidloes & Newtown from the western end of the line, in 1855. For a brief period of a few weeks, he took a farmer/surveyor named Parry into partnership, but the association did not endure. By the end of 1857 the rails extended as far as Penstrowed, when a local landowner known as 'old General Proctor, would not allow them to enter upon his land until it was paid for.'[1] As this impasse was the direct result of a shortage of funds, work came to an immediate halt and remained suspended throughout the whole of the following year. Fortunately, Davies was able to keep his men in employment elsewhere for he left in the Autumn of 1857 to construct the Vale of Clwyd Railway, between Denbigh and Rhyl, this time in partnership with Thomas Savin (1826-89), of Oswestry. The Vale of Clwyd line presented comparatively few construction problems, and Davies in particular, worked long, strenuous hours each day to enable the opening to take place in August, 1858.

Early in 1859, as well as making preparations to start work on their latest venture, the Newtown & Machynlleth line, Davies & Savin offered to

Llandinam, the Manning Wardle 0-6-0 1T (Works number 33), purchased by David Davies especially for work on the Newtown & Machynlleth line. It was delivered 'at the Railway, Leeds' on 3 October 1861. The bill for £1200 was dispatched within just five days, and the receipt for full payment was dated 11 October 1861; details which speak eloquently of the contractor's character and business acumen. *GBJ Collection*

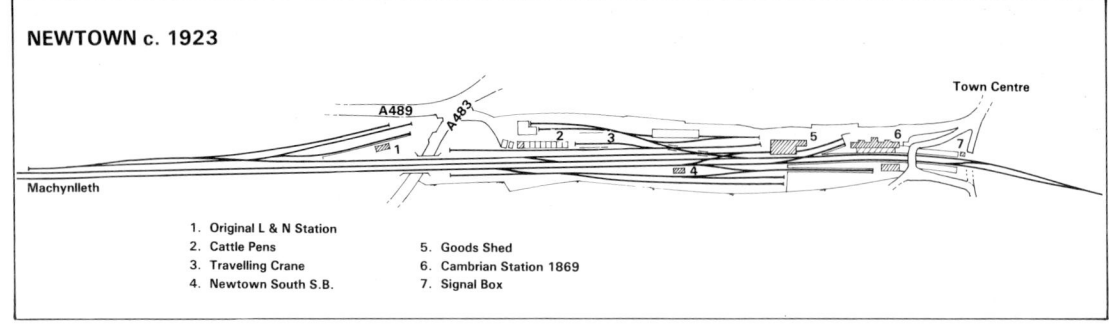

NEWTOWN c. 1923

1. Original L & N Station
2. Cattle Pens
3. Travelling Crane
4. Newtown South S.B.
5. Goods Shed
6. Cambrian Station 1869
7. Signal Box

complete the construction of the L&N in exchange for all unissued shares and debentures. Later in 1859, and in addition to these commitments, they were invited to complete the construction of the second of Montgomeryshire's railways, the Oswestry & Newtown, after that company had already failed with two previous contracting firms. On 30 October, Davies & Savin started on the section between Buttington and Welshpool.

Progress on the N&M was retarded until completion of the Llanidloes line. Materials and supplies were reaching Newtown by barge, for the westernmost reach of the Shropshire Union Canal, opened to Newtown since 1821, carried considerable quantities of bricks, rails, sleepers, and coal for both the west Montgomeryshire railways. As late as 27 July 1860, when the rival Oswestry line was close to completion and threatening to monopolise all goods traffic in the area, David Davies paid the sum of £368.13.11 to 'David Morgan for a Canal Bill to 30 May.[2]

A quarter of a mile gap existed between rail and canal heads at Newtown and a connecting branch line was contemplated in 1859 but the high cost of building a further Severn crossing, and the resumption of work on the Oswestry line, resulted in the proposal being dropped.

The original station at Newtown was a terminus constructed for the L&N and, in common with most of the early stations in the area, was a temporary affair. Located at the western end of the town at the junction of the Llanidloes and

Newtown c. 1960, revealing well-used platforms and a busy goods yard. Barely discernable in this photograph, a BR Standard Class 4 4-6-0 stands at the entrance to the goods shed. Note also the original L&N station building (ringed), serving as a coal merchant's office on the low platform/wharf at the bottom of the picture. *WIMM*

Llandrindod roads, it lay in direct alignment with the canal head, probably in anticipation of the proposed extension. It was completed in good time for the opening of the Llanidloes line on 31 August 1859 although, rather surprisingly, the cost of this building features in the Machynlleth line's accounts. The entry reads;

> 25 July, 1859. Mr Lewis, for men putting up Newtown station . . . £3.5.3.[3]

An agreement for a Joint O&N and L&N station at Newtown dates from September 1859 and it was to this second station that the inaugural Machynlleth train eventually ran. The low platform of the old terminus later served as a coal wharf and the original wooden station building, complete with a small boarded-up ticket office window, was used by the coal merchant as an office; both survived until November 1989, when this unique site was cleared for development.

Amidst the intense activity of progress on the L&N at Newtown and elsewhere, work finally started on the Machynlleth line. No references have yet been discovered relating to the laying of the first N&M rails, nor to the commencement or effective completion of the junction at Moat Lane, but inscribed within the cover of one of the Llandinam account books is the legend:

> Machynlleth Railway Works. John Jones commenced Caersws Bridge crossing the Severn on the 23 of February 1859. Mr John Elkington commenced cutting the Diversion at Caersws and Mr Carnegie commenced Pontdolgoch Cutting.[4]

The Elkington and Carnegie works are undated but it is not unrealistic to assume that they

Montgomeryshire's first new engine, the L&N's 0-4-2ST *Milford*, was the first engine recorded at work on the Machynlleth line. Originally built without a cab, it was withdrawn after an accident in Oswestry yard in 1893 and cut up the following year. *Loco. Pub. Co.*

commenced at the same time: Mr John Holt is noted as commencing the fencing on the Machynlleth Railway on 7 March 1859. No records appear to survive of Thomas Savin's contribution to the work so we have David Davies alone to thank for recording that the 'great undertaking' was finally under way.

After surveying the route, the erection of the fencing was the first real indication of the course to be followed by the new line. Gangs of men were established at the major sites, each managed by gangers, who were key-workers responsible for the general efficiency and quality of the work. Most of these trustworthy young men, from Llandinam, were well known to David Davies. This proved an important contributory factor to his success as a railway contractor for, whenever possible, he endeavoured to employ local men and materials, and their names feature prominently in the records. Apart from some specialist tradesmen who immigrated, Davies was proud to rely on the men of Montgomeryshire. There is little wonder that he was hailed as,

> working his line by means of Welsh materials, drawn from inexhaustible Welsh mountains; his workmen are natives, the planning and workmanship is also native, and he himself a thorough and spirited Welshman.[5]

'Specification for Works'

One of the most interesting documents related to the line's construction is the *Specification for Works, Newtown & Machynlleth Railway 1860*.[6] Countersigned by Vane, D. Howell, David Davies, Thos. Savin and R. & B. Piercy, the twenty hand-written pages contain many details of the original construction which would otherwise have been lost for all time. Some information, relating to the construction of gates and fences for example, may perhaps seem esoteric yet there exists an almost insatiable demand for greater knowledge of our early railways and the instructions and specifications reflect clearly the materials and methods of a byegone age; scrutiny of a modern specification, for a motorway perhaps, could provide an interesting comparison.

The distance from the junction with the Llanidloes line, generally called Caersws Junction until about mid-1862, to Machynlleth, is stated as '23

Cambrian No. 9, former O&N 0-4-2 *Volunteer*, which shed a tyre near Derwenlas whilst working the 'down' Mail, in 1876. No. 5 *Montgomery*, one of the earliest workhorses on the N&M, was an identical engine. *LPC*

CAERSWS c. 1923

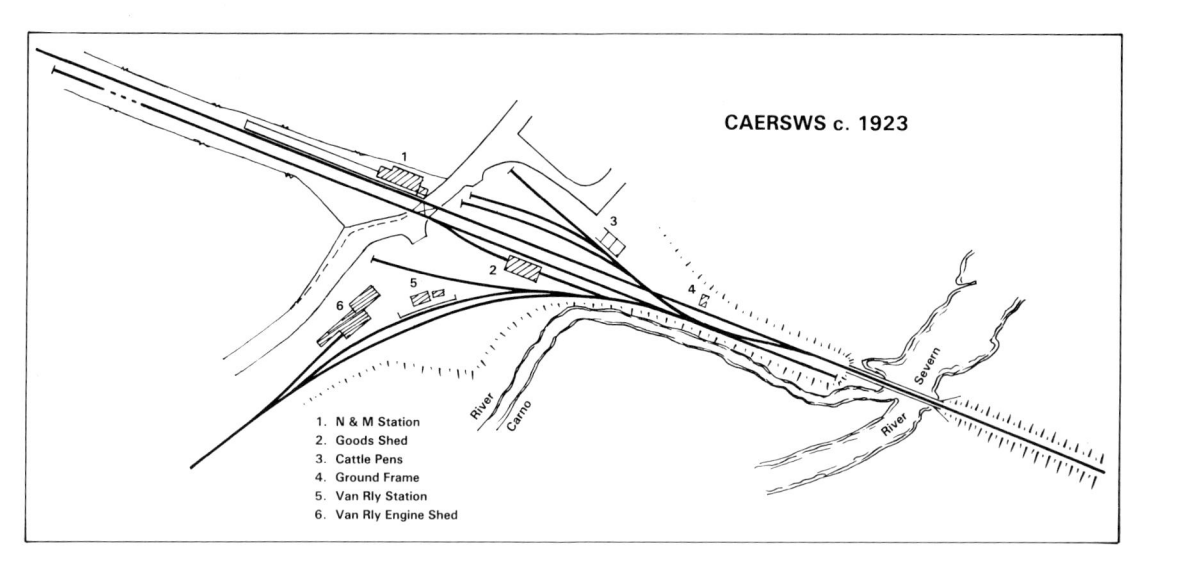

1. N & M Station
2. Goods Shed
3. Cattle Pens
4. Ground Frame
5. Van Rly Station
6. Van Rly Engine Shed

miles or thereabouts'.[7] For the purposes of construction this length was divided into two sections, with the initial nine miles to Talerddig (693ft above sea-level) being commenced first. It was originally estimated that completion to the summit would take approximately twelve months but the first locomotive and carriage trip over this section did not take place until 21 September 1861, some nineteen months later.[8]

The contract called for one line of railway with 3100 yards of sidings and passing places. Culverts, girders and timber work were to be for a single line of way, but bridge masonry was for double track. An element of quality control was introduced with the instruction that bridge masonry face stones were to be;

> ... square-jointed and the largest size that could reasonably be procured ... the mortar was to be fresh, every stone to be well bedded in the mortar and every joint flushed full therewith and not in any case be of an inferior description to the work put in the Park Gate turnpike road bridge under the Llanidloes & Newtown Railway at one mile, or thereabouts from Newtown.[9]

This bridge still carries the railway over the A489 Newtown-Llanidloes road, bearing silent testimony to the standard of workmanship and quality of materials used in its construction.

Permanent station buildings and signalling were not included in the contract. All buildings or trees on the land purchased for the line became the property of the Company; the sum of £40 was paid for a shed and pig-sty near Carno, for example.[10]

The boundary fencing was of oak or larch posts, 5ins x 3ins in section and 7ft long, with four mortices cut to receive the larch rails. These were set 3ft into the ground. A quickset hedge was then formed on the Company's side of the fence;

> except where rendered impracticable by the rocky character of the ground. The quicks are to be healthy plants of three years growth and ... they are to be set eight in a lineal yard in a single row ... and in a small bank as described by the engineers.[11]

A ditch a foot wide and eighteen inches deep was cut to drain away any surface water. Not much, it would appear, was left to chance.

The Company's landmarks, as the boundary posts are referred to in the specification, were of oak, 6ins x 4ins in section and 5ft long. They bore an identification mark which still calls for an explanation. The specification reads:

23

The portion above the ground to be painted four times in good oil colour, the last two coats with the initials RC in Egyptian Letters 4 inches in height deeply cut thereon and painted black.[12]

Why RC is not immediately apparent unless the Company, aware of the fact that they would amalgamate and change their title within the lifespan of their landmarkers, chose to refer to themselves merely as the 'Railway Company'. They could hardly have foreseen that these initials would correspond to 'Cambrian Railways' in Welsh!

Mile and gradient posts were also of oak and the mile and quarter mile posts were 'deeply cut

Caersws c. 1960, showing the old Van Railway station and engine shed, then used by the Engineering Department (Bridge Section). The old course of the river Carno is visible, as is part of the timber bridge over the Severn, scene of the 1868 tragedy.

WIMM

'Manor' No. 7810 *Draycott Manor* lifts the nine coach 9.45 a.m. Whitchurch-Aberystwyth train effortlessly away from Carno, on a rising 1 in 149 gradient, on 16 April 1960. *Ifor Higgon*

and painted in as large figures as practiable [sic] ... and fixed ... on each side of the railway'.[13] No examples of these items of lineside furniture remain; the earliest known survivor is the wooden Cambrian Railways boundary post with the initials 'C R' recovered from Newtown and now in the care of the Cambrian Railways Society, Oswestry. This example could well date from the mid-1860s.

The track formation itself was to be 18ft wide through the cuttings and 'should the excavation be in excess of the embankments then the embankments shall be made continuously to a width of 29ft at the formation level till such overplus is absorbed.'[14] This did not occur frequently for the excavated material was barely enough for the single line of road and the yield from the great cutting at Talerddig, because of its quality, was more useful for constructing the many bridges en route to Machynlleth than as infill. Later, the permanent station buildings were also built of Talerddig stone.

At the outset, the permanent way throughout was to consist of flat-bottomed rails, nominally of 22ft lengths, laid onto sleepers of good sound larch 'or other timber of approved quality not less than eight feet ten inches long, half round, nine inches by four inches and a half.'[15] Each 22ft length of rail was to be supported by eight sleepers which had to be 'faced or grooved with a machine, half an inch deep and six inches wide to receive the rails.'[16] The fastenings for securing the rails to the sleepers were five and a half inch 'dogs' or spikes, six being used to each sleeper. The weight of the rail was 65 to 70 pounds per yard, according to the gradient or 'as the engineers may direct'.

Oswestry's No. 3202 leans through a reverse curve near Commins Coch with the 1.50 p.m. Class 'K' Machynlleth-Oswestry Freight, assisted in the rear by 2-6-2T No. 5541. Despite slight variations of the departure time over the years, this train was nearly always referred to as the '2 o'clock Goods'. 12.4.58.   *Ifor Higgon*

By 1860, the engineers did indeed direct otherwise for, in a report to the Directors on 20 August they stated that;

> The nature of the gradients between Talerddig and Machynlleth, requiring a heavier permanent way than the portion between the Llanidloes & Newtown Railway Junction and Talerddig, the section of rail for that part of your railway has been changed, and the double-headed rail with cast-iron chairs adopted instead of the flat-bottomed rail used between Caersws and Talerddig.[17]

The track on this latter section remained in situ for around twelve years, until relaid with double-headed steel rails from Dowlais during the 1871-2 relaying programme.

The specification stipulated that the materials were to be neatly stacked at the various sites before construction commenced, while one of the clauses called for the rail fastenings, the dog-spikes, to be stored 'in such a manner as to prevent their being injured by rain or damp';[18] rather a strange stipulation for any ironwork destined for use at open locations in the uplands of Montgomeryshire. The ballast specified was of two varieties although, unlike the rails, it was not suggested that one was more suitable for the grades between Talerddig and Machynlleth. It could consist of either 'good, clean rough gravel', of a quality to be approved by the engineers, or of broken stone, and in each case was to be trimmed to within one inch of the rail level and 20 inches above the formation level . . . 'the whole of the sleepers to be well and properly covered over by the ballast.'[19] The stone ballast had to be transported into the area, but the 'good, clean rough gravel' was available locally alongside the

CAMBRIAN RAILWAYS

SECTION OF LINE

— *Horizontal Scale 3 Miles to an Inch* —
— *Vertical Scale 100 Feet to an Inch* —

1889

Newtown and Machynlleth Gradient Profile.   *NLW*

route at Pontdolgoch, for example, and near the Dyrn, between Llanbrynmair and Commins Coch, where traces of a large ballast hole are still clearly visible on the 'down' side of the line. In later years, the Cambrian obtained ballast locally from Penstrowed Quarry and from the waste tips of the Van Lead Mines.

Up to 600 navvies are reported to have worked on the L&N alone; a greater number, probably a thousand or more would have been necessary on the more arduous Machynlleth contract. Precisely how this large body of workers was deployed, housed and fed does not appear to have been recorded in any detail but it is known that men were drafted from one contract to another as circumstances dictated.

Many who undertook the construction of the N&M were drawn from the locality, returning home at the week-end, a factor which may have contributed to fewer instances of drunkenness or misbehaviour being reported than were normally associated with railway construction, although some of the credit must be attributed to the example set by David Davies and his gangers. In an account of progress at Machynlleth in 1862, the *Shrewsbury Chronicle* praised,

> ....the head Ganger here (Mr D.Owen) for the energy which he displays, not only in the active prosecution of the works on the line, but in the moral supervision of his men, whose steady example goes far to restrain within decent bounds the natural vivacity of the sons of toil when at 'leisure' . . . [20]

The men, however, were not a peculiar breed of non-transgressing navvies, for sporadic instances of misbehaviour were reported in the press, and they are known to have enjoyed plentiful, if illicit, supplies of roast lamb and mutton pie to relieve their diet when away from home: the willingness of the local sheep to surrender their freedom by jumping the newly erected railway fences seems to have been a contributory factor. The Company, nevertheless, took precautions against possible trouble, by stipulating that 'suitable Policemen

Benjamin Piercy, 1827-1888

shall be engaged at the contractors' expense when ever it may be ordered by the engineers or Justices, for the protection of the property of residents along the line'.[21]

All workmen were paid in cash at least once a fortnight. Payment took place on Friday evenings and as near as possible to the site of the works, but 'not at any house where intoxicating liquors are sold'.[22] No Sunday work was sanctioned unless the engineers certified in writing that this was necessary for the safety of the works. Moral values were again upheld in another of the general conditions of the contract when it was decreed that 'If any person in the employment of the contractors, in any capacity whatsoever, conduct himself in an improper manner or behave with insolence to any Officer of the Company, he shall on proper representation of the circumstance to the contractors, be dismissed by them'.[23] David Davies, as a fervent Methodist, must have been happy to endorse such high-minded principles.

Construction commences

Bridgeheads of stores and plant were established along the N&M route whilst the contractors' main depot was located in the Caersws area, probably on the site later occupied by the Central Wales Division Civil Engineering Department. The first engine shed on the N&M may have been situated here or, possibly, at nearby Moat Lane. At the outset, all supplies reached the various sites by road. Not only was this slow and tedious but also expensive due to the toll charges. When news broke that a new toll-gate was to be built between Caersws and Carno, to capitalise on the large amount of railway material expected to pass that way, David Davies immediately took counter-measures and mobilised his workforce. The men were sheltering from heavy rain at the time but they responded instantly to the challenge and set off to collect extra sleepers so that, before the new toll-gate could be built, the rails stretched all the way to Carno. Construction of the first nine miles to Talerddig was encouraging. According to an announcement in the *Advertiser* for Wednesday, 30 November 1859, the Severn had been crossed and the line to Pontdolgoch, 'was opened for general traffic' on Monday the 21st. The line most certainly had not been approved by the Board of Trade but the Company seemed content with this rather ambiguous announcement which seemed to suggest, perhaps, that a goods service was in operation and if any intending passengers presented themselves, it was not likely that they would be turned away. The brief report ended on an optimistic note: 'We hope shortly to be in a position to announce the opening of another instalment of this line', but there is little doubt that the Company was ill-prepared at this time to operate any kind of regular service, for it

The single platform Pontdolgoch Station, looking toward Caersws. c. 1960. *Lens of Sutton*

possessed neither locomotives nor carriages of its own.

The accounts of the various contracts during this period are frequently intermingled and not easily unravelled, but they graphically illustrate the interchange of plant, men and machinery according to local needs. The only locomotives available for operation over the N&M, up to June 1861, would have been the engines of the Llanidloes line, but after that time completion of the track from Oswestry through to Llanidloes would have enabled the O&N engines also to come onto the section. Of these, the 0-4-2 *Montgomery* was most prominent and was probably assigned to the Machynlleth line throughout 1862.

The Board was confident of rapid progress from the outset, for it announced in the summer of 1859 that the terrain as far as Talerddig, at least, appeared to present few problems. Sadly, this optimism was ill-founded for the decision to open out the tunnel at Talerddig, combined with some atrocious weather during the autumn and winter, as well as difficulties regarding the purchase of certain lands, delayed matters considerably. It was to be August 1860 before the engineers reported to the Board that the railway would be open for public traffic as far as the Wynnstay House, Llanbrynmair, a distance of 12 miles, 'by the spring of next year,' and the whole line to its terminus at Machynlleth 'will, we are assured by the contractors, be ready for the summer traffic of 1862 . . .'[24]

Such optimism was not reflected by subsequent events. In addition to the problems of construction, which seemed to multiply at this time, the period 1858-60 proved significant for the contractors as it became increasingly apparent that the two men no longer agreed over general principles. Talerddig was a watershed in more than the topographical sense and as plans were prepared for development west of Machynlleth, it became obvious that the Davies & Savin partnership was entering a critical phase.

Carno (known as 'Sarn' during the construction period), looking in the 'down' direction, towards Talerddig. Note the low platforms and the very basic accommodation on the 'up' side. c. 1960.

Lens of Sutton

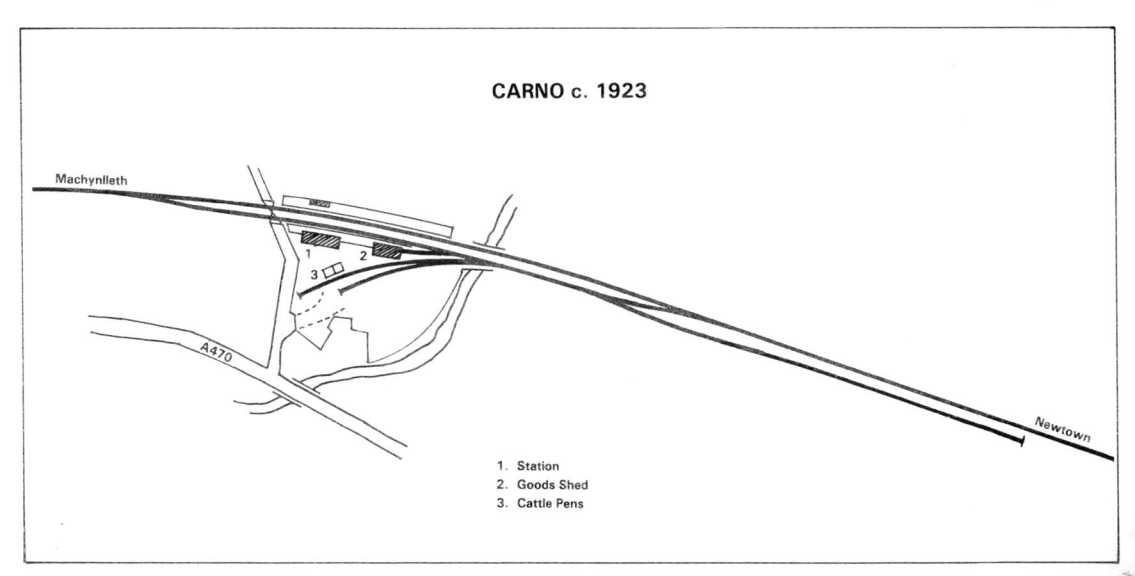

CARNO c. 1923

1. Station
2. Goods Shed
3. Cattle Pens

The parting of Davies & Savin

The climax came when the Machynlleth Company, led by David Howell and supported by David Davies, announced a scheme on 1 November 1860, for the Machynlleth, Aberystwyth and Towyn Railway (MA&TR). This extension of the N&M, always one of the Machynlleth Company's ambitions, had had to wait until the initial objective of a line through Talerddig was achieved; its principal aim was to reach Aberystwyth as quickly as possible. Savin, however, favoured a rival scheme, promoted by the Aberystwyth & Welsh Coast Company, which was drawn more toward the distant *lorelei* of Porthdinllaen, although there were to be branches to Machynlleth, Dolgellau and Caernarfon. Rather surprisingly, David Howell appears to have been involved with this rival scheme also, in partnership with his brother Abraham, as Solicitor to the Oswestry & Newtown.

Although the rock at Talerddig had yet to be breached, Savin, in his own mind at least, was already planning his way along the coast. In addition to supporting the more ambitious of the two schemes, he proposed a series of railway-owned hotels along the route which were to offer combined hotel and rail tickets in an early package scheme. This idea failed dismally at the time although it has since been applied successfully elsewhere. Savin's ambitions seemed boundless during this period for he also envisaged the transformation of vast tracts of the Dyfi estuary, near Ynyslas, into market gardens, producing fresh vegetables and fruit for his hotels and for transportation to England.[25]

The more cautious Davies, unhappy with Savin's grandiose and apparently limitless ambitions, was not prepared to jeopardise his hard-earned capital in what he regarded as a series of reckless ventures, and matters came to a head when the matter of bridging the Dyfi at Ynyslas was raised. Both the MA&TR and the A&WCR schemes of 1861 called for a bridge at this location, but this was initially of secondary importance to the MA&TR, whose principal objective was to carry the line directly to Aberystwyth. The A&WCR, on the other hand, saw the crossing of the river at Ynyslas as central to their whole scheme. Suddenly the question of the bridge and the location of the railway in the Aberdyfi/Ynyslas area became a highly contentious issue. Objections were raised by nautical and other interests along the Dyfi and the controversy raged for several years. The debate was not resolved until the A&WCR finally sought to abandon the idea of a bridge in 1865, but even that proposal also met with resistance!

The real significance of the bridge, perhaps, is that it became the main instrument of dissolution of the Davies-Savin partnership. During the Parliamentary debate on the A&WCR's Bill in

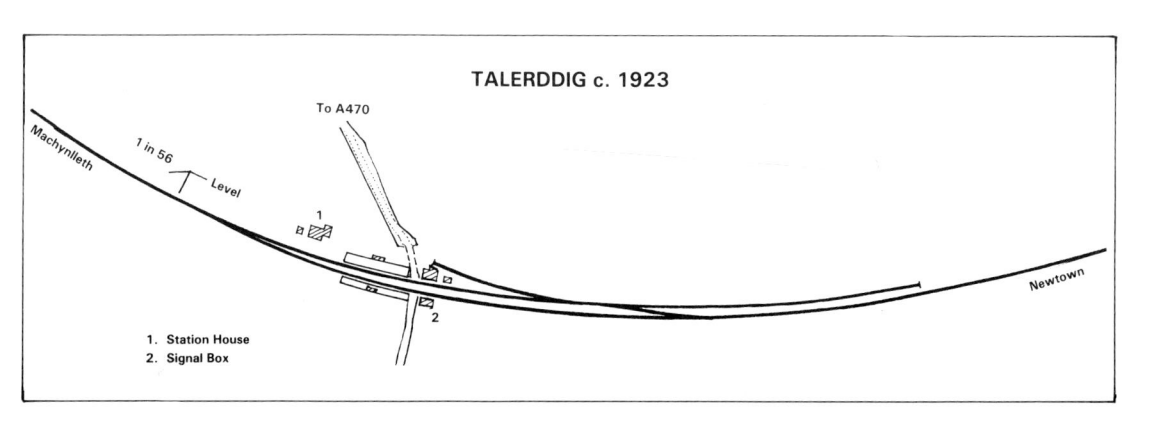

TALERDDIG c. 1923

1. Station House
2. Signal Box

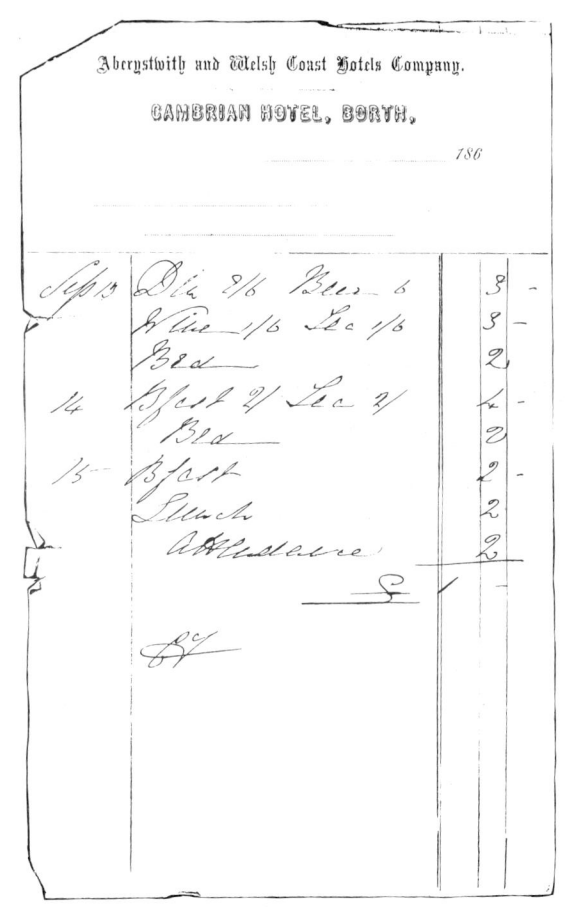

An interesting early bill from the Aberystwyth & Welsh Coast Company's Cambrian Hotel at Borth. Two night's accommodation with ''attendance'' for 20 shillings, provide a good illustration of the strength of the pound during the 1860s. Sadly, the client's name and the date were omitted. *PRO*

Fireman J. B. Pugh picks up a token for Dovey Junction near Machynlleth West Box, the border of former Davies & Savin territories. The broken white line represents the most tangible reminder, in recent times, of the disregarded N&M and A&WCR junction. *GBJ*

1865, David Davies stated, in typically forthright manner;

> I did not see the good of the bridge at all and dissolved the partnership in consequence.[26]

Whether this was indeed the case, or whether Davies merely used the bridge as the final excuse to rid himself of Savin and the risky pace with which he prosecuted his schemes may possibly never be known, but there is little doubt that David Davies was anxious to terminate the arrangement. Savin's tendancy to start new schemes before the initial objectives of current ventures had been achieved placed great stress not only upon the partnership but also on his personal finances, a factor which eventually contributed to his downfall.

Davies dissolved the partnership on 29th October, 1860, but the N&M Company was not formally informed until a document was drawn up on 30 January 1861.[27] In the opinion of many at that time, Davies got the poorer bargain by electing to complete the Machynlleth line, whilst Savin, in partnership with his brother John, and supported by those happy to abandon Davies and the N&M, chose to construct the 'easier' A&WCR. A Heads of Agreement was signed on 9 February and David Howell withdrew simultaneously from the Welsh Coast scheme to concentrate on N&M affairs. Thus the end-on junction at Machynlleth, besides signifying the boundary between the N&M and the A&WCR, also became a point of demarcation between the Davies and Savin empires.

Meanwhile, renewed progress on the Oswestry & Newtown had reached a stage between Welshpool and Abermule when the dissolution caused Davies to withdraw from that venture, leaving Thomas Savin to complete the O&N contract in a new partnership with his brother-in-law, John Ward of Whittington.

On 26 August 1861, the N&M engineers reported to the Board that the first nine miles would not be ready for a further eight weeks and on 21 September, the *Advertiser* despatched a correspondent to report on progress.[28] Although he was able to travel as far as Llanbrynmair, only the initial section to Talerddig was achieved in a carriage drawn by 'the ballast engine'. At the summit, a change of 'train' was necessary as work at the cutting was not complete and, after a short walk, the final section down the bank was covered in an open wagon powered by gravity! The 'ballast engine' and carriage would have been Llanidloes or Oswestry rolling stock as Davies's own ballast engine did not appear until mid-October; the N&M locomotives arrived during December and the first N&M carriage was probably not delivered until the following January.

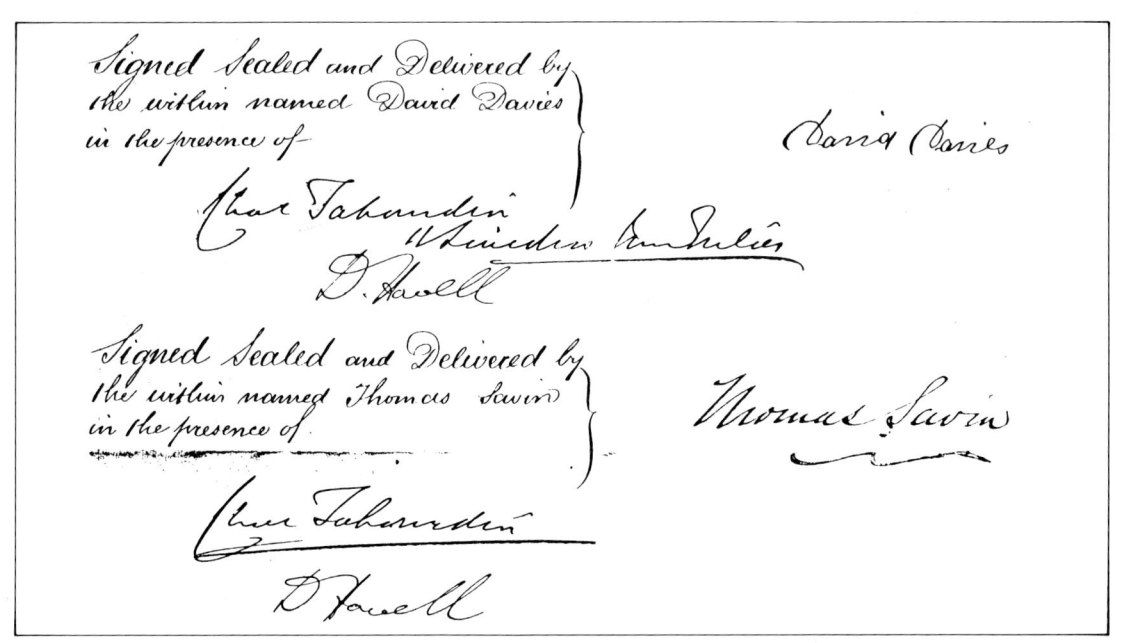

The signatories of the Heads of Agreement dissolving the Davies & Savin partnership, dated 9 February 1861.
WIMM

Piercy's most able lieutenant throughout the contract was George Owen, whose sphere later encompassed all the Cambrian territory. Owen surveyed the levels of the line through Talerddig whilst the opening up of the cutting itself has been credited to David Evans, one of the most trustworthy of the young men of Llandinam. Although David Evans did, indeed, work at Talerddig, another ganger, David Hughes of Caernarfon, must take credit for the initial excavation at the 'big cutting', as it was often referred to during construction. It is recorded that Hughes started work at Talerddig as early as 4 June 1859, less than four months after construction commenced at Caersws Bridge and he worked at the big rock until 26 February 1861, at which date David Evans is recorded as commencing at Talerddig.

At various times, between 200-300 men worked at this site alone and, at the time of its excavation, the remarkable 115ft high cutting was the deepest in the world. Measured by today's standards it is possible to underrate the task of cutting through solid rock using only primitive equipment and explosives, and to dismiss the Llandinam men's achievements too readily.

Though the rock presented the most obvious challenge at Talerddig, it was by no means the only obstacle. Before the cutting itself could be tackled, the boggy, eastern approach created by the little river Carno also presented problems. Davies' solution was bold and effective; he diverted the infant Carno, admittedly not much more than a stream at that point, to flow due west to join the Dyfi on its way into Cardigan Bay,

Two rather 'winded' 4-6-0's Nos. 75026 and 7823 *Hook Norton Manor,* breast the summit at Talerddig with a heavily laden Cambrian Coast Express on 9.6.1962. Some measure of the scale of the cutting may be had by comparing the height of the rock and the train in the distance.
Ifor Higgon

Pioneer 'Manor' No. 7800 *Torquay Manor* prepares to leave Talerddig with the 8.20 a.m. Oswestry-Aberystwyth train on 2.9.1961.

Ifor Higgon

rather than its previous easterly course to the Severn and the Bristol Channel. An entry in one of the account books reads;

> 23 February 1860, Parry and Pritchard, Settled for river diversion, Talerddig, . . . £10.[29]

Whoever Messrs Parry and Pritchard were is no longer known but their efforts proved successful for the bog around Talerddig remains most effectively drained, over a century and a quarter later, representing a sound return on the modest sum invested.

A small amount of gold was reputedly found at Talerddig, but it is more likely that the stone quarried was far more useful and more immediately profitable than any small quantities of rare yellow metal which may, or may not, have been found. Immediately to the west of the cutting itself, the railway shares a narrow defile with the main A470 road and the turbulent Afon Iaen, sometimes referred to as the Wynnstay. At this point, the railway had to be carried over the Iaen for a distance of some 150 yards; the 12ft wide 'big culvert' is not immediately apparent but it still performs the function for which it was constructed over a century and a quarter ago. Just beyond, the line crosses the A470 by means of a 60ft high bridge known to legions of Cambrian men as Pont Bell, (Bell's Bridge). It was probably named after one of David Davies's masons, George Bell, but the full significance of the name is no longer apparent.[30]

The next few miles down to the Dyfi at Cemmes Road called for further heavy engineering and the stone obtained locally was of inestimable value to the contractor; moreover, it was quickly and economically transported down the line as the easier sections were completed. Davies had predicted the arrival of the first engine at Machynlleth by 1 May 1862, a promise which was eventually kept, but only with great difficulty. The main problem occurred when one of the bridges at Commins Coch collapsed a few days before the engine was due to travel through. The vast

'Duke' No. 3259 *Merlin* and former 'Earl' Class No. 3213 *Earl of Powis* (name allotted but never carried), attack the final 1 in 56 to the summit at Talerddig with the 10.25 a.m. SO Aberystwyth to Birkenhead and Crewe train, on 6 August 1938. One of the Big Culvert's entrances can just be discerned amongst the vegetation in the right foreground; it extends beneath the line, emerging approximately opposite the 7th carriage.

Ifor Higgon

Bell's Bridge, Talerddig; surely one of the most familiar photographic locations on the GWR. 'Earl' No. 3204, formerly *Earl of Dartmouth*, is glad of assistance from 0-6-0 No. 892 at the rear of the 2 p.m. Machynlleth-Oswestry Goods, on the most difficult part of the climb. The extra width of the bridge, for the expansion which never materialised, as well as the track later raised to parapet height, are clearly seen from this angle. 24 April 1939.

Ifor Higgon

majority of the bridges have given exemplary service over the years; only the one at Glyntwymyn (sometimes referred to as 'the Glyn'), caused concern during construction. Initially, most bridges were temporary, wooden structures, in order to make the fullest possible use of the completed sections of track for transporting raw materials to site; they were built quickly and usually alongside the permanent structure. To minimise costs they were often not at the same height as the permanent rails on the embankments either side, which meant that they were approached from either direction by descending an incline from the permanent formation. Such was the case at the Glyntwymyn bridge, to the west of Commins Coch, which collapsed when Driver Henry Clough drove *Llandinam* and wagon loads of sleepers on to the temporary structure at too great a speed. This occurred on 25 April 1862, just six days before the engine was due to travel through to Machynlleth.[31]

With an essential bridge destroyed, his seven-month-old locomotive in the river and its driver killed, a lesser man than David Davies would have accepted that the pledge could no longer be honoured, but if David Howell's fortitude had kept the scheme intact during its difficult course through Parliament, it was now David Davies's opportunity to prove his own mettle in more practical terms. Such was Davies's personal example and rapport with the men that two hundred of his workers were sufficiently inspired to drag the little *Llandinam* out of the river the following day. After examination, it was discovered that the damage to bridge and locomotive was reparable; with renewed determination and

Glyntwymyn Bridge. A clear illustration of the method of carrying the embankment directly across single-arched 'culverts' on the Talerddig-Cemmes Road section. The incline down to the first, temporary, bridge at this point is indicated by the boundary fence. English Electric Type 3 No. D6984 on a Pwllheli-Paddington Express. 9.7.1966.

Ifor Higgon

LLANBRYNMAIR c. 1923

← To Machynlleth
A470

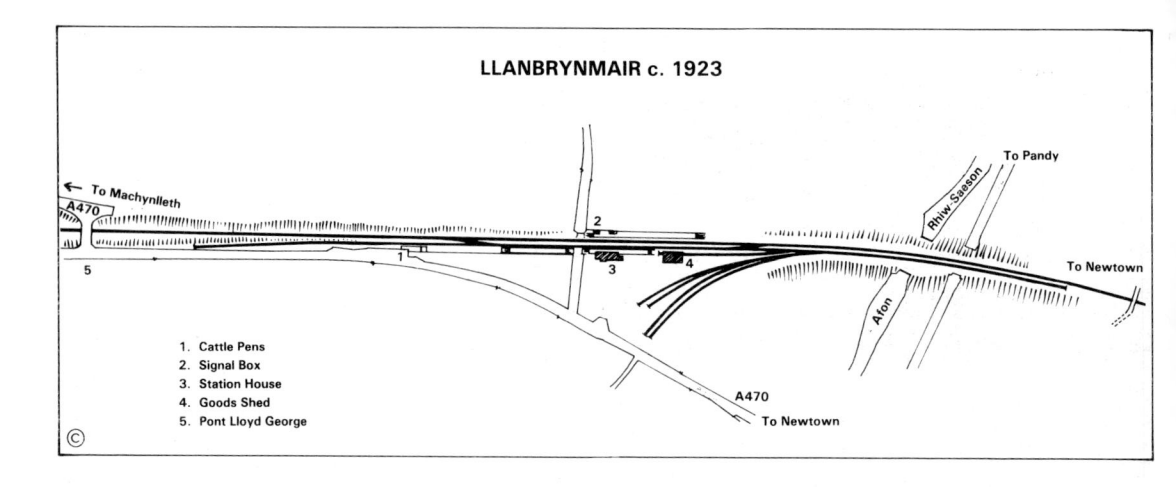

To Pandy
Rhiw Saeson
Afon
To Newtown
A470
To Newtown

1. Cattle Pens
2. Signal Box
3. Station House
4. Goods Shed
5. Pont Lloyd George

considerable physical effort, the promise was kept and Manning Wardle's *Llandinam* proved to be the very first engine to steam into Machynlleth, as predicted, on 1 May 1862.[32]

Work in the Machynlleth area had started a year previously in June 1861 at Craig-y-bwch, a rocky promontory about half a mile to the east of what later became the site of the station.[33] The cliff here had to be cut back to enable the line to squeeze between the rocky cutting and the Dyfi. Being located near the town, this activity caused great excitement and curiosity and it became quite fashionable to take a stroll on a summer's evening to view the works and inspect daily progress. Work at the station site commenced in a field called Cae Ty'r Bugail, (The field of the shepherd's house), colloquially known as Cae Tatws, (The potato field), about a week after that at Craig-y-bwch. The station site was the province of ganger David Owen, who was also responsible for making the ceremonial wheel-barrow used during the ceremony of cutting the first sod. The work required here was again of heroic proportions, for a considerable part of the rocky mountainside was removed to create space for the station and yards. The advantages of such a scheme were two-fold, for the engineers created a firm and broad shelf, well above the Dyfi's flood plain, and the spoil produced was invaluable both for building the embankment down the valley toward the coast and for providing material for constructing the engine and goods sheds, platforms and wharves.

As soon as work was underway at the western end of the line, Davies brought raw material in by sea through Aberdyfi, thereby advancing the work on two fronts. Rails from the Aberdare Iron Company arrived from Cardiff Docks; some came through Newport. Points, crossings, chairs, wedges, bolts and a variety of other railfixings came from Darlington, via Middlesborough. Sleepers came direct from the Baltic and all manner of tools, blasting powder and smaller artefacts also arrived by sea.

In his evocative account of the demise of coastal shipping at Aberdyfi,[34] D.W. Morgan refers to the coming of the railway as 'the enemy ashore', and there were undoubtedly many in the area who were not enchanted by the prospect of progress in the form of the steam locomotive. Yet, if the railway appeared to drive the final nail into the shipping trade's coffin, the Dyfi river boats seized the extra business eagerly, for all the materials which came by sea were transhipped at Aberdyfi into the smaller river sloops and 'flats' which discharged finally at the quays of Morben or Derwenlas. From Cei Ward and Cei Ellis, rails, sleepers and other heavy materials were hauled

Driver J. Ll. Pugh accelerates 4-6-0 No. 7811 *Dunley Manor* through Cemmes Road with the 'up' Cambrian Coast Express on 6.1.1956.

GBJ

Cemmes Road, looking west, showing the awkward connection between the mainline and the Mawddwy Railway, on the right. c. 1930.

M. M. Lloyd Collection

laboriously to the required sites; at Machynlleth station yard perhaps, or Abergwydol cutting; Gwastadcoed station, (later named Cemmes Road), Commins Coch or the various sites *en route* to Talerddig.

The old bills and receipts at the National Library of Wales make fascinating reading and together with David Davies's account books, provide rare detail relating to the construction of the line. It was Davies's policy to support local tradesmen whenever he could and as much material as posible was purchased in the area where the work took place. Candles, oats and beans; hay, oil and nails; all are itemised in precise detail, and priced to the final half-penny. This, after all, was an era when ha'pennies and farthings had some value and were not dismissed lightly. Not only did these local supplies help to keep costs to a minimum, but they engendered goodwill and created, albeit in a modest way, a degree of the prosperity expected with the coming of the railway.

The most prominent local supplier was the Machynlleth firm of Jones & Griffiths, who had timber yards at Derwenlas, Aberdyfi, Tre'r ddol and Ynyslas. They served as agents for importing many of the essentials, including the rails. In October 1861, for example, there is a reference in one bill to the schooner *Hope*, (Master, John Jenkins of Aberystwyth), which entered Aberdyfi with a cargo of 417 iron rails from Newport. On 7 October some of this cargo was transhipped into the sloop *Caradock* and the 'flat', *William*. Two days later, on the 9th, the remainder of the cargo was loaded onto the *Jenny, Blue Vein* and the *Caradock*, again, which had obviously enjoyed a quick turn-around up river. Within days another schooner, the *Charlotte Ann* (Capt. Richard Felix) of Aberdovey, discharged;

> on the beach at Aberdovey, in proper order:- 413 rails 24ft.0ins long; 1 rail 23ft.9ins long; 99 rails 21ft.0ins long; and 3 rails 18ft.0ins long.[35]

A bill dated 15 October mentions Capt Robert Roberts of the schooner *Ann*, of Barmouth, which entered Aberdyfi with 343 iron rails from Cardiff and another bill, under date of 21 October refers to a 'freight of rails' from Cardiff to Aberdyfi in the schooner *Capricorn* (Capt. John Hughes).[36]

John Harris, Iron Founder, of the Hope Town Foundry, Darlington, supplied many of the permanent way fixings for the Machynlleth - Talerddig section. These are interestingly itemised in a series of notes attached to one bill showing that;

> Walter Jones took on board the boat *Jenny*, from the

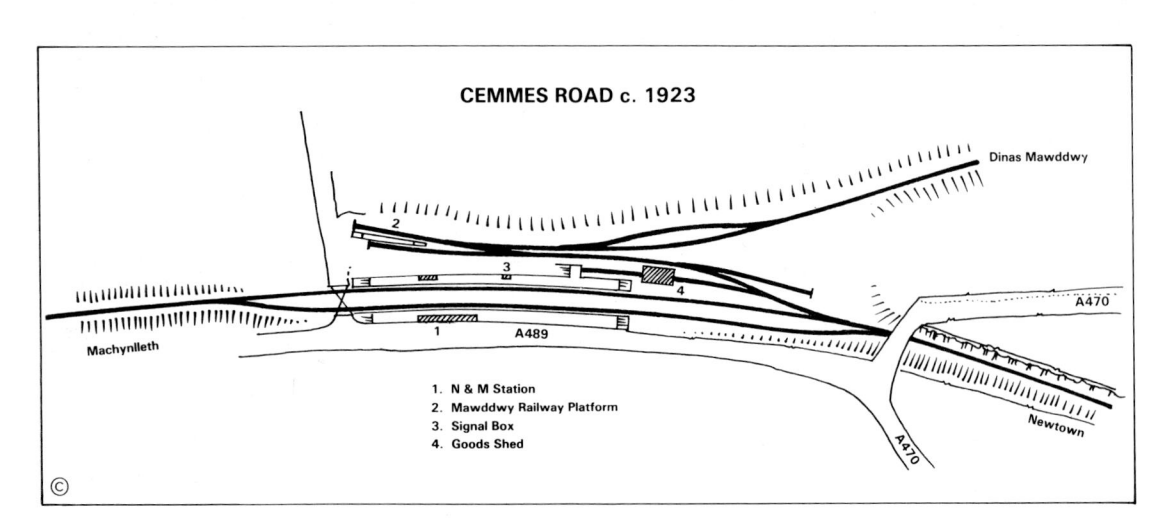

CEMMES ROAD c. 1923

1. N & M Station
2. Mawddwy Railway Platform
3. Signal Box
4. Goods Shed

schooner *Prince of Wales,* 22 casks of railway wedges and 22 railway chairs, on the 2nd of November 1861.[37]

Some further transhipments which took place around this time were listed by William Lloyd of Aberdyfi:

> Nov 20 loaded the boat *Jenny*, (Walter Jones) with 1300 railway chairs, 57 bags of Boults [sic] Nov 21st. loaded the *Patriot*, (David Davies) with 1200 chairs, Nov 21 loaded the boat *Britannia* (Richard Jones) with 800 chairs, Nov 21 loaded the 'flat' *William* (David Jones) with 2,100 chairs, Nov 29 loaded the boat *Jenny* (Walter Jones) with 2,043 chairs. Signed, William Lloyd, Agent, Aberdyfi.[38]

Many of these smaller items did not come ashore, but were transferred directly into the river boats.

Railway construction is normally thought of as a predominantly male occupation but, rather surprisingly perhaps, the N&M received some

Three Machynlleth Private-owner coal wagons. The firms of Pugh and Lumley remained in business until the 1950s; little is known of Edward Davies, other than the building date of his wagon No. 3, which was December, 1888.

M. M. Lloyd

essential supplies from a lady merchant also. Catherine Morgan, of Machynlleth, was the executrix of the late Hugh Morgan from 30 September 1861; she continued the service offered by her late husband and supplied David Davies with considerable quantities of a variety of materials and implements: a bill dated 18 December 1861 amounted to £619.3.4 and by 13 January 1862, another bill for a further £361.6.1 had been accumulated.

It would seem that by 1861, the unofficial goods service had been extended beyond Caersws to Carno, and the first truck-load of coal was taken through Talerddig and delivered to the *Wynnstay Arms* at Llanbrynmair, during the first week of December, 1861. Although this demonstrated that wagons, at least, could negotiate the rocky defile, the contractor was not then anxious to operate a regular service over the section as this would have impeded the removal of stone to the bridges near Commins Coch and Cemmes Road. By June 1862, however, sufficient rock had been extracted to allow the goods service to operate through to Llanbrynmair. The *Shrewsbury Chronicle* reported that it extended 'throughout the entire line' at this time, although the *Advertiser* was more cautious, and did not carry advertisements to this effect until the end of that year. The ever-optimistic *Chronicle*, even as early as October, had reported, 'The line is expected to be opened in the course of this month . . . Notices have been given to the Board of Trade and an Inspector will be down in the course of a few days . . .'[39]

The optimism of several press accounts during the final year of construction probably did no more than reflect David Davies's own projections and aspirations at that time: he was particularly anxious to complete the contract, for his attention was already being drawn toward the Pembroke & Tenby and the new Manchester & Milford schemes.

Early Great Western involvement

Whilst construction was proceeding apace, the piecemeal development of the railway system in Montgomeryshire had created a degree of distrust amongst the individual companies, as each sought to protect its own particular interests. In 1861, the N&M attempted to exploit its position as a link line to the coast by promoting a Bill to amalgamate with the O&N and L&N but this proved somewhat premature and the Bill was withdrawn. The Oswestry and the Llanidloes lines chose instead to liaise more closely with the London & North Western Railway; the publication of an integrated time-table, under a joint heading, emerged as a tangible indication of this association.

These moves were not appreciated by the N&M, which was also omitted from further talks on working arrangements, and the proposals proved particularly abhorrent to David Davies who opposed any collaboration with Euston. The N&M then turned toward Paddington for support and, with the Great Western ever alert to the possibility of extending its empire, an agreement was quickly reached that the GWR would work the line for 40% of the gross earnings. N&M shareholders were to be guaranteed an annual dividend of 5%. Heads of Contract and Agreement were drawn up and exchanged finally on 8 August 1861 although the original draft, dated 20 July called for the gross earnings to be divided on a 50/50 basis.

The documents were signed on behalf of the N&M by Earl Vane (Chairman), Sir Watkin Williams Wynn, R. D. Pryce and John Foulkes (Directors), and David Howell (Secretary); the signatories on behalf of the Great Western were Lord Shelbourne, as Chairman, Viscount Barrington, Spencer H. Walpole, J.W. Miles (Directors), and the formidable Charles A. Saunders (Secretary). It was agreed that the Great Western would 'take possession of and . . . work the line . . . for 10 years, to commence on the public opening of the line throughout to traffic'.[40]

The N&M declared the total cost of the line to

be £215,000, this sum to include £23,000 expenditure for stations, and valued the rolling stock at that date at £7000. When this agreement was announced, the Open Column of the *Advertiser* carried an anonymous letter warning of the difficulties which would arise as a result of the break of journey at Newtown and referring to the N&M as the worst-managed railway in the course of formation. The Board, however, confident of its new ally, took little heed of this outburst and promptly put the proposals to the shareholders at a special meeting on 31 August 1861. In marked contrast, the GWR appeared reluctant to proceed with the arrangement, despite clause 17 of the Agreement which stated that they were 'to use every reasonable and proper effort to obtain the sanction of the Shareholders of both Companies . . . at the earliest possible moment'.[41]

The Great Western continually failed to place the proposals before their own shareholders and over a year elapsed before they took any positive interest in the matter but, on 9 October 1862, it was deemed prudent to undertake an inspection of the line. This was carried out by;

> Mr Grierson, the talented Manager of the GWR . . . and other Gentlemen and Officials . . . They left Caersws about 2 o'clock in a carriage drawn by the *Countess Vane*, a new passenger engine, which took them as far as Sarn station (Carno), where the engine was changed and the *Talerddig* . . . was attached to the carriages. The latter took the party through to Machynlleth.[42]

Just four days afterwards, on 13 October a Board meeting was held at the Rectory House, Newtown, which referred to the agreement with the Great Western and moved that;

> . . . with a view to preserving present friendly relations with that Company, the following offer shall be made as regards the first year from the opening of the line . . . . Dividend on £150,000 to be at 4½%. Dividend on £50,000 to be 5%. The remaining £15,000 Capital provided for by the Heads of Agreement of 8 August 1861, to remain unproductive in consequence of the non-erection of permanent stations. At the end of the first year the dividend at 5% to become payable on the £215,000.

> A goods station to be built at Machynlleth in 2 months from the opening and an engine shed at the same place within 5 weeks of the opening.[43]

The N&M was obviously anxious to maintain Great Western goodwill and interest, particularly as construction difficulties which occurred during the period preceding the inspection would further delay the opening.

In addition to the rock-cuttings and embankments necessary on the Commins Coch-Cemmes Road section, four substantial river bridges were also required. One of these, the bridge at the Glyn, created a further problem for, in addition to difficulties with the temporary bridge at this point, a second major set-back occurred when the permanent arch collapsed during construction.

The method favoured by the engineers for bridging streams and rivers on the Talerddig-Commins Coch section, particularly where high embankments prevailed at the approach to the bridging point, was to construct a single arch culvert along the course of the river, as at Talerddig, and to carry the embankment directly across it. This appeared to offer several advantages, including comparative simplicity of construction, minimal maintenance and easy adaptation for possible doubling of the track at a later date. The method had worked well at several points west of Talerddig but on Wednesday 6 August 1862, at the Glyn;

> . . . the fall of what was intended to be the permanent structure took place . . . the brick arch giving way . . . by the weight of soil which had been placed upon it. The loss to the Contractor is estimated at about £500, besides the delay which it involves in the opening of the line . . . The vast quantity of lime which was used in the structure has been the death of thousands upon thousands of fish, and lots of salmon, sewing, [sic] and trout have been destroyed . . . . We understand that the re-construction of the bridge will shortly be commenced.[44]

The fact that so much of the lime was still active after the collapse suggests that the arch was placed under load before the mortar had cured; an indication, perhaps, of the desire to complete the

The P.W. Gang trundle a load of rails past the Machynlleth East Box, c. 1920.　　*J. P. Richards*

work as quickly as possible. Re-construction must have occupied all the hours of daylight during the ensuing weeks, for the completed bridge was ready for Mr Grierson's inspection of 9 October, and by the 15th of that same month Davies had sufficient confidence in the whole of the works to organise a pleasure trip for the 'good folk' of Llandinam to Machynlleth, where,

> after enjoying the beauty of the picturesque scenes along the route, . . . the company sat down to Tea at the Station-house where tables, well loaded with provisions, were temporarily put up for their entertainment. Mr Davies [sic] superintended this department and was most kind and attentive to all.[45]

This was not the only occasion for passengers to be carried to Machynlleth before the line had been approved by the Board of Trade, for the same report concludes that the Llandinamites returned home 'on the arrival of an excursion train from Newtown, conveying the Earl and Countess Vane home from the Yeomanry meeting'. Although these excursions were probably the first to venture as far as Machynlleth, they were not the first through Talerddig, for David Davies had sanctioned a Temperance Excursion from Oswestry and Newtown 'to the celebrated cutting of Talerddig and adjoining embankments at Llanbrynmair and Commins Coch', for 25 September 1862. The line may not have had the approval of the Board of Trade, but the local press were happy to advertise the excursion. It was to leave Oswestry at 10.10 a.m. (return fare 2/6), Newtown at 11.32 a.m. (1/- return), and at Moat Lane a connecting excursion from Llanidloes, (dep.11:10, fare 1/3), was to join it for the final haul over Talerddig.

> When the excursion arrived at Newtown it was found that the train, with 2 or 3 carriages added, was well-filled. In anticipation of the event, 5 carriages

No. 9017 had a knack of being around for the camera; it hauled the last GW train to leave Oswestry in 1947 and was much in evidence during the final steam years. On 1.9.1956, it worked the 7.35 a.m. Aberystwyth-Whitchurch service and judging by the excess steam at the front end, may have had to stop at Commins Coch Halt, just visible in the distance, which was normally a conditional stop.

Ifor Higgon

had been forwarded to Newtown station, which had been well filled by the time the excursion arrived . . . . .and there were hundreds on the platform for whom no accommodation was provided . . . Through the exertions of Mr Cuckson, Mr Baird and the officials of the Company, the dilemma was solved by ramming and jamming the excursionists right on the back of each other.'[46]

At Moat Lane, a re-arrangement of the train became necessary as the Llanidloes portion was added, before it was 'handed-over' by Mr Cuckson to Mr Richards, the Superintendent of the Machynlleth line. When this was achieved, 'the whistle blew and the train proceeded and . . . as may be expected, attracting from their dwellings hundreds to whom a well-freighted train was a perfect novelty.'[47]

De-training at Commins Coch must have presented the excursionists with another novel experience, due to the lack of a proper platform at that spot. They had been warned in the advertisements to provide their own refreshments, but on alighting were offered cups of tea for a penny, a bun for a half-penny or soda-water at two pence a bottle. Some dispersed to climb Commins Hill whilst others were content to play nearby or visit the site of the Glyn Bridge. The newspaper accounts make no reference to the railway arrangements, but it is probable that the empty train would have proceeded to Machynlleth where the engines could have been serviced and turned on the newly set-up turntable, completed only days previously. The locomotives for the return working, named as the *Montgomery* and *Talerddig*, were reported as pulling away 'gloriously' from Commins Coch towards

45

Talerddig, where a short delay occurred as men were still working and some time was taken removing obstacles from the line.

> This having been got through and the locomotive [sic] changed, the train was driven away at a rattling pace . . . .without mishap or casualty of any description.[48]

There were, doubtless, other occasions when passengers were conveyed before the opening, particularly over the various stages east of Talerddig which had seen goods traffic since 1859. Carno served as a rail-head from June 1862 but might well have fulfilled this role up to a year earlier and a Newtown & Machynlleth Railway Traffic Statement endorses the opening of the line for goods as far as Llanbrynmair, certainly by March 1862.[49] Occasional loads were also worked to and from Machynlleth during the summer, over the temporary bridges, as it appears that each section of track was put to commercial use at the earliest opportunity. Confirmation is provided by David Kinsey, a Llandinam monumental mason and contemporary of David Davies, who noted in his diary, under date of 22 June 1862, the delivery of 'a truckload of Flags and slates from Machynlleth, by rail, the first load that ever came (by rail).'[50]

By late autumn, 1862, the Great Western showed further interest in the project as a result of Mr Grierson's visit and, at a Board Meeting held in Machynlleth on 28 October, correspondence was read from C.A. Saunders which outlined new and unacceptable conditions for working the line. It was immediately resolved that;

> . . . the terms on which the GW offer to work the railway temporarily be declined . . . . .The communication to be sent to the GW Company is left to the discretion of the Chairman and Secretary . . .[51]

The new terms are not defined but, although the disappointment must have been acute, the Company then knew that it stood alone and would have to make fresh arrangements: the Secretary was instructed to give notice to the Board of Trade to secure the Government Inspection of the line 'as soon as the Contractor is ready.'[52]

The inspection was arranged within weeks, although it required two visits, the first being a part inspection only as Capt. H.W. Tyler of the

An interesting N&M way bill, showing the charge for transferring David Davies's earth wagons to Carmarthen, for work on the M&M line.

NLW

Royal Engineers had insufficient time to complete his scrutiny in one session. Reporting from Shrewsbury on 25 November, the day of the inspection, Capt. Tyler indicated that Caersws Junction was a single line junction only and he recommended a doubling of the line at this point. The only clue as to the station accommodation at the Junction is provided in the statement;

> A very good stage has been erected but could be improved by glazing around the exterior.[53]

The report described the works as 'heavy'; the steepest gradient was noted as 1 in 52.87 and the sharpest curve was of 10 chains radius. The recommendation of a 'check or guard' rail on a curve of 15 chains radius at 7 miles from Machynlleth, appears to apply to that part of the Commins Coch curve lying in the rock cutting immediately west of the A470 road bridge. A footbridge was recommended at the Chapel Crossing, Llanbrynmair and an indication that signalling was in its infancy, and not very prominent on the N&M, is found in the statement:

> The point signals, which are of good description, require to be altered so as to act in a reverse way to that in which they act at present . . . . . .A platform signal and conveniences are wanted at Machynlleth, and the latter at other stations also . . . temporary accommodation only is available at the stations and for the gatemen at the public road crossings . . . I understand that the points to the ballast sidings are not to be used at present. If they are used again.. signals and a signalman should be provided.[54]

The sidings mentioned were, presumably, at the Dyrn ballast hole, west of Llanbrynmair; the

Llanbrynmair station, looking toward Machynlleth. Note *l-r;* Token setting-down post; original short, low platform and the first permanent station building; 'down' platform extension beyond the level crossing; the abrupt down gradient emphasised by the bridge levels in the distance; original stone-faced 'up' platform, raised and extended in brick by the GW; signal box and small passenger shelter, typical of the early period. 30.4.1966.

GBJ

Pontdolgoch site would hardly be convenient for the works west of Talerddig and the other ballast sidings at this time, at Machynlleth, caused no concern in this respect. The only eye-witness account of the inspection is provided by the ever attentive *Advertiser*, which reported in its issue of 3 December 1862, that Capt. Tyler:

> . . . arrived at the Caersws Junction by the 11:44 a.m. train, where a train, consisting chiefly of two very powerful engines, about 80 tons weight, properly arranged for the occasion, was awaiting his arrival. The Inspector, accompanied by Capt. Pryce, Mr Howell, Mr Davies (the Contractor), Mr George Owen C.E., Mr Webb and others, then commenced his inspection, minutely examining every point and severely testing every bridge, from the Junction to the Glyn Bridge which, as it had been the scene of one or two accidents, was closely inspected and found in a most satisfactory condition. Capt. Tyler expressed himself highly satisfied with the works and especially with the permanent way, of which he highly approved. He suggested the alteration of the points at the junction with the Oswestry and Llanidloes line at Moat Lane, which will devolve upon that Company and some slight alteration in the working of the signals along the line, which will not involve more than a week's delay. As these alterations will necessitate his return, the official examination was not carried further than the point stated, but the Inspector was driven thence rapidly through to Machynlleth where he looked over the station arrangements and expressed himself fully satisfied. As he had to leave by the 5:20 p.m. train from Moat Lane, the train at Machynlleth was got into readiness and the entire distance, Machynlleth to Moat Lane, run over in the space of 40 minutes, the distance being 23 miles . . . .As soon as the alterations at the Junction have been carried out by the Llanidloes Company, Capt. Tyler will return and finish his examination of the line from the Glyn to Machynlleth. Meanwhile, as will be seen from an advertisement, the line is opened throughout for goods and mineral traffic; and before long, will be for passengers also.

An advertisement which duly appeared in the *Advertiser* for 10 December listed the intermediate stations as Caersws, Pontdolgoch, Carno, Llanbrynmair, and Cemmes Road; it was issued from the General Manager's Office, in Caersws at that time, during November 1862.

By the last day of the year, Capt. Tyler was able to report that the junction at Moat Lane had been doubled and the exterior of the Junction stage had been glazed. The check-rails had been added, as recommended, a footbridge constructed at Chapel Crossing for the benefit of youngsters attending the nearby British School[55] and more rock removed from the cutting of Talerddig. Capt. Tyler then drew attention to the many bridges, adding that 'they will have to be very carefully watched regarding settlement, especially the bridge at Cwmbychan.'[56]

He also recommended a 'bell and arm' communication between the passenger platforms at Machynlleth and the signalling outside the station,[57] as well as the removal of yet more rock from the cutting. Continuous brakes were recommended for the passenger carriages and the Company was also urged to 'establish the telegraph upon the line as soon as possible . . . This being done,' concluded Capt. Tyler, 'I am sure the line can be opened to the public with safety'.[58] It appears the fullest advantage was immediately taken of Capt. Tyler's verbal approval on the day of the inspection (30 December 1862), for even before his report was written, preparations were rapidly made for the first approved passenger service to commence the following day.[59] The last day of the year, traditionally a Market Day at Machynlleth, marked the beginning of a period of celebration which embraced a more formal Grand Opening and extended over the weekend, with some of the festive atmosphere being revived after the Sabbath, for the service trains on the following Monday, 5 January 1863 also arrived and departed to the accompaniment of the anvil guns.

Chapter 3: Notes & References

1. Hamer, D. Lord Davies Papers, NLW.
2. Llandinam Papers, NLW.
3. ibid.
4. ibid.
5. Gasquoine, C.P.
6. Specification for Works (1860): WIMM.
7. ibid.
8. OA 25.9.61.
9. Specification for Works (1860): WIMM.
10. RAIL 517/1 p.49.
11. Specification for Works (1860): WIMM.
12. ibid.
13. ibid.
14. ibid.
15. ibid.
16. ibid.
17. RAIL 517/1 p.128.
18. Specification for Works (1860): WIMM.
19. ibid.
20. SC 21.2.1862.
21. Specification for Works (1860): WIMM.
22. ibid.
23. ibid.
24. RAIL 517/1. p.103.
25. S&MT 29.8.1865.
26. OA 10.5.65.
27. Davies & Savin, Heads of Agreement (1861): WIMM.
28. OA 25.9.1861.
29. LDMP:NLW.
30. Bell's Bridge was strengthened by locating iron ribs beneath the arch in 1868 and later, in 1889, a 'false' arch was constructed below the original, which was showing signs of flattening at that time. RAIL 92/58. p.202.
31. OA 30.4.1862.
32. OA 7.5.1862.
33. LDMP:NLW.
34. Morgan, D.W. *Brief Glory* (1948) Brython Press.
35. LDMP:NLW.
36. ibid.
37. ibid.
38. ibid.
39. SC 3.10.1862.
40. Heads of Agreement N&M and GWR (1961): WIMM.
41. ibid.
42. OA 15.10.1862.
43. RAIL 517/1. p.163.
44. OA 13.8.1862.
45. OA 22.10.1862. A contemporary account in the *Shrewsbury Chronicle* indicates that Mrs Davies supervised the tea arrangements.
46. OA 1.10.1862.
47. ibid.
48. ibid.
49. LDMP:NLW.
50. Kinsey,D. (1838-93). Scrap-album/diary, NLW.
51. RAIL 517/1. p.167.
52. ibid.
53. PRO MT6/26/25.
54. ibid.
55. The British School was re-located lower down the valley in 1874.
56. Most of the N&M bridges were strengthened as a result of the inspections which followed the storm of February, 1868.
57. A platform hand-bell was rung at Machynlleth, on the approach of passenger trains, up to the early 1920s. Whether this was part of the 'bell and arm' recommendation is not known, nor indeed, what became of the bell itself (which could well have borne some interesting evidence of ownership), but from all accounts the warning was taken as a timely reminder by the local gentry to abandon the privacy of their carriages and make for the platforms.
58. PRO MT6/26/25.
59. Based on the evidence of the unofficial conveyance of passengers by goods train from and to Carno, from the summer of 1862, it would not be unreasonable to assume that passengers were also conveyed unofficially from Machynlleth when goods services were extended there during the autumn that year. It might thus be as appropriate to suggest that the conveyance of passengers was resumed on 31 December!
    ME 15.2.1916. *The Romance of Montgomeryshire's Railways*. Ald. David Hamer stated the railway was opened on the last day of 1862.
    ME 29.2.16. *Peeps into the past*. 'Old Reader' stated the last day of the year [1862] was a day of rejoicing for thousands of inhabitants of western Montgomeryshire owing to the opening of the railway between Machynlleth and Moat Lane.
    'On December 31, 1862 the town of Machynlleth was *en fete*', and a train left Machynlleth for Newtown on that day with 1500 passengers.

Chapter 4

The Grand Opening

Saturday, 3 January was the day chosen for the Grand Opening, despite some who felt that the following Monday would be more appropriate, as the Saturday was considered 'the day of preparation for holy rest and worship'.[1] This argument, however, did not impress the Directors; the enterprise had been subjected to too many delays since inception and the official opening was arranged for the first opportunity. Ways and means of operating the new railway were discussed at a meeting of the Board at *Plas*, Machynlleth, as late as Friday the 2nd, although, because of rapidly changing circumstances, the resolutions passed at this meeting were soon destined to become obsolete. It was decided that the GW matter would 'stand in abeyance until another Board meeting' and that David Davies would, in the meantime, 'carry on, on behalf of the Company, all such arrangements as may be needful and legal for the working of the railway.'[2] The maintenance of the railway for the first twelve months was to be undertaken by Mr Davies for the sum of £2000 and it was resolved that he be employed to build the stations, (excluded from the original contract), '. . . at the valuation of Mr Poundley and that he be instructed to furnish plans for the consideration of the Board, say to cost about £6000.'[3]

Within weeks, the Directors were compelled to reappraise these arrangements but, happily, such difficulties were not generally apparent at the time and did not interfere with the long-awaited celebrations.

Unaffected by such matters, the townsfolk had started that same Friday to decorate the streets with flags, banners and impressive floral arches, whilst a large body of navvies prepared the station approaches. As banners, slogans and mottoes played such a prominent role in the festivities it is regrettable that none appear to have survived as souvenirs of such a momentous day in the history of the little town.

NEWTOWN AND MACHYNLLETH RAILWAY.

STATIONS.	WEEK DAYS.			STATIONS.	WEEK DAYS.		
	1,2,3 a.m.	1&2 p.m.	1,2,3 p.m.		1,2,3 a.m.	1,2,3 a.m.	1,2,3 p.m.
Newtown	9 0	1 43	3 51	Aberystwith (coach) d.	0 30	11 0	..
Moat Lane Junc { arr.	9 25	1 53	4 3	Machynlleth......dep.	9 0	1 30	4 15
dep.	9 30	2 0	4 15	Cemmes Road	9 22	1 52	4 08
Caersws	9 25	2 5	4 20	Llanbrynmair	9 40	2 10	4 03
Pontdolgoch	9 45	2 15	4 26	Carno	10 0	2 30	5 12
Carno	10 0	2 30	4 35	Pontdolgoch	10 12	2 42	5 23
Llanbrynmair	10 24	2 54	4 53	Caersws	10 18	2 48	5 29
Cemmes Road	10 40	3 10	5 10	Moat Lane Junction	10 25	2 54	5 35
Machynlleth	11 0	9 30	5 30	Newtown	10 45	3 2	5 55
Aberystwith (coach) ar.	2 0	8 15	..				

The first Time Table, January 1863

DEMONSTRATIONS TO CELEBRATE THE
Opening of the Newtown and Machynlleth Railway
On SATURDAY, the 3rd day of JANUARY, 1863,
AT MACHYNLLETH.

PROGRAMME:—

At 8 o'clock a.m., a PROCESSION will be formed at the Town Hall, and proceed to the Railway Station in the following Order:—

The Band of the Machynlleth Rifle Corps	FLAGS AND BANNERS
The Machynlleth Volunteer Rifle Corps	The Machynlleth Second Friendly Society
FLAGS AND BANNERS	The Machynlleth Brass Band
The Machynlleth National School	FLAGS AND BANNERS
FLAGS AND BANNERS	The Chairman, Directors, and Officers of the Company
The Machynlleth First Friendly Society	FLAGS AND BANNERS
	Shareholders and well-wishers, four abreast

A TRAIN will be ready at the Station at Half-past 8 o'clock, a.m., to go to NEWTOWN and back.

RETURN TICKETS will be issued at the following Rates:—

First Class, 2s.   Second Class, 1s.   Third Class, 6d.

TIME TABLE.

TRAINS will run as under, and stop at the intermediate STATIONS:—

a.m.		p.m.	
Machynlleth - - dep. 8 30		Newtown - - - dep. 11 50	
Newtown - - - ar. 10 45		Machynlleth - - ar. 2 15	

Machynlleth dep. 5 45 p.m. in time for Trains to Llanidloes, Newtown, Welshpool, &c.

No Children will be admitted under the age of Twelve.

An hour will be allowed at Newtown. The Train will leave for Machynlleth at 11 50 precisely.

On the return of the Train to Machynlleth at 2 15, the proceedings will be opened

BY THE RIGHT HONOURABLE EARL VANE

After which the REV. GEORGE GRIFFITHS, Rector, will invoke the blessing of Almighty God upon the Undertaking. The Railway will then be formally Opened

BY THE RIGHT HONOURABLE COUNTESS VANE

The PROCESSION will afterwards reform in the same order, and proceed to the Town Hall, where a Cold Collation will be provided, at which EARL VANE will preside.

Collation Tickets at Three Shillings and Sixpence each, to be had at the Wynnstay Arms Hotel

ADAM EVANS, PRINTER, MACHYNLLETH.

The programme for the Grand Opening. The blue paper chosen by the local printer provided little contrast, making photography more difficult.

WIMM

Near the old Town Hall, located on the site of the present Castlereagh Memorial Clock,

> an arch was suspended with a number of banners bearing appropriate mottoes. At the junction of Penrallt Street with the Dolgelley Road another arch was erected, bearing on one side the words, 'Long life to the Earl and Countess, and success to the family of Plas, Machynlleth', and on the other, 'Long life to Sir Watkin and Lady Williams Wynn'. Another arch with appropriate motto was placed over the gateway to the station, while from the side of Penrallt Street, and from the Wynnstay Arms and Unicorn Hotels, strings of mottoes were suspended.[4]

When the Saturday morning finally dawned the townsfolk were up and about from an early hour, ready for the great day. The bells of the church rang out merrily and soon drew a response from the Band of the Fourth Montgomeryshire Volunteers who had appeared on the streets, helping to increase 'the sounds of merry-making which, by this time, early as it was, were becoming pretty general'.[5] Supporters, interested onlookers and the merely curious had travelled into town on foot or horseback, by trap, carriage or wagonette, to wish the venture well and to see the first train on its way. By 8.00 a.m. the streets were thronged with spectators and the official procession to the station was marshalled outside the Town Hall, ready for the great exodus to Newtown.

Down at the station, the final touches were put to the railway's preparations, under the guidance of Mr Richards, the Traffic Manager and Mr Hamer, Machynlleth's first Station-master. The Company, possessing a total of only four passenger carriages and a brake-van, was obliged to the Oswestry and Llanidloes Companies for the

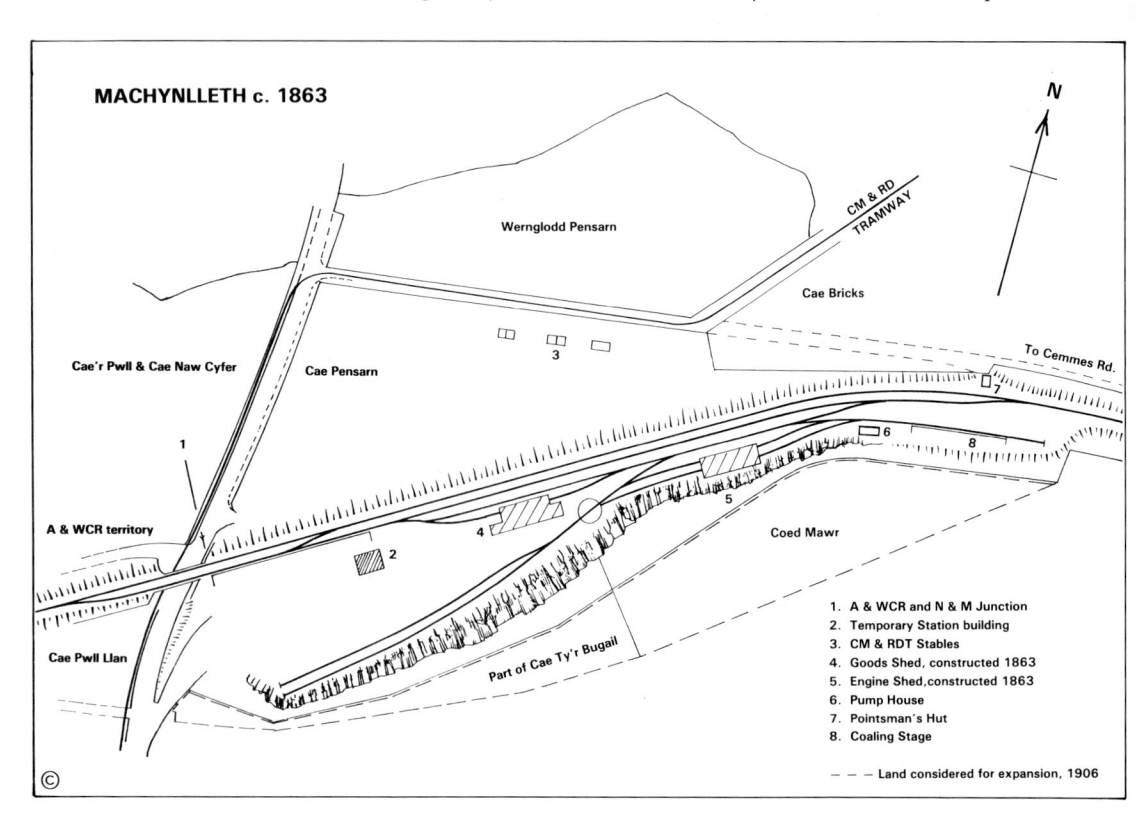

MACHYNLLETH c. 1863

1. A & WCR and N & M Junction
2. Temporary Station building
3. CM & RDT Stables
4. Goods Shed, constructed 1863
5. Engine Shed, constructed 1863
6. Pump House
7. Pointsman's Hut
8. Coaling Stage

- - - Land considered for expansion, 1906

The Opening Ceremony at Machynlleth—from a photograph by J. Owen, of Newtown.   ILN

loan of additional vehicles that day, which was just as well, for over 1500 passengers were booked on the inaugural train. A total of twenty-two carriages provided adequate accommodation for the excursionists to be seated 'comfortably', although this happy state could only have been achieved after much shunting, as the solitary platform (on what later became the 'down' side) would not have accommodated the whole train at once. This could account for the half hour delay at the start, for it was 9.00 a.m. before the Newtown & Machynlleth's only locomotives, the highly polished and gaily decorated *Countess Vane* and *Talerddig*, drew away for the first official assault on Talerddig Bank.

So the train sped on its way, 'sometimes slowly and sometimes quickly according to the nature of the incline'.[6] Progress up the final section of the bank, from Llanbrynmair to Talerddig, must have fallen sharply into the 'will we or won't we?' category for, even allowing for stops at each of the intermediate stations, arrival at Newtown, due at 10.45 a.m., did not occur until 'about noon'.[7] *En route,* the train passed under several arches, particularly in the Caersws area, including one at Moat Lane which bore a wheel-barrow with the motto 'The way to the gold fields.'

As it arrived at Newtown, the train was greeted by booming cannon, ringing bells, brass bands and cheering crowds, to which must be added the sight and sound of the young Marquis of Blandford[8] riding on the footplate of the leading engine and playing 'See the Conquering Hero Comes', on a *cornet-à-piston.*

The return train was timed to depart at 11.50 a.m., so the stay at Newtown was but brief, being barely adequate in fact to receive the speech of welcome. This was delivered by the Rector, the

53

Machynlleth Branch of the Associated Society of Locomotive Engineers & Firemen, January, 1924.
Top: Edmund Jones, O. B. James, I. Hughes, Emlyn Evans, Gomer Edwards, Evan J. Holt, Owen J. Davies, Will Jones (Towyn), D. Owen (Borth).
Middle: Charles Goodyear, Price Davies, Bob Pugh, Ernie Owen, Ted Cudworth, Ben Jarman, Ellis Owen (Talsarnau), John Evans (Rhydymain), R. Ingram, Ted Pugh, Evan Humphreys.
Seated: Henry Caffrey, Dick Jones (Pontdolgoch), J. Vaughan Owen, Hugh Humphreys, John Edmund Jones, Dick Thomas, Philip Lewis & son Glyn, Humphrey Evans, Bill Field, J. Graham.
Front lower: Richard Williams and Llew Roberts.
Photograph courtesy the late D. Vaughan Owen and Len Evans

Rev. John Edwards, who apologised that it was their intention 'to have made more demonstration than circumstances permitted, but it was only last night we were enabled to assemble . . .'[9] Earl Vane responded on behalf of the visitors as, briefly, did Mr Charles Wynn, M.P. for Montgomeryshire, the most recent member of the Board. Departure from Newtown was at 12.30 p.m., a most creditable achievement considering that several carriages had been added, to increase the total to thirty-six. There is also the probability that the locomotives were turned for the return journey, assuming that a suitable turntable was in operation in Newtown at this time.[10]

As the 4-wheel carriages of the period were approximately 25 ft long, the total length of the 36-carriage train would have been around 300 yards; or equal in length to fifteen GW 60ft. bogie coaches of the 1930 era. Little wonder, therefore, that during the celebrations later that day at Machynlleth, David Davies called it 'a monstrous train', adding;

> I do not think you would see any of the great companies running such a train. It is a considerable risk to run forty carriages, loaded as they were, and it is something to be able to say that all who were in them felt perfectly safe during the whole journey.[11]

However many vehicles were actually in the train, it must have been a most memorable journey for those on board and would have presented an unforgettable sight to the crowds who lined the route, as it laboured over the summit at Talerddig and quickened its pace through the cutting on its way down the bank, towards Llanbrynmair and the Dyfi valley.

On arrival at Machynlleth, the train was greeted with the firing of anvil-guns and the cheering of the crowds. The passengers, now numbering close on a thousand more than had embarked in the morning, spilled out onto the short, low platform; the carriages were shunted clear and the throng gathered around a temporary dais for the opening ceremony, performed by Countess Vane. Amongst those who spoke was Earl Vane, who introduced the proceedings, and the Rev. George Griffiths, the Rector, who invoked the blessing of Almighty God upon the undertaking. The opportunity was also taken by David Davies to present a silver spade to Countess Vane to mark the ceremony of cutting the first sod, some four years previously. On that occasion, Countess Vane had to use an iron spade but David Davies now made amends, ending his speech by remarking that 'If the noble lady likes to return the iron spade to me I shall keep it as a valuable memorial of that event'.[12] As the Seventh Marquess of Londonderry presented an ornamental wheel-barrow and *two* spades to the Machynlleth Urban District Council in 1948, it would appear that David Davies's request was not granted![13]

There were further speeches by Sir Watkin, Capt. Pryce and John Foulkes before the procession re-formed and headed for the Town Hall, where a 'cold collation' was provided to both celebrate the event and, doubtless, to satisfy and sustain the inner person during the countless toasts and speeches. It was a time for reflection and self-congratulation; in the light of the achievement, many of the problems seemed to diminish in size and importance although David Davies, forthright as ever, was quick to remind the assembly that the past three years had been amongst the wettest he could recollect; 'If it had not been so, I should have had the railway made much sooner, and £10,000 more in my pocket'.[14]

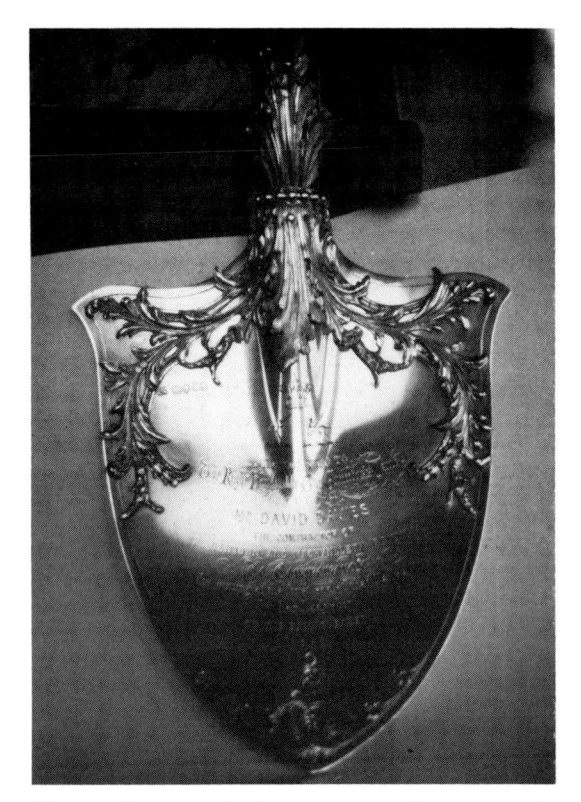

The inscription on the Ceremonial Spade, presented to Countess Vane on the occasion of the opening of the railway, 3 January 1893, reads: 'Presented to the Right Honourable The Countess Vane by Mr. David Davies the Contractor of the Newtown & Machynlleth Railway to commemorate the cutting of the first sod of that railway by her Ladyship on the 27th November 1858'.

On the afternoon of Monday, 5 January Lady Vane entertained around 200 children from the National Schools for 'Tea and Plum Cake' at the *Plas*. Led by the Rifle Corps Band, they went in procession from the school and were met by the Plas family who had assembled at the lodge gates to greet them. The local youngsters were to benefit again in March when, at an 'influential meeting.. held at the Town Hall . . . it was decided that the children of the National & Vane Schools should be treated with a railway trip to

55

Fund-raising Railwaymen, at Machynlleth c. 1958, alongside the former 1st Class Refreshment Room on the 'down' platform. *l-r:* 1 John Humphreys, 2 Oswald Davies, 3 Leonard Edwards, 4 J. Bonner, 5 Ted Gates, 6 Griff Evans.

GBJ

Talerddig and on their return, should be regaled with tea and plum-cake etc . . .'[15]

The date of this particular treat is not recorded but as it was in honour of the marriage of the Prince of Wales it could well have taken place that same day, Tuesday, 10 March.

By the end of January, the Town and District were anxious to record their appreciation of David Howell's valuable services as Secretary. A Testimonial was arranged with subscriptions finally reaching around £250.0.0 and the presentation of a 'splendid silver candelabrum and massive salver, manufactured by Smith & Nicholson, of Lincoln's Inn Fields'[16] was made on 17 June, 1863. The illuminated list of subscribers displayed at the *Plas* Machynlleth, alongside the other N&M mementoes, serves most interestingly to emphasise the rather surprising omission of David Davies from these commemorations. Davies did not attend the presentation ceremony although the presence of his secretary, Thomas Webb is noted. As the success of the N&M venture was undoubtedly the result of close co-operation between Howell and Davies, it is most surprising that this occasion was allowed to pass without some formal appreciation of the Llandinam man's contribution. Davies's other railway ventures were marked by several presentations, both by his workers and those who derived more lasting benefit from his endeavours, making this omission all the more regrettable, and enigmatic.

. . . And the Pioneer Days

Thoughts of the agreement with the Great Western may have receded as the Company proceeded alone during the early months of 1863, but the matter returned into focus with the announcement that the GWR had finally declined to take up its option to work the line,

The earliest surviving photograph taken at Machynlleth, probably dating from the opening decade, 1863-73, shows former O&N *Cambria* (CR No. 27) shunting in the top yard. *Cambria* did not see GW ownership, being withdrawn in 1919.

WIMM

citing the incomplete nature of the permanent buildings as the main reason. Clause 2 of the Agreement of 1861 had stipulated that;

> In addition to Mr Davies's contract, the Newtown & Machynlleth Company shall expend not less than £23,000 in the construction of permanent stations, sidings, turntables and signals at Caersws, Pontdolgoch, Carno, Llanbrynmair, Cemmes and Machynlleth in manner to be approved by the Great Western Company.[17]

Even by the time of the Board of Trade Inspection in December 1862, the signalling and siding accommodation were minimal and the building of the permanent stations had not even started in most instances. The Great Western withdrawal was publicly announced at the N&M's Half-yearly General Meeting of Ordinary Shareholders on 7 March 1863:

> It is with a feeling of deep regret that we find ourselves unable to fulfil the promises contained in our recent half-yearly reports; namely, that as soon as the railway should be opened, the Great Western Company would work it under their agreement and pay a dividend of £5 per cent on our capital. Their refusal to do so, being as we conceive, a violation of their plain intention of the agreement, shook our confidence in the reliance to be placed upon their fulfilment of any of its terms. Our disappointment was aggravated by the fact that they rested their refusal on the circumstance that the permanent stations were not completed . . . . In the difficulty in which we were thus so unexpectedly placed we, under great disadvantages, made temporary arrangements for the working of the line . . . .[18]

The N&M had little option but to transfer its allegiance nearer home, to the more friendly O&N, which was also working the Llanidloes line by that time. Meanwhile, the draft of an interim

Working Agreement with the O&N Company had already been approved by 28 February, and steps were taken for carrying it and the formal Amalgamation Agreement into full effect. In just two months, therefore, the resolutions of the Board on 2 January, were largely invalid. The Machynlleth column in the *Advertiser* of 11 March, carried news of the Amalgamation with the O&N 'and the working of it by Mr Savin has given universal satisfaction to all the District around.'

By 1 April, it was reporting:

> We are glad to see that the Montgomeryshire system of railways is becoming cemented . . . and the Newtown & Machynlleth—separated for some time by false friends—has allied itself to the system.

The Agreement, although backdated to 1 March 1863, was not signed until 31 August.

The evidence of the Illustrated London News print of the Opening supports the Great Western case regarding the lack of permanent buildings. Although building of the engine-shed had been started, construction of the permanent station had not commenced. Despite the demoralising blow of the Great Western indecision and final withdrawal, the Railway endeavoured to consolidate its position and provide a service for the community. The Company coped with operation of the inaugural but very limited time-table but knew that with only two locomotives, four passenger carriages and one brake van, it was ill-equipped to deal single—handed with the expected expansion of passenger traffic during the coming months. As a consequence, the authorisation of David Davies to spend up to £20,000 on

The exhaust bark of 'Duke' No. 3259 *Merlin* and Dean Goods 0-6-0 No. 2432 reverberates amongst the hills between Cemmes Road and Commins Coch as they storm their way up the bank with an Aberystwyth-Leicester Return Period Excursion. 7.8. 1937.

Ifor Higgon

additional rolling-stock was a matter of great urgency.[19]

Davies, as may be expected, responded promptly; notwithstanding preparations for the opening of the railway and also monitoring work on his other contracts, he found time to place an order for four new 0-6-0 Goods engines with Messrs Sharp Stewart, by 10 January 1863, as well as ordering further passenger carriages from Messrs Ashburys of Manchester.

The initial service to appear under the banner of the Newtown & Machynlleth Railway consisted of three 'up' and three 'down' trains per week-day, with connections by coach for two of these to and from Aberystwyth. No Sunday trains were time-tabled.

The first Machynlleth Fair of 1863, held on 4 March, provided a good opportunity to assess the benefits bestowed by the new transport. A special train arrived at 8.00 a.m. and the service train followed around 11.00 a.m. with a further 300 passengers who had travelled from the different stations on the line from Newtown. The farming community anticipated better times to come, as did the local consumers who 'hoped that railway accommodation will have a tendency to equalise, in the course of another year, the prices of eatables in this country'.[20]

Fair Day traffic of this nature, however, whilst being encouraging, was local in character and hardly the stuff of which dividends were made; the Company anticipated greater things with the opening of the Welsh Coast line to Borth, for they appreciated they would not derive full benefit from their line until the coast railway had been completed. The seasonal but highly lucrative summer traffic eventually emerged as the line's most profitable source of revenue, and fully lived up to the promoter's expectations, but the brevity of the season was a distinct disadvantage.

The N&M continued to advertise its time-table independently until early April, but by the following month it was listed in the *Advertiser* under the 'London North Western, Oswestry & Newtown and Llanidloes and Machynlleth Railways'. Old rivalries were being put aside and a new emphasis on co-operation and inter-dependence emerged with the approach of the first holidays of the year. The success of the new alliance was amply demonstrated when:

> Two monster trains arrived at the station here on the morning of Friday last (Machynlleth, Good Friday, 3 April, 1863) . . . .the first train consisting of about thirty carriages conveying passengers from Shrewsbury and the intermediate stations, and to which was attached at Moat Lane a number of carriages from Llanidloes, arrived here at 11:30 . . . and about half an hour later another train appeared in view of about an equal number of carriages . . . from Oswestry and towns en route. Each train was drawn by two powerful locomotives . . .[21]

The Newtown column in the same issue claims that the Shrewsbury train was 'the largest ever seen in this county upon any occasion, for when it left Moat Lane Junction (where it had been joined by the Llanidloes portion), it consisted of four locomotives, sixty passenger carriages and six vans.'[22]

It would have been prudent for this train to have run in two (or more) portions, but it must be remembered that during those heady, pioneer days virtually anything could happen when decreed by the need of the moment; the opportunity may well have been seized to extend the experience of the operators and test the capacity of the line. It would be fascinating to have confirmation that such a train actually ran.

The new combined time-tables of May 1863 indicate that the through trains were re-arranged to run between Oswestry and Machynlleth, for the Moat Lane-Llanidloes service was listed separately. As the rail-head at Machynlleth was then the nearest to Aberystwyth, the coaches which formerly plied between that town and Llanidloes were diverted to Machynlleth. Two 4-horse coaches left Aberystwyth daily (at 6.30 a.m. and 11.00 a.m.), to arrive at Machynlleth in good time for trains leaving at 9.00 a.m. and 1.30 p.m. These coaches then returned from Machynlleth at 11.00 a.m, connecting with the 6.00

MACHYNLLETH c. 1925

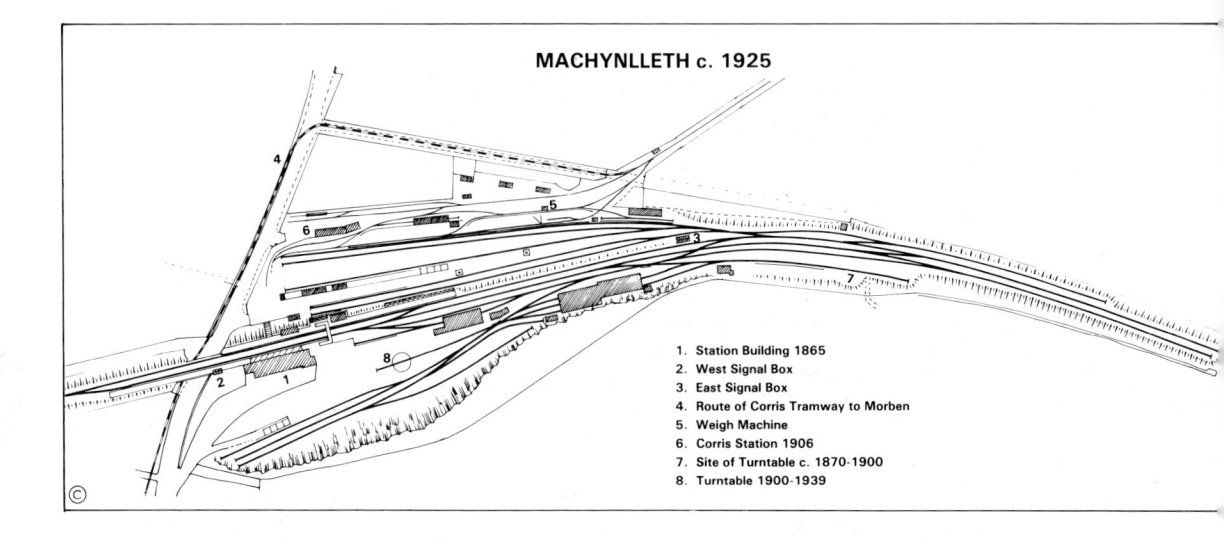

1. Station Building 1865
2. West Signal Box
3. East Signal Box
4. Route of Corris Tramway to Morben
5. Weigh Machine
6. Corris Station 1906
7. Site of Turntable c. 1870-1900
8. Turntable 1900-1939

a.m. train from Oswestry, and at 3.30 p.m., or on arrival of the 6.15 a.m. train from London. A similar service from Barmouth (Cors-y-gedol Hotel) and Dolgellau (Ship Hotel) was offered by the *Harkaway*, 4-horse coach, which left Barmouth daily at 8.45 a.m. and Dolgellau at 11.00 a.m., also arriving at Machynlleth station in time for the 1.30 p.m. 'up' train. The *Harkaway* left Machynlleth daily at 3.30 p.m., or upon arrival of the 6.15 a.m. departure from Euston. Dolgellau was reached by 5.55 p.m. and Barmouth by 7.10 p.m. By July, the opening of the Machynlleth-Borth section of the Aberystwyth & Welsh Coast Railway saw the withdrawl of the Aberystwyth coaches, but a second Dolgellau coach, the *Euston*, was featured in the lists and a coach left Mallwyd to connect with rail services at Cemmes Road.

As with the period of decline in coastal shipping, the coach operators made the most of their final opportunities. From the summer of 1862, before the line was opened, a coach called *The Express* was advertised to run daily from Machynlleth;

> ... to Sarn station, on the Machynlleth & Newtown Railway, [sic] starting every alternate day from the Wynnstay Arms and the Herbert Arms, at 6:00 a.m., and returning to the above named hotels every evening at 6:15.p.m., thus bringing railway accommodation within 16 miles of Machynlleth. We may sincerely congratulate 'Mr Coachy' for his great pluck this year, and patting him on the back, we would wish him every success this season, as he appears to be on his last leg, [sic] and the breath just out of him, still shewing fight to the last.[23]

This account clearly indicates the operation of a regular, if limited, passenger train service between Carno (Sarn) and Moat Lane, fully six months or more before the line was inspected by the Board of Trade.

Machynlleth station yard must have presented a fascinating sight after the line was opened, as horse-drawn coaches, private carriages, traps or wagonettes awaited the arrival of the London train. To complicate matters, the yard was still a construction site with its own noises, clamour and smells, and the addition of the general hustle and bustle of those fortunate enough to be travelling by the new transport must have created an atmosphere of excitement, progress and advancing prosperity.

Although the through traffic was to be the line's main source of revenue in years to come, the fragmented nature of the system presented many problems which are not easily appreciated today.

Platform staff at Machynlleth for the Royal Visit, 1911

Photograph Courtesy of the late Mrs. E. Evans

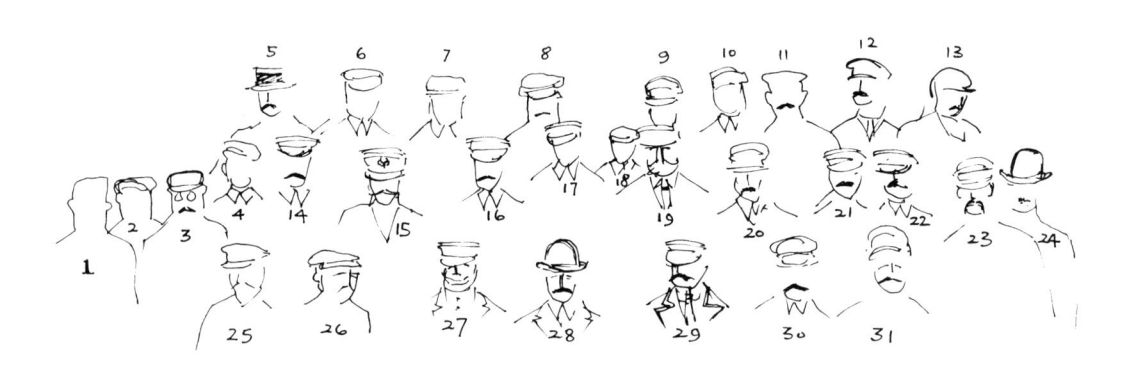

1. Moore
7. J. R. Evans
10. Evan John Lloyd
11. George Weaver
12. Bill Venables
26. Evans, Manager of Bookstall
27. Pat Jenkins, Station Foreman
29. T. R. Morgans, Station Master
30. Evan Rees, Foreman Porter
31. J. Blayney

61

Difficulties of working out the charges, for instance, were only overcome with time and experience.

In March, 1863, for example, the N&M sued one Thomas Brumford for the sum of £1.6s.5d. Brumford had forwaded 18 bags of onions to Machynlleth from Evesham on 5 December 1862. Upon arrival at their destination it was discovered that the final bill, which was an accumulation of the charges of the individual railways which had handled the consignment, had not been received. As the defendant was anxious to collect the onions, he was allowed to have them on payment of £2.11s.0d. on the understanding that if carriage came to more, 'more should be paid';[24] if less, the excess would be returned. When the bill arrived, it was found that the charge was £2.12s.9d. to Montgomery alone; by the time the onions had reached Moat Lane, this had increased to £3.5s.5d. ... 'at which point the Company took possession of them'.[25] The N&M charge was 12 shillings for carriage between Moat Lane and Machynlleth, making £3.17s.5d. in all, leaving a balance of £1.6s.5d. Because through rates had not been agreed, the common practice was to make the last company traversed responsible for the collection of the bill: this company would then pay the previous carrier/s. The case was adjourned whilst the question of the rates was decided by enquiring of the different companies, but by 19 May, his Honour gave judgement for the plaintiff as 'the claims made by the (N&M) company were below those of the other companies.'[26]

The problem of damage sustained by parcels or goods sent by rail was evident from the outset, but appeared to have been solved by at least one customer who, perhaps, had suffered at the hands of the railways previously but profited by the experience. He placed the onus squarely upon the railway companies and their servants by addressing a parcel to;

> Mr Ruben Peake, Llanfihangel, Gennie Glyn [sic]. To be left at Borth Station till called for. On route from Ellesmere Port, Chester, Wrexham, Ruabon, Gobowen, Oswestry, Newtown, Machynlleth, and thence to Borth. Should this parcel be delayed at any of the above named stations, damages will be lay'ed upon the Companies servants for the detention of such parcel, value, 20 shillings.[27]

Not surprisingly, perhaps, the parcel was handled carefully and delivered to Borth promptly and intact.

Summer excursion traffic rapidly established itself as the mainstay of Cambrian finances. In addition to services from the midlands and the north of England, the opening of the Mid Wales Railway brought south Wales excursionists to Cardigan Bay in 1865. The first train, bound for Aberystwyth, arrived via Moat Lane on Good Friday:

> There were no fewer than thirty carriages, propelled by two engines. The South Walians were, in most cases, quite strangers to our North Wales scenery, and they appeared mightily gratified with their trip.[28]

Later that summer, 'immense excursion trains from the LNW line passed through' (Newtown), bound for the coast.[29]

Excursions in the reverse direction, from mid Wales to the midlands and London were also popular, although a 'day' excursion to the capital bore greater resemblance to a marathon than a pleasure jaunt. Despite being hailed as;

> ... the latest marvel of the excursion world .... most excursion trains from the neighbourhood occupy a day in passing the journey to London, the train having to stop at nearly every station on the line; but the arrangements in this case are such that the journey will only occupy six hours, and no passengers will be taken after Shrewsbury.[30]

Undoubtedly, one of the major advantages of the coming of the railway was the dramatic improvement brought about in the postal arrangements. In 1807, for example, Machynlleth was served by only three horse posts a week during winter; in summer, one delivery was by horse post whilst the remaining two were by mail coach. The incoming mail did not arrive until 3.00 p.m. whilst the outgoing service left at 5.00 a.m.[31]

The mail coach was withdrawn for a period, being re-instated c.1838 when a Machynlleth eye-witness later recalled the arrival of the first coach of the new service;

> I recollect the turn out there was to see it. The coach was new, and the horses picked and high-mettled, and their harness all new and bright. Previously, letters were conveyed on horseback. Mrs Lewis, the Shop, kept the Post Office, assisted by Miss Breese. The post ride between Aberystwyth and Machynlleth was a very severe one for both man and horse . . . Letters before the introduction of the penny postage were few in number and were delivered by the shop apprentice, who carried them about in his apron.

The general town delivery was made about 8 or 10 hours after the arrival of the post from Mallwyd with the London letters, which was about 11 o'clock at night.[32]

Plans for transferring the Machynlleth, Aberystwyth and coast mails to the new rail service were instigated by Earl Vane, who personally dispatched a memorial to the Post Master General on 26 March 1862, extolling the advantages of the Machynlleth route. It was therefore decreed, soon after the rail service was established, that the mail would travel by goods train, 'on the road early in the morning . . . it will arrive at Machynlleth about 7:00 a.m . . .'[33]

War-time Prizewinners at Llanbrynmair, 1941
l-r: Lengthman A. Morris; Patrolman D. G. Hughes; Lengthmen R. Jehu and J. Morris; Trolley Driver E. Davies; Sub-Ganger E. C. Jones; Lengthman A. Hughes; Ganger W. Evans; Inspector T. Harrison and Sub-Inspector W. George. Note the blackout measures: shaded platform lamps and white paint on lamp standards.

Geoff Charles Collection, NLW

The initial service, from Shrewsbury to Borth, commenced on 1 January, 1864, and the *Advertiser* quickly reported that, '... the new postal arrangements come lately into force, by which letters are delivered by 9 o'clock in the morning and are again conveyed at 6 o'clock in the evening of the same day, is productive of great advantage'.

From 1 January 1865, LNWR rolling-stock was used for carrying the mail, and on 20.3.1883, the first specialist vehicle, a Sorting Carriage of 1860 vintage was provided for use between Shrewsbury and Aberystwyth. Within five years, however, the Cambrian had built its own Mail coach, a combined Parcels and Letter Sorting Carriage. No. 200 was a 32ft long, 6-wheel vehicle constructed at Oswestry Works which served until 1902, when it was replaced by a larger and improved vehicle, the 42ft bogie carriage, No. 293.[35]

In 1926, the GW introduced their own vehicle No. 863; old No.293 was re-numbered No.811 in the GW lists and became the spare vehicle, later allocated to the Moat Lane—Brecon service. In 1933, two new GW Sorting Carriages appeared on the service; No. 797 was equipped with a net and four arms for exchanging mail at speed, (although this apparatus was never used on the Cambrian), and No. 796, (sans net and delivery apparatus), which was normally the spare vehicle.[36]

The last operation of Sorting Carriages between Shrewsbury and Aberystwyth took place on 22 September 1939. The service was suspended during the period of the war and not restored afterwards. Mail trains, however, continued to run until 1977, when greater use was made of road transport although some mail continues to go by rail.[37]

At Aberystwyth, a 'Late Fee Box', known locally as the 'ten-minute box', was fixed to the railings at the station. Letters posted here required a surcharge, were hand-stamped on the spot just before departure of the Mail and always displayed the time of '6.00 p.m.' This service continued up to 1977.[38]

An old round-topped, wooden Victorian post box located at Machynlleth in 1883 was removed by the postal authorities in late 1987 and relocated at Llandrindod Wells, in an attempt to enhance the Victorian atmosphere of the station at the mid Wales Spa. Although it has been positioned beneath a small new roof, the old box is currently under threat from the elements for the first time in 105 years for, unhappily, the Llandrindod rain rarely falls obligingly in a predictable, perpendicular fashion. Only one other (incomplete) example is thought to exist in Wales, at Rhyl Station where, mercifully, it resides under cover. Attempts to restore the Machynlleth box to its rightful location have proved fruitless, providing a sad footnote to the story of Mails on the Cambrian.

Chapter 4: Notes & References

[1] OA 7.1.1863.
[2] RAIL 517/1. p.169.
[3] ibid. Poundley was a Montgomeryshire Surveyor.
[4] OA 7.1.1863.
[5] ibid.
[6] ibid.
[7] Kinsey, D. makes an uncorroborated claim that the train failed to stop at the intermediate stations to pick up navvies who had tickets. The generous time of nearly 3 hours taken for the 30 mile journey suggests that stops were made, scheduled or otherwise, (perhaps for the purpose of raising steam), but contemporary reports make no reference to any such incidents.
[8] George Charles Spencer Churchill (1844-92), Earl Vane's nephew, became the 8th Duke of Marlborough in 1883. His brother, Randolph Henry Spencer Churchill, (Sir Winston's father), was also a frequent visitor to *Plas* Machynlleth.
[9] OA 7.1.1863.
[10] The Shrewsbury Chronicle (5.8.1859) noted, at the opening of the Llanidloes line, that 'locomotives *Milford* and *Llewelyn* reversed on the turntable' at Newtown. Two turntables of suitable length were ordered for the N&M from John Ashbury of Manchester, but these were located at Machynlleth and Moat Lane. The first to arrive, (bill dated 21.8.1862), was a new 40ft turntable, 'similar to those supplied to the Oswestry & Newtown Railway' and was sent to Moat Lane initially, although it seems that this was the table installed at Machynlleth in September that year; it cost £255.0.0d. A bill dated 3.2.1863, for 'One 42ft Turntable as per contract. Delivered at Shrewsbury. £160.0.0d.' shows this to be a cheaper, slightly larger table which was probably the

one installed at Moat Lane, the only other point on the N&M which required a table of this size. LDMP/NLW.

The original Moat Lane turntable was made of wood, (which could account for the lower cost); it was difficult to operate and required four men to turn an engine. It survived at Moat Lane until replaced by a 50ft turntable, formerly at Birkenhead Central, which was purchased second-hand from the Mersey Railway in 1909 and installed a year later. RAIL 83/367.

[11] Thomas I. (1938) *Top Sawyer*, Longmans, Green & Co, London. p.69.
[12] ibid. p. 68.
[13] These valuable mementoes are currently on display at *Plas Machynlleth* although, regrettably, the first ticket issued on the Opening Day, previously preserved in a small glass case, was lost when these artefacts were stored at the Owain Glyndwr Institute. Should this item ever appear in the future, it is the undoubted property of the Machynlleth Town Council.
[14] Thomas I.
[15] S&MT 3.3.1863.
[16] OA 24.6.1863.
[17] Heads of Agreement, N&M and GWR, (1861): WIMM.
[18] MH 7.3.1863.
[19] RAIL 517/1. p.169.
[20] S&MT 9.3.1863.
[21] S&MT 7.4.1863.
[22] ibid.
[23] OA 2.7.1862.
[24] S&MT 17.3.1863.
[25] ibid.
[26] ibid.
[27] OA 27.11.1863.
[28] S&MT 18.4.1865.
[29] ibid. 25.7.1865.
[30] N&WE 24.8.1869.
[31] Scott Archer, M.(1970) *Welsh Post Towns before 1840*. Phillimore & Co. p.78.
[32] Note by TWH. 1.1.1890. *Bygones*. Woodall, Minshall & Co., Oswestry. p. 289.
[33] S&MT 15.9.1863.
[34] OA 13.1.1864.
[35] Cowell, R. Private Notes & Papers.
[36] Hosegood, J.G.(1983) *Great Western Travelling Post Offices*. Wild Swan. p.56.
[37] Cowell, R.
[38] ibid.

Chapter 5
Railways Related to the Newtown & Machynlleth Railway

Three short branch-lines were established along the 23 miles of the N&M, (Corris, 1858; Mawddwy, 1865 and Van, 1870). These generated much additional traffic but, undoubtedly, the most important line for the survival and success of the Machynlleth venture, apart from the obvious lines to the east, was the Aberystwyth & Welsh Coast Railway, (1861). No history of these ventures is attempted here, merely the registration of a few salient facts not readily available in published form.

The Machynlleth Company had nurtured ambitions of extending toward the sea from the outset but completion of the line over Talerddig was obviously the first priority. The N&M was not the first nor the only promoter to cast envious eyes on the potential of the Cambrian coastline for even after Holyhead and Fishguard had claimed the Irish trade, Porthdinllaen still attracted some speculators whilst others saw equal promise in the development of Cardigan Bay holiday traffic. Although not directly related to developments in the Dyfi valley, a line of uncertain title which called itself, variously, the West Midland & Welsh Coast Railway, the North Wales & West Midland Railway, or the Shrewsbury, Barmouth

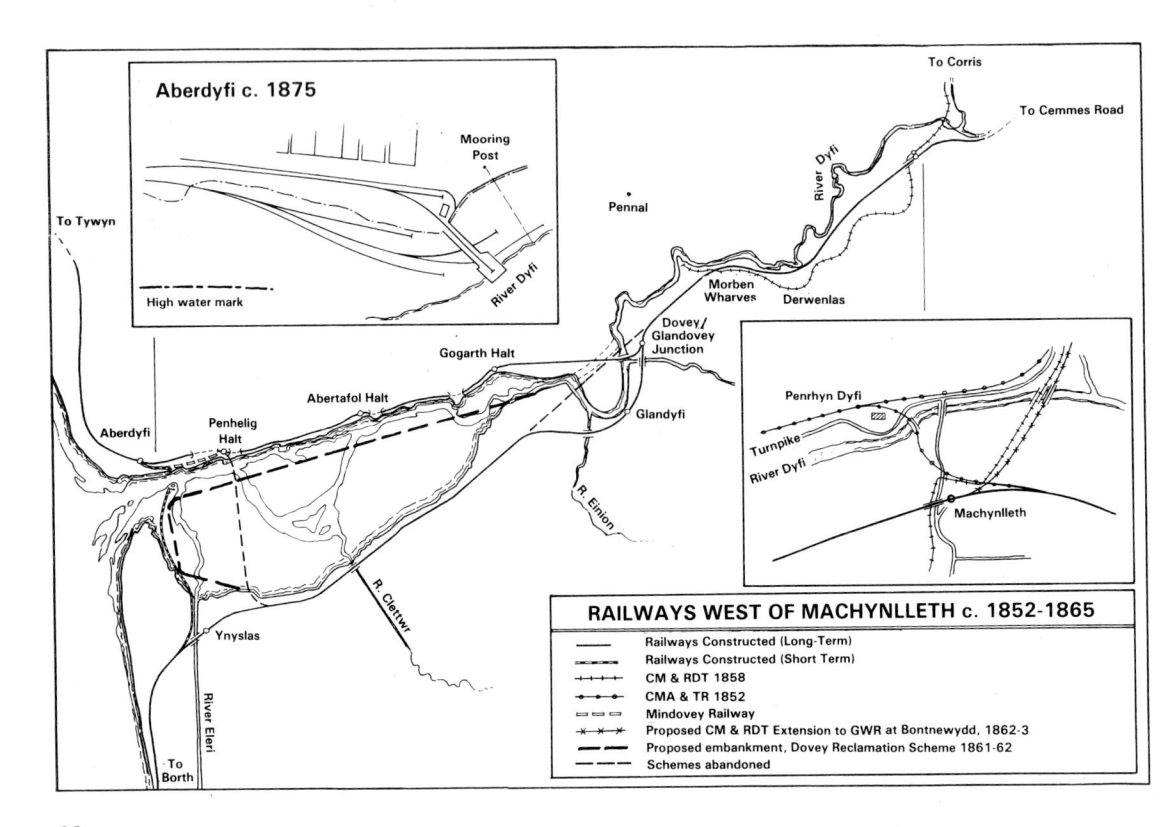

RAILWAYS WEST OF MACHYNLLETH c. 1852-1865

- Railways Constructed (Long-Term)
- Railways Constructed (Short Term)
- CM & RDT 1858
- CMA & TR 1852
- Mindovey Railway
- Proposed CM & RDT Extension to GWR at Bontnewydd, 1862-3
- Proposed embankment, Dovey Reclamation Scheme 1861-62
- Schemes abandoned

and Portmadoc Railway, (1860), illustrates well the magnetism of Porthdinllaen. Planned to leave the Shrewsbury & Welshpool Railway near Hanwood and run via Porthywaen to Llangynog, it was to penetrate the Berwyn Hills by means of a 1¼ m tunnel. Near Llandrillo a branch was to connect the line with Corwen whilst the main line followed the course of the Dee to Bala, before proceeding to Dolgellau, Barmouth and northward 'along the sea-shore, at the foot of beautiful hills abounding in minerals'[1]. It was envisaged that the entire coast between Barmouth and Porthmadog would 'in the process of time, become one large watering-place.'[2] but, the engineering difficulties alone were sufficient to inhibit financial support. By this time, however, the first rails had already reached the valley of the Dyfi. They originated not as part of any grand scheme but from an attempt by local quarry owners in the Corris area to improve transportation for their products from the quarries down to the sea.

THE CORRIS, MACHYNLLETH & RIVER DOVEY TRAMROAD, 1858.

The earliest plans date from 1850, when a tramway from Corris was projected along the Dulas and Dyfi valleys to a wharf at Pant Eidal, on the north side of the estuary. By 1852, the proposals for a Shrewsbury—Aberystwyth line inspired the Corris promoters to up-grade their scheme and adopt the standard-gauge for a railway from the quarries to Penrhyn Dyfi, near Machynlleth.[3] It was then to proceed independently of the Aberystwyth line, along the north bank of the Dyfi, to Aberdyfi and Tywyn. A connecting line was to be constructed at Machynlleth to link the two routes. This would have been an impressive affair laid in the form of a reverse 'S' and carried mainly on a 462 yd viaduct in order to clear the river and flood plain. Two short tunnels were to be located lower down the valley near Pumwern (198 yds) and Llugwy (158 yds) and there was to be a further viaduct of 572 yds on a curve as the line skirted Pennal. Had this

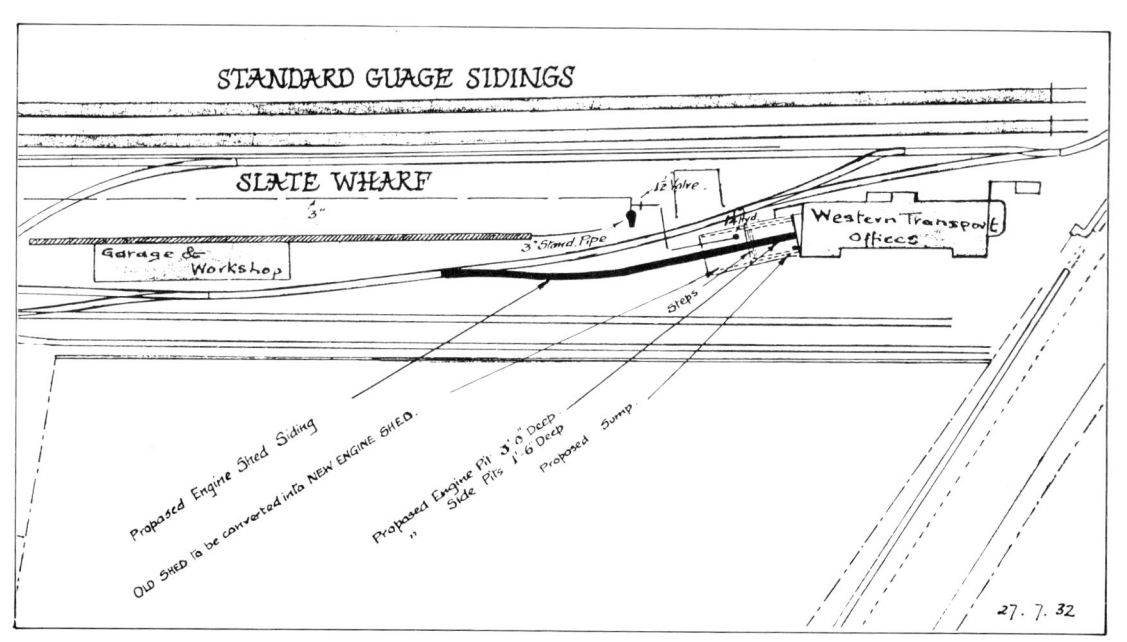

A Great Western proposal for Corris Railway Engine shed at Machynlleth, 1932.   *GBJ Coll.*

ambitious and costly scheme been adopted, Machynlleth would have become the natural junction for the coast line from the outset and its importance further increased by a later Corris scheme to extend eastward from Aberllefenni to meet the GWR at Bontnewydd, near Dolgellau. Plans for this standard-gauge line, drawn up a decade later, indicated a junction with the N&M near the site of the later Machynlleth East signal box. The line would then have crossed the valley on an embankment before bridging the Dyfi by means of three masonry arches, each of 40ft span and 13ft high. The route to Corris was re-surveyed to ease, as far as was possible, some of the inevitably tortuous curves; typical gradients to Corris were to be 1 in 70, 1 in 87, and 1 in 60. At six miles from Machynlleth, near Aberllefenni, the grade stiffened to 1 in 35 for three miles, until at nine miles it eased somewhat to 1 in 42 through a 1958 yd tunnel. The summit of the line would have been encountered immediately on leaving the tunnel, at 10 miles 1 furlong; here the gradient was to change abruptly downwards at 1 in 35/36, to the 15 mile post, where a short, sharp rise (1 in 57) would have been required to reach the intended junction with the Bala & Dolgelly Railway,(GWR). With the use of these 15 miles, 2 furlongs, 5 chains of line, the Great Western could have monopolised the traffic between the north-east of England and Aberystwyth, but the prize was not considered sufficient compensation for the outlay and the line remained on the drawing board.[4]

This scheme, however, was ten years hence. In 1852 the failure of the Shrewsbury-Aberystwyth project caused the quarry owners to abandon their standard-gauge ambitions and to amend their scheme a third time, for there was little point in constructing a line to Tywyn without the promise of through tourist traffic. When talk of another main-line to Machynlleth was revived, this time by the N&M in 1856, the Corris scheme was modified finally to a 2ft— 3ins gauge feeder tramway to run from Aberllefenni to 'the terminus of the N&M Rly, and its further extension to a small sea-port in a creek on the Cardigan Coast, on the River Dovey'.[5] The Act for the horse-drawn Corris, Machynlleth and River Dovey Tramroad was passed on 12 July, 1858, and the line opened as far as Machynlleth, on 1 April 1859, reaching the quays at Morben by November that year.

Yet again, the press present the only eye-witness account when a reporter from the *Shrewsbury Chronicle* visited Machynlleth and noted that:

> Friday afternoon (1 April) was observed as a holiday in this neighbourhood and thousands of persons were assembled on the hills and in the valleys to witness the first transit of goods by railway to this town, a novel sight truly to the natives, and which forms a new epoch in the history of Glyndwr's native place. Among the company on the grounds were the noble family of *Plas,* Machynlleth, and all the elite of the neighbourhood. We beg to congratulate Mr Causton and the Company on the steady progress of the work and hope soon to have to report its final inauguration by the setting up of the gates 'ere long at the water's edge.[6]

Although the first rails to reach the town, therefore, were narrow in gauge and light in section, the standard-gauge was soon to follow, for work had started earlier that spring on the N&M between Caersws and Talerddig. With materials, plant and labour available in quantity along the Severn, the initial construction was concentrated in that area and there was little evidence of progress at Machynlleth for a further two years. Possibly the first indication that 'y lein fawr' (the big line, as opposed to 'y lein fach'—the little line) was about to enter the valley, was a diversion of the Corris tramway away from the N&M station site in 1861. The natural lie of the Corris line into Machynlleth, together with the official Plans & Sections for that line, (as well as the later A& WCR), suggest that it could originally have cut directly across the site of what later became the N&M's goods yard. If actually built in this manner, the direct route across the yard could have lasted no more than two years, from April 1859 to May 1861, when work commenced

The hikers' footpath at Machynlleth marks the trackbed of the former Corris Tramway extension to Derwenlas; it crossed the road on the level at the distant bend. The trackbed was raised slightly, particularly at the town end, in order to increase its usefulness during the valley's frequent floods, and it served this purpose long after the tramway had been lifted. Consequently, it was repaired and raised slightly c. 1946, but this only served to retain a greater depth of water on the road after the height of the flood had passed. The problem was overcome when Montgomery County Council raised the level of this section of the A487 in 1951.

S. W. Baker

on the N&M at Machynlleth. The route of the diversion around the N&M site certainly possesses the characteristics of an afterthought.

One of the few maps to show the diversion clearly is the 1862 extension plan for the link line to Bontnewydd, and evidence that the tramway followed the diverted route is provided by the location of three wooden stables, constructed parallel to the diversion, at a point where the gravity worked section between Corris and Machynlleth gave way to the more intensely horse-worked section westward to Derwenlas.[7] Operational criteria suggest a loop-line could have been located alongside the stables, to enable 'up' and 'down' trains to pass whilst horses were being changed. No evidence has yet emerged that the Corris ever operated 'dandy cars', as did the Festiniog, so it would appear that the horses worked 'light' from Corris back to Machynlleth along the neighbouring road whilst the heavy loaded wagons were capable of running down by gravity. Such a working was called a 'run', when up to twenty-five or thirty loaded wagons were controlled by a team of brakesmen who exercised considerable skill to ensure steady and undramatic progress of the heavy cargo of slate down the valley. These continued to be operated even after the introduction of steam locomotives in 1878,

69

Corris Railway No. 2 lying derelict behind the carriage shed at Machynlleth Low Level on 16 April 1927. On 20 October, it was hauled to Maespoeth by Loco No. 4 and stripped for suitable parts to re-build engine No. 3.
Ifor Higgon

No. 3 about to depart for Aberllefenni with loaded coal wagons. 5.4.1948.   *T. A. Hughes*

The thin coating of alluvial silt deposited on the rails after a flood in the Dyfi valley obligingly emphasises the high standard of the Corris track, even at this late date. Such a flood could have been negotiated by the engine, but had the level reached the culvert, from which the photograph was taken, the service would have been temporarily suspended. Note the GW's concession to the ferocity and frequency of the Dyfi floods, namely fencing consisting of the three upper strands of wire only, allowing most debris to pass without damaging the fence. 7.6.1948.

GBJ

particularly during busy periods; the date of the last 'run' is not recorded but probably none was required after the First World War.

From the stables the tramway proceeded westward along the lane, before crossing the main Machynlleth-Dyfi Bridge road on the level; it then turned sharply south and ran parallel with the road to the outskirts of the town. This section of the tramway was carried on a low slate wall which survived in its original form until re-built by Montgomeryshire County Council c.1946. Two tragic accidents which occurred at this location during the early days highlight some interesting facts. The first recorded accident, to a middle-aged woman, reveals that the tramway carried passengers unofficially but through payment, from as early as 1860; the second mishap, in 1865, confirms that the Machynlleth to Morben section of the CM&RDT did not close immediately the A&WCR was opened to Borth[8].

On reaching the town, the tramway proceeded through the area known as the Garsiwn and followed the contours of the land, just above flood level, past Ogo-fach, Nawlyn and the Derwenlas Lime kilns to the Morben Wharves.

It is most probable that the Morben section survived at least until 1867, when the Glandovey Junction-Aberdyfi deviation was opened, and it is not impossible for it to have lingered some years again, as the cost of transhipment to the standard gauge for the short journey from Machynlleth to Aberdyfi could well have been greater than the slower tramway/river-boat alternative.

The encroachment of the river at Dyfi Bridge finally caused the closure of the Corris. Services continued at the time of this photograph and afterwards, after further erosion had taken place, undermining the boundary fence, but were suspended when the final encroachment reached the sleeper ends. Ironically, the track was never undermined and, with an abundance of quarry waste at the railhead at Aberllefenni, repair of the damage could have been quick and economic. 7.6.1948.

GBJ

THE ABERYSTWYTH & WELSH COAST RAILWAY, 1861.

Construction west of Machynlleth was not as straightforward as might, perhaps, have been imagined, and what should have been a comparatively easy stage to construct suffered because the initial scheme proposed for Garreg, (the contemporary name for Glandyfi), together with a Dovey Reclamation scheme prepared for 1861-2, caused considerable controversy and delay, and threatened to change the shape of the estuary almost beyond recognition. Furthermore, difficulties and debate escalated around the thorny question of bridging the estuary between Penhelig and Ynyslas.

A viable standard-gauge plan to reach the coast did not emerge until November 1860, with simultaneous announcements in *The Aberystwyth Observer* of rival Aberystwyth & Welsh Coast Railway and Machynlleth, Aberystwyth & Towyn Railway schemes; it was intended to submit both to Parliament in the following session. Both planned to follow much the same route to Aberystwyth, but the MA&TR scheme had to be dropped when the lithographers employed by the engineers failed to finish the Plans & Sections in time.[9] The corresponding drawings for the larger A&WCR scheme were only obtained 'in a confused state', which meant that they were, in fact, deposited late; 'a few hours after 8 o'clock',[10] on 30 November, the time indicated in the Standing Orders.

Despite opposition by the N&M and the West Midland, the A&WCR scheme was adopted, receiving Royal Assent in July 1861. As some small measure of compensation, the unsuccessful Machynlleth Company managed to add a clause to the A&WCR's Bill that if it failed to complete the Machynlleth-Aberystwyth section by 1 August 1864, the N&M would be sanctioned to complete the line. When construction finally commenced on the A&WCR, the Machynlleth-Aberystwyth portion was tackled energetically and opened to Borth by 1 July 1863. The original intention to open this section simultaneously with the N&M was foiled largely by the delays incurred at Garreg. The final stretch from Borth to Aberystwyth was inspected by the Board of Trade on 11 June the following year, and just seven weeks before the dead-line; it opened to passengers on 23 June 1864.

The Welsh Coast at Machynlleth

Although it was essential for Savin to complete the Machynlleth-Aberystwyth section quickly, he regarded establishing a base in the Aberdyfi-Ynyslas region as his first objective. As soon as Royal Assent was gained in the summer of 1861 and throughout the autumn, he concentrated his operations at Aberdyfi, where plant and materials were brought in easily by sea and independently of his former partner and the Montgomeryshire lines. By January 1862, Savin was ready to start work on the A&WCR at Machynlleth, even though the N&M had yet to be told formally of his withdrawal from their contract. He commenced at the end-on junction with the N&M, near the location of what later became the West signal box, precisely 22 miles, 7 furlongs and 5 chains from the Llanidloes line at Moat Lane. This junction was almost directly above the Machynlleth-Dyfi Bridge turnpike, some twenty feet or so below the rails at this point: the first task of the Welsh Coast Railway at Machynlleth, therefore, was to bridge this road. By 28 March 1862, the foundations were laid for what was euphumistically hailed as 'a great viaduct', although what transpired was but a modest bridge, with one opening for the road and a second opening for the tramway to Morben.

A great number of men were employed 'and many more would be quickly engaged if they were forth coming'.[11] The main disadvantage of relying so much upon local labour, it would seem, was its limited nature, but by May 1862 the work was proceeding with great vigour and 'but very few weeks will elapse before the services of a locomotive will be required and that part which lies between the junction at Machynlleth and Aberdovey (sic) will be completed.'[12] Either journalistic optimism was again running high or Savin had acted once more without proper authority, for he was not authorised by the N&M to excavate and remove spoil at Machynlleth station, to form the embankment, until August 1862.

By that time, the *S&MT* expressed the opinion that the line would

> ...ere long be ready for the transit of goods as far as Borth at least. The viaduct at Machynlleth is now completed and is in every respect a substantial and highly ornamental piece of architecture. The embankment along the Vale of the Dovey will be soon ready for ballasting and railing'.[13]

From the evidence of the ILN print of the Opening of the N&M, it would appear that the main span for the bridge was still lying on the station platform at Machynlleth on 3 January 1863, in which case it is most probable that a temporary wooden bridge served here until after the N&M opening, to enable Savin to transport spoil from the nearby Rock. After installation in early 1863, the wrought iron girders and timber decking served until 1927, whilst the foundations and stone abutments, credited to one R. Roberts, survive today.

Work on the embankment continued throughout autumn and winter of 1862 but the simultaneous opening with the N&M line was not possible. By the following February, a month after the opening of the N&M, the *Advertiser* carried more positive news in its Machynlleth column:

> Great progress on the Welsh Coast Railway between this town and Aberystwyth. The embankment along the Vale of the Dovey from the terminus of the N&M line, to Derwenlas has just been completed and railed over. An engine for the ballasting purpose is to be used upon it this week for the first time.[14]

Railway construction at Derwenlas isolated two of the busy wharves which lay near the village, on a sheltered bend of the river; this was severed twice by the new line, sealing the old course at one point with an embankment whilst a small timber bridge effectively restricted the other: a new channel was cut to take the river to the north of the railway. This arrangement still permitted water alongside the old quays but there was no longer a sufficiently strong flow to prevent silting and the Derwenlas quays fell into disuse after 1862/3. A third quay lower down the river at Morben, (Cei Ward) was more favourably positioned and continued to function, quite possibly, well after 1870.

From Morben, the original intention of the Welsh Coast company was to strike directly for Ynyslas, necessitating a second and much larger diversion of the Dyfi at Garreg. The route would have touched Merionethshire briefly and provided a long, straight and level section of line, a rare luxury within the restricted confines of mountainous central Wales. Representations from the ship-building and fishing interests at Garreg, as well as considerations of expense, caused the A&WCR to apply to Parliament during the 1862-3 session for a deviation to bring the line south in a sweeping curve, between road and river to Cei Coch, the location intended at one time as the terminus of the Corris Tramway. This diversion avoided the need to disturb the course of the river and became one of the reasons for the delay in opening the Machynlleth-Borth section.

The Dovey Reclamation scheme, intended for presentation to Parliament during the 1861-2 session, called for the construction of a substantial embankment nearly 6½ miles in length from the vicinity of Ynys Edwin, in a direct line, almost to Cerrig-y-Penrhyn, then curving back to rejoin the southern shoreline east of the Eleri/Dyfi confluence. This massive earthwork was intended to contain the Dyfi within 3 or 4 furlongs of the Merioneth bank and an extension of the Lerri cut/embankment would obviously have been necessary for the smaller river to reach open water[15]. Vast tracts of the estuary would have been reclaimed and the projected bridge between Penhelig and Ynyslas could have been a much more modest and viable proposition. The Dovey Reclamation scheme was dropped but the recent study of a series of aerial photographs of this area (taken after a fall of snow in January 1963,) revealed that work on the direct line at Garreg was

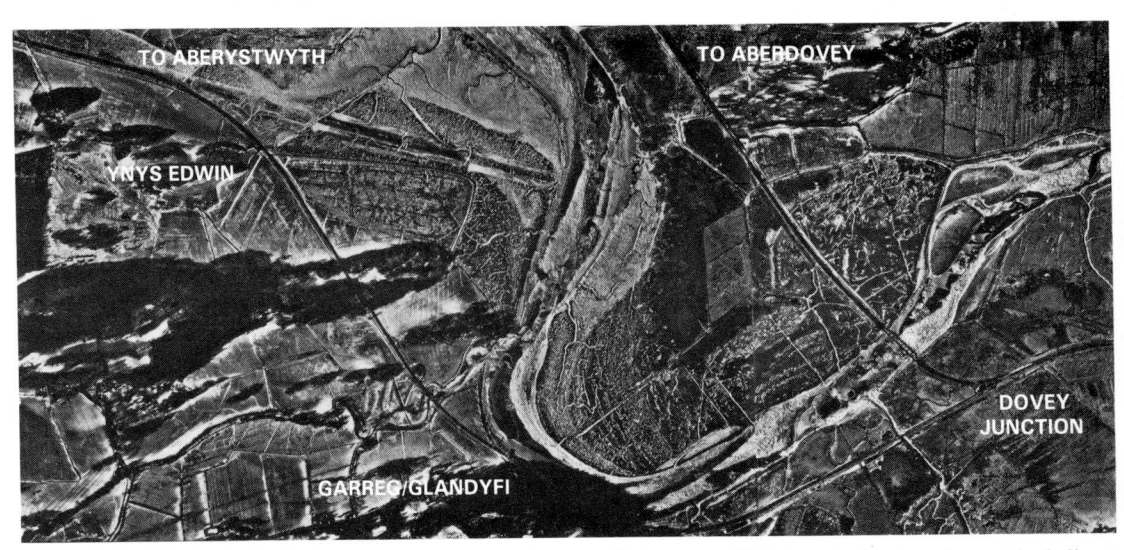

Vertical aerial photograph of the Glandyfi area, taken on 22 January 1963, but indicating the original direct alignment of the A&WCR 1861, avoiding the congested location at Garreg. *Crown Copyright*

The conglomeration of buildings which evolved at Dovey Junction is apparent in this undated photograph of the 1950s period. The original junction was a little to the left of the station name-board.

OPC

actually started in late 1861/early 1862. The 1963 snowfall was accompanied by high winds which swept much of the surface snow aside, revealing clearly that a start had been made on boundary ditches at the Montgomeryshire (Dovey Junction) end, and an even greater effort had been expended across the county line in Cardiganshire, in the vicinity of Ynys Edwin.

Beyond Ynys Edwin the line skirts the northern boundary of Cors Fochno at the very water's edge, providing fine views across the estuary, with occasional glimpses of red shanks or waders on the mud-flats and sandbanks during periods of low water. This stretch of line has provided engineers with a succession of problems over the years, particularly after stormy weather. The many hundreds of tons of rocks which now protect the line are adequate for all but the severest of conditions and provide a good illustration of the way the railway's sea defences benefit the hinterland.

Both the A&WCR and MA&TR schemes planned to bridge the estuary between Ynyslas and Penhelig. Savin intended developing Ynyslas into an important resort and accordingly purchased most of the land surrounding the Eleri's confluence with the Dyfi. In addition to the station and wharf, Savin erected some dwellings and established a market garden nearby to supply fresh produce for his hotels at Borth and Aberdyfi. He obviously intended his lead to encourage further development in the area but this did not materialise. The main difficulty was the soft, boggy nature of the ground, which could not adequately support even the most modest building. In due course, the houses had to be demolished and even the permanent station was reduced to a single storey structure. On 22 August 1873, George Owen reported:

> I regret to state that the newly erected building shows signs of subsidence and I am fearful, from the boggy nature of the soil, that it will not stand through the winter[16].

He recommended that the inhabited portion be partially taken down and re-built to one storey height, to correspond with the other part of the station and, in commendable Cambrian fashion, utilising the same materials 'so far as they will go'.[17]

Savin was more successful with the market garden venture, however, and the walled plot known as Ynyslas Gardens, whilst not actually located on the bog, continues to serve this same purpose today. Progress west of Borth toward Aberystwyth was virtually non-existent in 1862 and it was thought that 'no active measures will be taken until the hay harvest has been secured'.[18] A characteristic Cambrian perspective was evident even in the very earliest days! Cambrian hay was never a prominent feature of the railway but, for many years, that grown on embankments and spare land was harvested and stacked at strategic positions along the line. The stacks were numbered, in best railway tradition and, apart from reducing fire hazards and controlling the environment, the sale of hay made useful contributions to Cambrian finances. In 1870, for example, Stack No.9 near Llanbrynmair yielded between 9 and 10 tons, Stack No.10 at Ynyslas produced 16 tons and Stack No.12 at Aberdyfi contained 19 tons.

The Aberdyfi Viaduct

Perhaps the main reason Savin did not persevere with different building techniques to defeat the problem of settlement at Ynyslas was the failure of the scheme for a viaduct. The view has long been held that the bridge was abandoned because the surveyors, for one reason or another, failed to find an adequate foundation, but contemporary newspaper accounts report to the contrary:

> Operations have been going on for the last fortnight by one of the most experienced borers in England, in the channel of the river, to ascertain the exact nature of the bed of the river for the foundation of the viaduct, and the last operations have ascertained the same to be what the engineer calls a capital bottom.[19]
>
> The Railway Viaduct. The Board of Admiralty and the A&WCR Co., have at last come to a definite settlement about this structure. The Company are

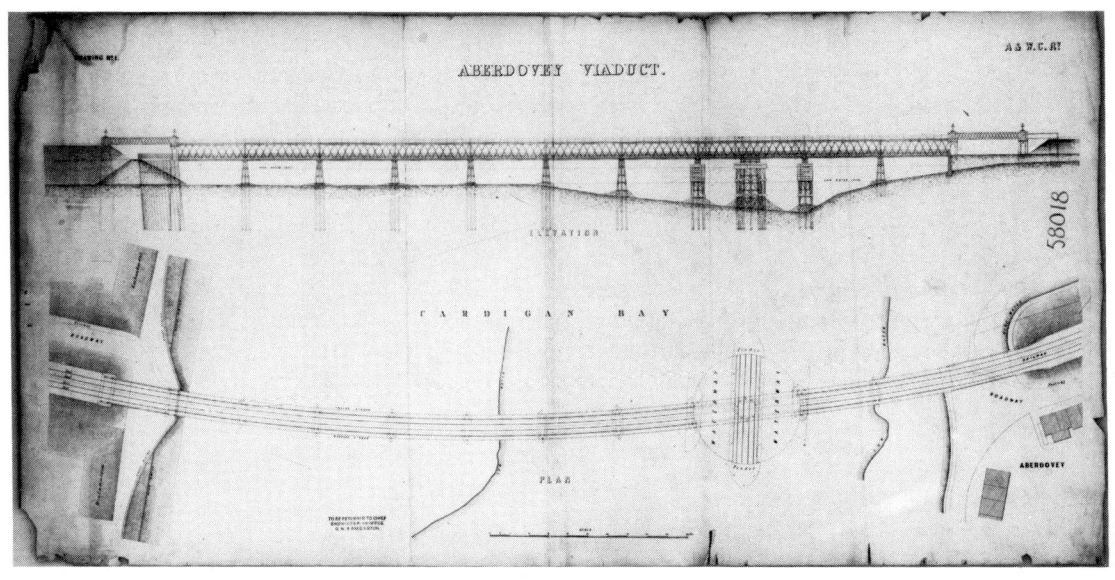

The second (1863), scheme for a bridge at Aberdyfi, showing clearly its alignment on a curve, the opening section and the roadway located beneath the double-track railway. *WIMM*

at liberty to commence its erection. The site is at Penhelig, as originally proposed.[20]

—We understand that foundations at 60ft below water have been found, and that the Board of Trade have sanctioned the undertaking—one of the greatest ever accomplished in Wales . . . [sic][21]

From information currently available,[22] it would seem that two different sets of plans were considered before the idea of a bridge at Aberdyfi was finally abandoned in 1865. Little is known of the original scheme (1861), apart from the sketchy indications of the deposited Plans & Sections for a viaduct with a 26ft opening, evidence presented before Parliament in 1865,[23] and a newspaper report which begins:

> Two stone bridges crossing the public road at the extremities of the town . . . are in an advanced state of construction . . . There will be some heavy rock cuttings at the back of Aberdovey and several houses will have to be pulled down. The foundation for the bridge across the Dovey has, as is well known, been fixed upon, and the works therewith are on the eve of being carried out. The bridge will be of cast-iron and will consist of three spans, one of 120ft and two others of 75ft each, the former so constructed so as to be enabled to act as a drawbridge when necessary. On the Cardiganshire side of the river, the bridge will be continued by an embankment of a very extensive character, which, it is believed, will have the effect of re-claiming vast quantities of land in Gorsfochno now covered by water.[24]

The measurements and the number of spans here quoted, however, do not appear to tally with those suggested by the Plans & Sections, and create something of an enigma without sight of the original drawings. Although they compare with the 110ft swing span and 75ft fixed spans of the second scheme (1863), they appear to have little in common with the initial drawbridge schemes planned for the Dyfi crossings nor, as it happens, with the later drawbridge constructed across the Mawddach in 1866, where the opening span was 47ft, (effective opening of 36ft, due to protective fenders), and the fixed spans were of 30ft or 40ft.

The initial reference to a drawbridge at Penhelig, however, is quite specific and is supported by no less an authority than Piercy, who, in answer to a question raised at an A&WCR meeting at Aberystwyth in 1861, refers to 'a drawbridge over the Dovey'; adding, 'that the engineering difficulties of crossing that river have been greatly exaggerated.'[25]

Evidence offered before the 1865 Parliamentary Committee by Brunlees, a civil engineer familiar with drawbridge design, estimated the cost of the 1861 bridge and embankments at £62,267. He indicated the bridge would have been 30ft wide, allowing either double track or a single line of rail with a 15ft roadway alongside. However, the Brunlees evidence was not always explicit as he appeared to quote both the 1861 and 1863 schemes at random, causing even the experienced chairman of committee, Mr Schofield MP, to remark at one stage:

> But the plans have the roadway under the line, so it is useless suggesting what we have not got before us. We must confine ourselves to the plans of 1863.[26]

Indeed, the 1863 plans show that the bridge appears to have been completely re-designed, presenting a longer, more versatile (and more expensive) structure. Fortunately, a full set of working drawings for this bridge are held at the Ceredigion Museum, Aberystwyth and although these are undated, they correspond with the description of the 1863 design quoted in the Inquiry. Provision was made for double track at an upper level and a 30ft roadway beneath, which would have created a taller structure than in the preceding scheme, in order to keep the roadway clear of high water.

The evidence provided by Brunlees before committee, together with the *S&MT* description and the hints within the A&WCR's Plans & Sections, may be regarded as less than satisfactory in many respects but they serve to make the absence of drawings for the 1861 scheme all the more regrettable. The 1863 plans reveal that the largest span was to swing open, creating two openings each some 28ft wide, as opposed to the drawbridge of the earlier scheme which, if similar

77

to the original Barmouth Viaduct, would have provided one opening for shipping of around 36ft. The swing span incorporated the only straight section of track on the 1863 plan: the remaining eleven spans were to be built on a curve, the line passing through the site now occupied by Penhelig Terrace, over the existing roadbridge, and into the Craig-y-don tunnel. This intention became the principal reason for the reverse curve and rather tight alignment which later evolved at Penhelig when, as a result of the deviation, the second tunnel became necessary.

Travel patterns along Cardigan Bay would undoubtedly have been transformed had either bridge been built for, in addition to a direct north-south rail link, the provision of a road would have shortened the Ynyslas-Aberdyfi journey by approximately 20 miles. However, quite apart from any local misgivings about the principle of a bridge, the railway authorities themselves were divided. The engineers were confident that a bridge would answer all needs but some Directors disagreed. Piercy, who had always been strongly in favour of the plan was, perhaps, less concerned

The distant platform seat marks the location where the line from Ynyslas would have joined the existing route, having entered the picture from the left, through the site now occupied by Penhelig Terrace, before crossing the road bridge to follow the original sweep of the curve into Craig-y-don tunnel. The platform seats, which do not appear to be of Cambrian pattern could well be former Barry Railway seats, possibly from Pontypridd (Graig) station, which was closed in 1930; Penhelig was opened by the GWR on 8 May 1933. *GWR/WIMM*

about cost and political difficulties, seeing only a rare opportunity to create a major work. Speaking at the Inquiry in 1865, against the proposal for a bridge and in favour of the alternative plan for the construction of a new line along the north bank of the Dyfi between Aberdyfi and Morben, David Davies commented:

> I know Mr Piercy wanted the bridge sadly [sic]. He looked to the honour of the thing but I looked to the money . . . . If there was any chance of the bridge being really built I should not oppose it. I know engineers spoke in favour of it, and I also know with them that it is only a question of pocket[27].

Referring more specifically to those who opposed the deviation, as the alternative scheme became known, Davies said,

> If this was a bona fide opposition, I am the man who ought to support it for I am making a line (M&M) which will be better served by the bridge, but we have waited four years for the bridge . . . I offered to make the deviated line for £45,000 in six months, but the bridge would cost £100,000 . . . it would take £20,000 to erect scaffolding to build the bridge, and that may be washed away in a month . . . it would take four years to build.[28]

It is not difficult to appreciate that many of the maritime fraternity would have been against the big bridge because of restrictions imposed on shipping, yet the project had local support and not all of those with nautical interests opposed the scheme. John Evans, *Y Morben*, for example, was a particularly vociferous supporter of the viaduct and much opposed to the deviation. He made strenuous efforts to defeat the construction of the line which would bridge the upper reaches of the estuary at Glandovey, but his efforts proved unsuccessful. His thriving shipbuilding and wharfage business at Morben duly suffered and eventually succumbed to the inevitable: John Evans became disconsolate and died soon afterwards.

From as early as June 1862, it was expected in some quarters that construction of the bridge was imminent[29] but nothing tangible transpired and the idea lingered until abandoned by the eventual passing of the A&WCR (General) Bill three years later. In addition to seeking powers to abandon the bridge and build the deviation, this Bill contained a third controversial element, a proposal to construct the Mindovey Railway, from a junction at Penhelig and across the front of Aberdyfi by means of a wharf, to a second junction with the A&WCR at the western end of the town. It sought to improve facilities for the loading and discharge of vessels which would lie alongside and was not intended as a through route. If Aberdyfi was divided over the question of the deviation and the bridge, it was virtually unanimous in opposing the proposals for the Mindovey Railway. Concerted opposition in Parliament successfully defeated the scheme, whilst the proposals for the deviation and abandonment of the viaduct eventually carried the day, setting the seal on the development of the little port which has remained basically unchanged to this day. When news of the passing of the Bill reached Aberdyfi and Tywyn in May 1865, '. . . bells were set ringing, bonfires lighted, guns fired and some fireworks let off during the evening'.[30]

The Dyfi Ferry

Until such time as a rail connection was established between Aberdyfi and the rest of the system, the ancient ferry across the Dyfi estuary assumed a vital role in the construction and operation of the coast line to Llwyngwril.

A ferry between Aberdyfi and Cerrig-y-Penrhyn had, for centuries, provided an important link across the natural boundary between north and south Wales. It had been part of the Ynys-y-Maengwyn estate at least since 1494 and was certainly under the control of the Corbetts of Ynys-y-Maengwyn in 1808. During the 1860s the lease was acquired by the Welsh Coast Railway when the Company realised the ferry's importance in the construction of the new railway. The ferry no longer operates today, but a recent newspaper account indicated that steps could be taken to revive it.[31] Prior to the coming of the railway, it appears there were three ferry vessels to suit the particular traffic needs of the moment. These were referred to as:

> 1. Y Fferi Fawr—The Big Ferry, used for the conveyance of animals and heavy horse-drawn vehicles; 2. Y Fferi Ganol—The Middle Ferry, a general purpose vessel which could cope with some animals, riders on horseback, and passengers with luggage, and 3. Y Fferi Fach —The Small Ferry, used for passengers only. Sample tolls included, Foot passenger 2d . . . Horse & rider 6d . . . Carriage (2-wheels) 2/6d . . . 1 horse Phaeton 4/0d . . . 2 horse Phaeton 4/6d . . . Carriage & pair 7/6d . . . Double fare was charged on Sundays, and operation of the Ferry was restricted to the hours of daylight.[32]

During the pre-railway period the ferry was operated only at low water, crossing the short distance to Cerrig-y-Penrhyn just opposite Aberdyfi; here, wooden poles marked the path southward over the sands to Moel-Ynys, on the road to Borth and Aberystwyth. The main disadvantage of the Penrhyn site was that it became submerged during high tides. Such arrangements, though they had sufficed for several centuries, were totally inadequate for the railway constructors who immediately sought an additional landing place for use at high water.

As a result of the Gorsfochno Inclosure Act, the river Eleri had been diverted, circa 1826, to flow into the Dyfi estuary, instead of its previous course directly into Cardigan Bay near Borth. By the time the Welsh Coast Railway arrived on the scene, the little river was well established in its new cut and joined its larger sister near Ynyslas, a site which seemed to offer the contractor a new and convenient landing place. An advertisement[33] placed in the Oswestry paper by Messrs Jones & Griffiths suggests that this company already occupied a small wharf at Ynyslas, on the eastern bank of the Eleri, but whether this was the first to be established here is not apparent.

Savin built his wharf on the western bank of the river, served by a branch which gained access from the Machynlleth direction by means of a reverse junction. There was at least one siding here and also a small waiting shelter;[34] the branch then continued across the sands for over a mile to the ferry terminus at Cerrig-y-Penrhyn, where it was obviously not prudent to erect any kind of shelter. The Cerrig-y-Penrhyn ferry branch (1m. 5f. 3ch), was constructed in 1863 without the delay of a formal application to Parliament. Savin, later expressing regret that he had not applied to the Board of Trade before he commenced the ferry branches on both banks of the Dyfi, claimed that they were only temporary works;

> . . . created to meet the emergency of a sudden call for the use of the ferry by many hundreds of workmen and others, for whom the previous ferry accommodation was utterly unfit and dangerous.[35]

His plea was successful.

Savin's opinion of the primitive and unsuitable ferry can be imagined, and one can appreciate his enthusiasm for constructing a bridge. Even as a temporary expedient, the ferry was most unsuitable for its new role. The old vessels, dependent upon wind, tide or muscle power, were completely inadequate for towing heavy locomotives and rolling-stock across the windswept, tidal waters. By 1862, a steam tug called *Victoria* was operating in the estuary and another steamer, the *James Conley* was also reported at work in the area.[36]

Perhaps the most interesting vessel during this period, however, was the steamer *Elizabeth*, introduced by Savin late in 1863 to entice passengers from Ynyslas across to Aberdyfi and the isolated section of line to Tywyn and Llwyngwril. The opening of the first section of the A&WCR, from Machynlleth to Borth on 1 July 1863, emphasised the need for a reliable ferry connection and although most people initially appreciated the advantages of the new services, such progress was quickly taken for granted and critics soon emerged. One of the major areas of complaint concerned the irregular and tardy crossing of the river, now an essential component of the railway's time-table. In an attempt to rectify this deficiency, Savin announced the purchase of the new steamer at the time of the Machynlleth-Borth opening, promising its early arrival, but;

> From the first week in August, week after week, and day after day, she was expected at Aberdyfi. In September . . . the opening of the railway (to Llwyngwril) was advertised, a dinner ordered, guests invited; but no steamer came, and the opening was postponed. The same thing occurred the following week and the same postponement. At last a newly built steamer did arrive, but was found to be too long for the place in which she was to turn, and so, at present, for any regular traffic between the two sections of the railway, is comparatively useless.[37]

The delivery of the *Elizabeth* was not helped by the fact that the steamer was brought from London around the coast and was storm-bound at Milford Haven for several weeks. Such considerations were dictated by the vessel's shallow draught, but the delay cannot have appeased those who had to cross the estuary meanwhile, 'in an open boat, open to the western gales from the Atlantic'.[38]

Whether the *Elizabeth* was always better than an open boat was debatable for she apparently spent much of her time aground. To quote David Davies again, 'The steamer was little use, for the shifting sands left it on the bank every now and then'.[39] . . . or, to revert to a previous source on this topic:

> There is no regular communication by steamer from Pont-Ynyslas to Aberdovey; the steamer has been for a week high and dry, upon a bank near Pont-Ynyslas . . .[40]

The travelling public had little representation in the matter during the five years 1862-67, for the ferry was run principally for the convenience of the contractors. Nevertheless, by January 1864, the *Advertiser* was able to report an improvement in ferry services, largely as a result of the introduction of the *Elizabeth*, but carefully added, 'Still, however, there is room for improvement.'[41]

The same issue drew attention to storm damage suffered by the incomplete Penrhyn pier where early 'roll on, roll off' facilities, vital to the whole scheme, were being installed to enable Savin to transport the rolling stock across the river:

> Completion of the pile pier on the Penrhyn will be delayed some weeks. Eight of the piles were lifted up, some were knocked crooked and others were washed away.[42]

Eventually, the pier was stabilised with the help of between 30 and 40 tons of rails. As soon as work on the Machynlleth-Borth section was complete, Savin was able to bring rolling stock into the area directly by rail, so early completion of the improved ferry link assumed great importance. Eventually, locomotives and carriages made the journey across the Dovey, each towed on a barge by one of the steam tugs. By the summer of 1863 sufficient stock had reached the Merioneth shore to inaugurate the service from Aberdyfi to Llwyngwril, but the formal opening was delayed several times until 24 October, when the *Elizabeth* duly appeared to provide the passenger link across the estuary.

Development at Aberdyfi

Whilst, in one sense, it had been logical for Savin to extend from the existing railhead at Machynlleth, the little port of Aberdyfi gave him valuable independence and it became the natural springboard for all his early Welsh Coast ambitions. The 'unremitting and energetic' engineers,[43] had already taken levels and staked out the line from Aberdyfi to Tywyn by mid-August 1861. Contemporary reports claimed there was 'the certainty of immediate commencement of the works',[44] for unlike the neighbouring N&M, the Welsh Coast Company wasted no time after securing their Act, and work commenced as soon as the rails arrived by sea from Ebbw Vale, and probably from the very water's edge at the point of off-loading. The wooden sleepers for the line eventually arrived in quantity from the Baltic but at the outset much timber for the use of the WCR was purchased from the Tywyn area. As well as controlling and improving the ferry, Savin's main requirement at Aberdyfi itself was the provision of a wharf. Up to 1861 none is thought to have existed and boats discharged directly onto the beach, as evidenced by the unloading of rails for the N&M. A wharf was therefore quickly constructed, approximately where the later structure stands today, although it was much smaller and the river-side siding, parallel to the main landing-stage, was located below the level of normal high water. It would seem that this was done intentionally in order to facilitate the transfer of rolling stock on and off the barges. Commercial freight, such as slate from Tywyn, also went by this means.[45]

The practice at Aberdyfi of running boats directly onto the beach, both for unloading and for repair, was one of the major factors against the construction of a proper sea-wall and dock, as proposed in the A&WCR's General Bill of 1865. The first such proposal was introduced as early as 1852 by the Corris, Machynlleth, Aberdovey, and Towyn Railway, when the 'main-line' was to skirt Aberdyfi to the north, much as the existing route, but the plan also intended forming;

> ... Penhelig Bay into a dock by erection of a wall from Penhelig Point, extending westward for about 16 chains, and continuing in a north-western direction to the shore, with suitable gates for locking in the water at high flood.[46]

As the CMA&TR plan failed to materialise, largely due to the demise of the accompanying Shrewsbury-Aberystwyth project, the proposal was not put to the test at that time. In 1861, Piercy originally proposed to take the A&WCR main-line across the face of Aberdyfi but was disuaded by Brunlees.[47] The A&WCR's General Bill of 1865 therefore constituted the third and final threat to erect a line across the front at Aberdyfi. Significantly, most of the proposed wharf lay within the area where harbour dues were demanded, as was made apparent when the Board of Trade reported that;

The proposed railway in front of the town of Aberdovey interferes with, and in fact, monopolises the whole foreshore; which from time immemorial has been used by vessels discharging or loading cargoes in the Port of Aberdovey. It appears that nearly the whole of the trade of the Port is carried out in a very limited space, the western boundary of which consists of an iron mooring post, and that westward of the latter the only port charge, of one farthing per ton, called ringage, is not levied . . . On this account it appears to me that if any railway, quay, or wharf be allowed, it should be situated westward of the mooring post, or on the part now partially occupied by the jetty and railways.[48]

This suggestion, however, was at least three years late, for Savin had built the jetty and railways referred to, without the consent of Parliament, as early as the autumn of 1861. The jetty was mentioned by the *Advertiser* in the issue of 15 Jan 1862 when it reported:

> Considerable progress is being made by the contractors for the prosecution of the work. At their wharf at this port, a very large accumulation of 'plant' has already been made. About a thousand tons of rail are already in transit from the Ebbw Vale Iron Works.

Once plant and materials were discharged from sea-going vessels at Aberdyfi, Savin was anxious to transport as much as was relevant to the opposite shore and to the railheads on the Machynlleth-Borth line. The small Dyfi riverboats were obviously useful here and although their days were numbered, they were undoubtedly glad of the business. They discharged materials up-river at Derwenlas and also at Ynyslas, and at least one, the sloop *Mary Ann* was owned in its later days by the enterprising Mr Savin himself.

The A&WCR Bill of 1861 made provision for the railway at Aberdyfi to pass from Penhelig to the north of the town, through some considerable rock cuttings and the 533yd (Craig-y-don) tunnel. Work at both ends of the tunnel was under way during June 1862 together with the line to Tywyn; most of the route was fenced and a considerable portion of permanent way laid. The first station at Aberdyfi was a temporary wooden building located on the beach and close to the landing stage; it served throughout the period the ferry was in regular railway use until 1867, when Aberdyfi's second station was opened on the present site. This building, in turn, survived until the first decade of the present century, when the construction of a new station at Pwllheli released the original Pwllheli building for re-location at Aberdyfi. This survives today, although no longer serving its original purpose; the platform canopy, however, has found a new lease of life at Llanuwchlyn, on the narrow-gauge Bala Lake Railway. A small engine shed was established at Aberdyfi in 1862. At this time, Aberdyfi was a busy place and full of activity. *The Chronicle* noted:

> The Green, at the other end of town, on the Towyn road, which formerly was a promenade and cricket ground, is covered with sleepers, saw-mills, shops for smiths, wheelwrights, carpenters and joiners, engine houses, stables and cottages,[49]

whilst the *S&MT* had earlier announced that the business of the port had increased ten-fold during the last year. 'New quays, warehouses and wharves will be erected.. and the town is full of bustle'.[50] The work therefore seemed to be progressing satisfactorily but Aberdyfi presented Savin with a great many problems, problems which only five years previously must have been beyond the wildest conception of a modest Oswestry draper. Savin had emerged within that short space of time as a powerful figure, and during the years 1862/3, particularly, he was as much a speculator and financier as a contractor, and his power and influence were at their zenith. Land was purchased in great quantity, not always without dispute; hotels were built and Savin's ambitions generally knew little restraint. His first real set-back only emerged with the failure of the scheme for the bridge between Ynyslas and Penhelig: his second disappointment at Aberdyfi was the rejection of his scheme for a dock.

Throughout his career Savin had been adept at taking full advantage of the limited capital of the various schemes with which he became associated, by accepting payment in the form of shares.

Indeed, the railways of mid Wales would not have been built had not both Davies and Savin accepted this form of payment. Savin had thus emerged rapidly as a powerful figure and although he made good progress with construction toward Tywyn and Llwyngwril, development at Aberdyfi itself proved much more difficult. The resistance of the inhabitants to the development of a dock and construction of a viaduct, as well as the reluctance of some members of his own Board to support him, meant that Savin's ideas were under attack from several quarters. A certain amount of intolerance, sometimes noticeable when ambitious men deal with those of differing opinion, must have contributed to his problems at the estuary of the Dyfi. Apparently well aware that his plans would not find immediate support, he opened a Public Meeting at the Corbett Arms, Aberdovey, on 24 January 1865, in a cautious and reasonable manner by asking:

> Perhaps one of you gentlemen will be kind enough to let us know what you want? . . . .[51]

and later, after John Evans, *Y Morben,* had stated that the plans would be injurious to Aberdyfi, which would be better left as it was, Savin countered with:

> If you will convince me of that, I will not spend one shilling upon the place. There is no one more anxious than I am to benefit Aberdovey.[52]

Such equanimity, however, did not prevail, for as the meeting progressed, feelings ran high and when Capt. Owen Thomas declared that they were not going to be tyrannised like serfs in Russia, the meeting broke up before a vote of thanks could be passed to the chairman.

It became clear that no amount of blustering or brow-beating would succeed where reason and rhetoric had failed and it was not difficult, in such circumstances, to create enemies. Most prominent amongst these, perhaps, was George Whalley of *Plasmadoc*, and one-time MP for Peterborough. He was involved in many of the mid Wales railway schemes and a man who revealed many of the characteristics possessed by

Savin himself. A clash between the rival Railway Barons of mid Wales was inevitable. As chairman of the Board of the A&WCR, Whalley resented Savin's methods and the conflict reached a climax in November 1863 when Whalley and some of the Board tried to impose conditions to restrain the contractor. These were firmly rejected by Savin and although Whalley appealed to the shareholders as well as the O&N and L&N companies for support, it was without effect; Savin had his own supporters and Whalley and three other WCR Directors were compelled to resign. Benjamin Piercy had supported Whalley and was swiftly sacked, with his brother, Robert. Henry Conybeare of the Brecon & Merthyr Railway was then appointed Engineer, but he survived in the post only until November 1866 when, in turn, he also was dismissed, to be replaced finally by the ubiquitous George Owen. Owen brought some stability to the position, for he progressed as Engineer of the newly formed Cambrian Railways, and remained in post until 1898.

The Llanidloes & Newtown, the Oswestry & Newtown, the Newtown & Machynlleth and the Oswestry, Ellesmere & Whitchurch Railways fully realised that any hope of future success depended upon unity and co-operation. The way ahead had been indicated by the formation of the Oswestry & Newtown Joint Committee which undertook the day-to-day running of the individual companies in 1863, and a Bill for the amalgamation was presented to Parliament in March 1864. This was successful and the Cambrian Railways Company was formed on 25 July 1864 but, because it could not conform with the Standing Orders at the time, the A&WCR was excluded from the scheme. A year later however, on 5 July 1865, amalgamation of the A&WCR with the other Cambrian Railways became a reality and brought renewed hope of an early conclusion to the work at Aberdyfi. Yet, before the new regime was allowed time to settle, matters received a major setback with news of Savin's financial difficulties, announced on 5 February, 1866. Thomas Savin had adopted what may be termed a creative and flexible approach to finance; from the outset, he had undertaken to operate the railways for a percentage of the receipts and interwove his personal finances with those he served in a most adventurous manner. He was inclined to manipulate both hardware and finances for what he considered the greater good at any given time. The disadvantages of this approach to accountancy began to emerge.

Savin struggled to keep his financial empire intact throughout this difficult period, but his resources were fully extended. In additions to his problems along the Dyfi he was faced by construction difficulties further along the coast at the Friog and the Mawddach; elsewhere, the Mid-Wales, the Hereford, Hay & Brecon and the Brecon & Merthyr lines all had problems of their own. The failure of the London Banking firm of Overend & Gurney provided the final embarrassement for Savin who, although a wealthy man in theory, was unable to realise his assets in the short term.

The building of the deviation, which David Davies had offered to complete quickly and economically, suffered as a result of these machinations and although work continued spasmodically, construction proved to be a protracted affair beset by landslips, bailiffs, storm damage and a general lack of resources. Precisely when the first train made its way along the north shore of the Dyfi is not known, but the first locomotive to cross the river under its own power was the O&N's *Volunteer*. It had reached Aberdyfi by barge from Ynyslas and its journey across the river was significant in a broader sense also, as recorded in the *Merionethshire Herald*:

> On Monday last, (July 30), the *Volunteer,* driven by John Ward from Aberdovey to Ynyslas, crossed over the Dovey Bridge, thus completing railway communication between Oswestry and Caernarfon. A few weeks' ballasting is all that is required to make ready the Coast Section for Inspection and Public traffic.[54]

Yet again, optimism was mis-placed. Conybeare had earlier declared the line ready for inspection (June 1866), only for the Board of Trade Inspector to report (in September) that the deviation was not satisfactory. One of the problems concerned the restricted clearance of the four tunnels on this section, (Frongoch, 199yds: Morfor, 219yds: Penhelig, 119yds and Craig-y-don, 533yds.) The Board of Trade indicated that all opening carriage windows had to be fitted with bars. By the end of the year, the Company's trains are known to have used the line again although in February 1867, George Owen reported to his Directors that,

> ... works are not sufficiently completed for re-inspection because of large landslips, as the result of a rapid thaw, at Penhelig. The Glandovey Bridge also sustained some damage from a vessel being blown against it in the recent gales.[55]

The opening section of the Glandovey Bridge worked on a different principle to that employed at Barmouth, where the opening section was an over-drawbridge. The bridge at Glandovey was opened by moving the drawbridge back *beneath* the roadway of the adjoining superstructure; it had to be closed, lifted into position, and supported from beneath for the passage of a train. It had an opening span of 35ft and the scheme was devised and first used by Brunlees in the viaducts at Morecombe Bay.[56] [Diminishing river traffic eventually caused the opening section of the bridge to be closed and fixed permanently in 1914.]

Matters had improved gradually with the coming of spring, for by the end of March 1867, Owen was able to report that repairs to the permanent way along the deviation were all completed and that Mr Quilter, the Contractor for this section, had withdrawn his men enabling goods traffic to be resumed. Simultaneously, a request was made for extra platelayers to maintain the standard achieved by the contractor. By April, 1867, the Cambrian Board was sufficiently confident of the eventual opening of the Aberdyfi line to put many of the small items used in the construction of the deviation up for sale.

For disposal at Ynyslas, amongst baulks of timber, logs and piles of various sizes was; 1 x 16ft turntable in pieces, very rusty and nearly spoiled by exposure . . . £25.0.0[57]

At the same time, in Aberdyfi, the following were listed amongst other impedimenta for sale:
55 earth wagons ... @ £3.10 ea £192.10.0
1 Timber Carriage £10.10.0
1 Timber crane & cast-iron pillar..... £25.00.0
1 15ft Turntable, that has been used... £22.10.0
1 40ft Turntable, (Damaged)......... £45.00.0
50 Wheelbarrows ... @ 2/9d ea...... £6.07.6[58]

The Engineer was duly sanctioned 12 platelayers to cover the new works, working in three gangs of four men: each gang was responsible for two miles of formation[59] and the deviation was opened officially between Glandovey Junction and Aberdyfi from 14 August 1867.

Morben/Glandovey/Dovey Junction

With the benefit of hindsight, it is possible to suggest that the location of the junction was not particularly well chosen. Although the site could sometimes present the waiting traveller with views of great beauty, it more frequently emphasised a bleak and windswept aspect which, at the time of the opening particularly, was even more forbidding than in later years, for the solitary platform was without shelter of any kind. The only structure in the immediate area was the small cabin for the pointsman who controlled the junction. This was located at ground level near the levers, which were placed outside the wooden building and open to the weather. Over the years, the location of the actual junction has been moved progressively away from the west end of the station: originally, the coast line curved abruptly from the adjacent bridge, directly onto the mainline without, as in later years, running parallel to the Main before effecting the junction. In addition to employing a pointsman, the Company retained the services of a second man to operate the opening section of the bridge; he also benefitted from the shelter of a small wooden hut.

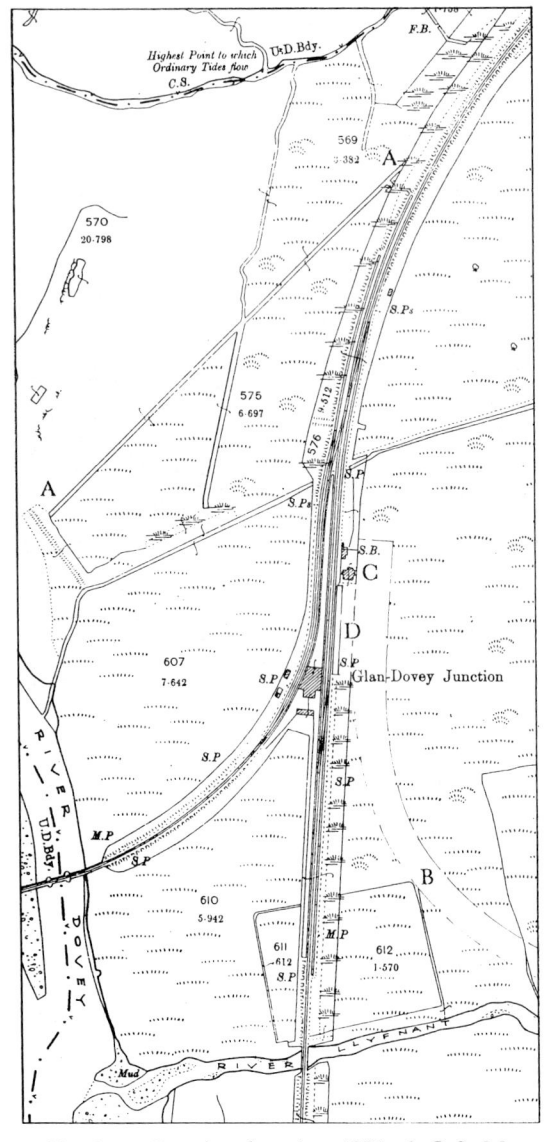

Glandovey Junction, based on 1901 ed. O.S. Map

A. Alignment of original 1861 scheme
B. Land required for road link to main Machynlleth-Aberystwyth Road (A487) 1884
C. Signalman's house
D. 'Down' platform pre c. 1885

The spartan conditions did nothing to encourage good public relations, but the Company was not entirely insensitive to the needs of its customers, for within a few months, George Owen had requested of his Directors;

> . . . .permission to extend the platform and to remove the old waiting shed from Ynyslas to this place; the passengers are now being turned out of the trains without the least shelter of any description—it being without exception the most dangerous junction possible.[60]

The men who had to work the junction, often under appalling conditions, also came in for some consideration, but only when it became apparent that their services to the Company were being impaired by the conditions.

During an inspection tour on 13 September 1871, Owen noted that a house was required for the pointsman at Glandovey Junction. He suggested this should be located as close as possible to the signal box; it was to be a wooden superstructure on piles and the old signal box was to be converted into a Waiting Room 'with Ladies w/c and a small place for the ticket collector'. By the 21st. the Engineer's notes had become a more urgent and formal request to the Directors, as the house for the pointsman was;

> . . . much required in as much as there are no lodgings to be obtained near here and the consequence is that the man in charge has to walk upwards of one mile in all weathers, thus often coming to his work in the morning wet through, in consequence of this no good man will remain here.[61]

It always required a 'good man' to survive the storms which could surround the junction[62] and the estimated cost of £250 was obviously considered a good investment, for the request was granted. A year later Owen requested a further dwelling, this time for the bridgeman, as it 'would effect a saving of the wages of one man as there being no residence, two men are employed for day and night, taking turn about in alternate weeks.'[63]

The signalman's house stood until the late 1920s but the bridgeman's house, constructed in

86

Elegant Cambrian signals still stand sentinel at the exposed and remote Dovey Junction on 4.8.1955.
V. R. Webster

1873, still survives in private hands. Over the years, flooding has occurred regularly in the area of the Junction, particularly when the river is high and periods of heavy rain are followed by westerly gales which prevent the tide from turning. In addition to problems of water reaching firebox level during steam days, or the electrical circuits on the modern 'Sprinter' units, (the latter only about 8 ins. above rail height), the danger of freak washaways of ballast is always present and the junction has often been blocked by debris, fouling points and signalling. Had the junction been located from the outset in the Morben/Derwenlas area, it could have been constructed above normal flood levels at no great expense; the bridge could have been built further upriver, above some of the wharves, thus removing the need for an opening span, and the villages of Derwenlas and Pennal could have had the direct rail communication which they sought, at various times, without success. An added advantage would have been the proximity of the main Machynlleth-Aberystwyth road. Doubtless, the railway authorities, together with the Machynlleth interests and the owners of *Llugwy* and *Morben Hall* saw to it that the junction was located in that no-man's land where it was out of sight and sound. It cannot have been fully appreciated at that time that the chosen location was so vulnerable during stormy weather. Although flooding is a recurring problem, re-siting the junction was not, apparently, given much serious consideration by the Cambrian, but the Company did contemplate the possibility of raising the existing site above flood level in 1889 and constructing an access road. There was also an earlier plan, of 1884, to provide a road to the junction but neither was implemented and the junction remained without a direct road link. As recently as April 1989, the principal turnout for

Storm damage near Gogarth Halt, c. 1936
Gwynedd Archives

the coast line was moved some 300 yards nearer Cei Ward, away from the area most prone to flooding, and the possibility of raising the trackbed some 2-3ft through the Junction may yet be reconsidered if suitable finance can be found.

The Board was provided with no fewer than three memorials from the people of the Pennal district for a station for the village. The first of these, in 1871, provided the company with an opportunity to re-assess station accommodation in the area and, perhaps, re-site the junction away from the troublesome marsh. The 1871 memorial requested the provision of a siding between Machynlleth and Glandovey Junction. The Engineer replied, on 19 January 1871;

> I have inspected the point referred to, it is called *Cae Wharf* and is situated about mid-way between Machynlleth and Glandovey Junction. There is already a signal-box with all requisite signals etc., in which a man is constantly kept by the Company for the purpose of protecting the road leading to the wharves and ship-building yard, in the occupation of the representatives of the late John Evans of *Morben*, but other accommodation such as a platform and an additional siding would be required involving an outlay of say £150-170. It is proposed to establish a ferry and to form a road by which Pennal could be reached by a little more than ¾ of a mile. I am of the opinion that if the station were constructed, no additional traffic would be placed upon the line and from an engineering point of view it would be objectionable as it would be on a sharp curve and the trains have to run over this section in quick succession and to stop them at this point in the summer or indeed at any time of the year would very materially interfere with the running and be a constant source of annoyance.[64]

The Engineer's response is quoted at some length as it reveals something of the railway's provision at this interesting site, as well as presenting that official's reaction to the possibility of attracting new traffic. It also provides us with another, rather intriguing, variation of the name of this location; *Cae Wharf*, or 'the field of the wharf'. The residents of Pennal and Derwenlas waited until 1913 before again submitting a request for a station; this time the Company 'promised to erect a Halt, at a cost not exceeding £100 at Derwenlas, should a bridge be constructed over the river'.[65] Sadly, and not for the last time, a public amenity was denied the local population because the Merioneth and Montgomery County Councils failed to agree. This also was the time when a Halt was proposed at Gogarth, together with a siding at Pil Gogarth. The Halt at Gogarth did not materialise for a further decade, when the Great Western constructed one in 1923; a siding was not included.[66] Services from Gogarth were suspended from May 1984, due to its unsafe condition; formal closure followed in September that year.

Largely as a result of the Regulation of Railways Act 1889, which placed upon all railway companies a statutory obligation to complete block working and interlocking arrangements,[67] the Cambrian was forced to improve its signalling equipment and up-date its procedures. Small stations were tackled in November 1889; plans for Machynlleth, Barmouth and Glandovey Junction were submitted in 1890, with the junction benefiting from 'provision .. made for increased platform accommodation sufficient to avoid the difficulties experienced last season.'[68]

In 1904, Glandovey became Glandyfi and the junction was re-named Dovey Junction. Thus it assumed the format it was to retain, with but minor alterations, until the station building had to be demolished because of subsidence and decay, and replaced by BR in 1957/8. Soon afterwards, in 1959, the signal box suffered the same fate; a new box was located on the island platform and the track layout modified. The introduction of radio signalling in October 1988 ensured that the final box at Dovey Junction was operational for under thirty years, whilst the most recent re-consideration of raising the level of the trackbed, first mooted a century ago, serves to emphasise the chronic lack of investment over the years.

THE MAWDDWY RAILWAY 1865

The third line associated with the N&M, the Mawddwy Railway, was incorporated in 1865 upon the instigation of Edmund Buckley, the lord of the manor of Dinas Mawddwy. At the outset, it was reported that 'the line is to be on the same gauge as the Talyllyn' i.e. 2ft-3ins.[69] but the standard gauge was eventually adopted and the 6m. 61ch. Mawddwy Railway was constructed. It served a sparsely populated area and ultimately failed to generate sufficient traffic to ensure any lasting success.

Along with its near neighbour, the Van Railway, it boasted the doubtful privilege of being opened and closed twice during its cash-starved existence. Both track and the very modest rolling-stock were badly worn by 1908, precipitating its closure. Despite the deplorable condition of the line, there were still those in the upper Dyfi valley who missed the facilities offered by the little branch and a fresh move was made to re-open it as a light railway. This was achieved with the help of

Engines based at Penmaenpool for the Barmouth-Dolgellau shuttle service returned to Machynlleth, usually at fortnightly intervals, for washing-out purposes, filling their time on the Mawddwy branch. GW 0-4-2T No. 1155 enters Dinas Mawddwy with 4w and 6w stock: no date. *Real Photographs*

Lord Davies of Llandinam (David Davies's grand-son), together with the financial support of several of the local authorities. The Cambrian took the little railway under its wing and in a report to the Board in 1910, the Engineer wrote;

> The smaller of the two engines is in the better condition. (Manning Wardle, *Mawddwy*, of 1865 vintage.) I took men to strip the engine of all possible removable parts to reduce its weight and on September 20th, allowed it to run slowly by its own gravitation down the grades and drew it by horses in a few places and over doubtful bridges, to Cemmes Road, whence it was brought on its own wheels by goods train to Oswestry Works. The estimated cost of repairs, including new cylinders, tubes and the greater part of a new firebox, will be £155. Work is proceeding. The other engine *Disraeli,* is of a larger type but from the inspection I have been able to make of it at Dinas Mawddwy, I do not consider it is worth repairing. This engine will also be brought to Oswestry Works as soon as the p.w. has been put in condition for it to be brought away by an engine.[70]

The branch was duly opened for the second time on 29 July 1911, to close finally on 6 September 1950.

The early promoters intended extending the line from Dinas Mawddwy, under Bwlch-y-Groes by means of a 1½ mile tunnel, to connect with the GWR at Llanuwchlyn. This scheme echoed the Corris's earlier ambitions to offer the Great Western a short-cut to Aberystwyth but, again, the rewards were thought insufficient and the project was not pursued.

THE VAN RAILWAY, 1871

The final branch to be opened along the N&M was from Caersws to the lead mines at Van (6½ miles). It was also the last railway constructed by David Davies, providing a local conclusion to the Llandinam man's great achievements. The line was opened on 14 August 1871, and the passenger service followed in December 1873, to

Mawddwy, in later guise as GW No. 824, rests at Moat Lane between duties on the Van Railway. 28.7.31.
V. R. Webster

last only until 1879. Owing to lack of business, the line closed to all traffic in 1893 but not before the Cambrian extracted much spoil from the mine workings for use as ballast or ground cover in goods yards. There was even some dispute over this matter as representatives of the Marchioness of Londonderry claimed that more wagon loads were being extracted than had been agreed, and George Owen had to travel to Machynlleth to meet Edmund Gillart, the solicitor acting for the Londonderry Estate, to resolve the matter.

All must have been settled amicably for by 1896 the Cambrian was again breathing new life into an old corpse and the line re-opened for a further period of modest activity on 1 August that year.

It is perhaps worth noting that a Van Railway Traffic Book used by John Ceiriog Hughes, the railway's manager and noted bard, rests at the Public Record Office, although it is probably fair to suggest that neither the railway nor lyrical entries possess much historic or artistic merit.

By 1940, traffic had dwindled and the line was closed finally in November. The drive for scrap metal benefitted a year or so later, when the track was lifted. The separate Van station, sidings and engine shed at Caersws remained in use until 1984, as the depot for the Central Wales Division Engineering and Bridge Department.

Further information on both Van and Mawddwy Railways, is contained in the excellent Lewis Cozens publications of 1954.

Chapter 5: Notes & References

[1] Suggested Prospectus, WIMM.
[2] ibid.
[3] Plans & Sections, CMA&TR, 1852, NLW.
[4] Plans & Sections, CM&RDT Extn. 1862-3, NLW.
[5] OA 13.4.1859.
[6] SC 8.4.1859.
[7] Two of these stables survived until the late 1940s, and one served its original purpose to the end when, during World War II, the GW re-introduced a horse-drawn cartage service to the town. The other stable was distinguished by having a hay-loft above the stalls, formed of two redundant roofs from a pair of the line's original four-wheel carriages.
[8] OA 25.7.1860 and S & MT 2.5.1865.
[9] AO 16.2.1861.
[10] ibid.
[11] SC 28.3.1862.
[12] OA 21.5.1862.
[13] S&MT 22.8.1862.
[14] OA 18.2.1863.
[15] Plans & Sections, Dovey Reclamation Scheme, 1861-2, DCA.
[16] RAIL 92/23. 22.8.1873.
[17] ibid.
[18] S&MT 13.2.1862.
[19] OA 15.1.1862.
[20] OA 17.6.1862.
[21] OA 8.7.1863.
[22] S&MT, 1862; A&WCR, 1861 & 1863; OA 1865.
[23] OA 17.5.1865. Brunlees, CE, evidence before Parl. Committee.
[24] S&MT 13.6.1862.
[25] OA 5.6.1861.
[26] OA 17.5.1865.
[27] OA 10.5.1865.
[28] ibid.
[29] S&MT 13.6.1862.
[30] S&MT 16.5.1865.
[31] WM 26.5.1989.
[32] Wynne Thomas, T. (1931) The Dovey Ferry, Cambrian News. p.3-6.
[33] 'Jones & Griffiths, having made an arrangement with the Welsh Coast Railway Company to run a siding to their quay at Ynyslas, are now in a position to deliver timber etc, along the Oswestry & Newtown and Newtown & Machynlleth lines, at reduced prices.' OA 9.7.1863.
[34] OA 17,2,1864.
[35] SC 19.5.1865.
[36] OA 13.8.1862. re. *Victoria*, and Green, C.C. (1977) *Cambrian Railways Album* Vol. I. Ian Allan Ltd., p. 16.
[37] OA 25.11.1863.
[38] OA 28.10.1863.
[39] OA 10.5.1865.
[40] OA 25.11.1863.
[41] OA 20.1.1864.
[42] ibid.
[43] OA 24.8.1861.

[44] ibid.
[45] S&MT 16.5.1865.
[46] Deposited Plans, CMA&TR, NLW.
[47] OA 17.5.1865.
[48] SC 19.5.1865.
[49] SC 12. 1862.
[50] S&MT 13.6.1862.
[51] ESJ 1.2.1865.
[52] ibid.
[53] ibid.
[54] MH 4.8.1866.
[55] RAIL 92/18.
[56] Higgon, I.A.
[57] RAIL 92/18.
[58] ibid.
[59] ibid. Inland on the N&M section, eight gangs of four men covered 2.40 miles per gang, with a ninth gang, of five men responsible for 2.60 miles at Machynlleth and Yard.
[60] ibid.
[61] RAIL 92/21.
[62] Frater,A.(1983) Stopping-train Britain. A Railway Odyssey. Hodder & Stoughton Ltd. pp.85-89.
[63] RAIL 92/22.
[64] RAIL 92/21.
[65] RAIL 92/89.
[66] ibid.
[67] The Signalling Study Group, (1986), The Signal Box, Oxford Publishing Company. p.24.
[68] RAIL 92/59.
[69] ESJ 28.6.1865.
[70] RAIL 85/414.
[71] RAIL 1014/14.

Chapter 6
Some Early Developments . . .

The primitive nature of the early stations soon brought complaints from the travelling public; the wooden huts were clearly unsuitable for any prolonged use and plans were quickly prepared to provide more permanent and worthy buildings.

Although grandly quoted in the title of no fewer than three of the four original constituent companies, Newtown seemed to suffer most in this respect, possibly because three separate companies were involved in any decision-making. It was clear from the beginning that the original L&N station was not easily adapted for through traffic, so a second station was provided near the present site. However, this also proved of a temporary nature and hardly met the needs and expectations of the Newtown public, particularly when it was seen that active measures were being taken elsewhere to provide better facilities; the complaints were many and prolonged. In January 1865, the *Shropshire & Montgomeryshire Times* took up the cause and pointed out;

> . . . the desirability of erecting the new station near the present cattle pens . . . as there is ample space . . . We have certainly never entered the town without being struck by the inconvenient and dangerous approach to and from the present temporary station; we sincerely hope the directors will soon carry out the wishes of the inhabitants, for nowhere is there a station so much needed.[1]

Later that month, George Owen reported to the Board that he had inspected sites for the proposed station and recommended that 'the space now occupied by the existing building be adopted as in every way the most suitable for the requirements of the Company.'[2]

This difference of opinion over the choice of location merely served to prolong the matter, for as the persistent *S&MT* later reported, 'Hope deferred maketh the heart sick', adding, 'Some hitch appears to have occurred with regard to securing a satisfactory site . . . '[3] The 'hitch' must have been considerable for, although Owen carried the day with his choice of location, he was not instructed to prepare plans until 1867. The contract was not let until November 1868, (to John Ward, for £1697), and the new station did not materialise until May, 1869.

Undoubtedly, a contributory factor to Newtown's dissatisfaction was the manner in which other stations had been built. By early 1865, for example, the Cambrian Board was able to meet 'in the spacious and handsome Board-room at the Welshpool railway station'[4] and most of the stations on the N&M, including Machynlleth's impressive headquarters of the line, were in the final stages of completion.

Plans for a permanent station at Machynlleth had been produced by George Owen in September 1863 although the architect quoted in the contemporary press was T.M. Penson of Oswestry.[5] It is probable that Owen planned the track arrangements, including goods and engine sheds, whilst Penson was responsible for the station building. Originally, the *Advertiser* had announced that,

> . . . the shabby wooden shed . . . the subject of much remark . . . will shortly be removed and a handsome structure is being reared from the plans of Mr George Owen of Oswestry . . . The contractor is Mr John Morgan of this town.

but in the Machynlleth column a week later it reported,

> New Railway Station. We are requested to correct certain errors which crept into a paragraph with the above heading in our last issue. The designs of the new station are Mr T.M.Pensons, [sic] and the works are to be executed by Mr Thomas Savin.[7]

93

Requiem for a shed: Moat Lane, with Cambrian stand-pipe, wartime paintwork and more fresh air than a sanatorium. 18.3.1952. BR/WIMM

A more positive note was struck by the *S&MT*, which reported that

> ... the foundations for our new gas works and a large and commodious station house have been almost simultaneously laid this week. The masonry for the former building has been contracted for by Mr Christopher, and the latter, as well as the station buildings at Cemmes Road, by Mr John Morgan, both inhabitants of this town ...

If it thus appears that Savin was responsible for Machynlleth station, John Morgan could well have been sub-contracted for the work as well as construction of the station house at Cemmes Road.

A delay occurred during the winter months for, after establishing the foundation, no further progress was reported until the end of March, 1864, when erection of the station house was 'resumed'. The penultimate N&M Board meeting, held earlier that month on the 10th, had finally approved Penson's plans subject to the following modifications;

1. The platform to be covered and a weatherboard placed at the Welsh Coast end of it.
2. A cellar to be provided.
3. Talerddig stone to be substituted for bricks in erecting the outer walls, with a dressing of free stone. The outer walls to be similar in style of workmanship to those of the other stations on the line which have been nearly finished. The woodwork on the outside walls, as now shown on the plans, are [sic] to be dispensed with.[9]

Regrettably, details of this woodwork are not known. Construction took about a year and it was not until the 30th March, 1865, that 'the station buildings were . . . nearly completed, and

The Cambrian's second engine-shed at Machynlleth, the low, three roof structure, which reflects clearly the Company's restricted financial straits at the time of its construction. 28.7.1931. *V. R. Webster*

although not too much can be said of its architectural beauty, yet the situation was delightful in the extreme . . .'[10]

The refreshment rooms were amongst the first sections to be completed for, according to the same issue, they had 'just been opened by Mr Rowlands, landlord of the *Wynnstay Arms*' and it is worth noting that Cemmes Road station also boasted a refreshment room at this time. No marked foundation stone is evident, nor has any reference been traced of a formal opening of the station; the town had probably experienced a surfeit of railway-based celebrations during the previous decade.

If Machynlleth station failed to stir the aesthetic senses of the *Chronicle*'s correspondent, the handsome old building is, hopefully, better appreciated today although the recent completion of new BR offices, and the collapse of an ambitious scheme for converting the old station into a gallery of modern Welsh art, may yet prejudice its future.

The more menial and purely functional buildings at Machynlleth are not without interest, however, and are worthy of brief comment.

The first to be built was the engine shed, completed early in 1863. Eventually, it comprised two sections although it was not always too apparent which 'half' was constructed first. The Company's records, however, confirm that the existing two-road portion was the original shed, despite the plausible theory that the three-road section would have neatly housed the N&M's complete locomotive stock of six 0-6-0 tender locomotives. Both sheds were built with narrow, arched entrances which had to be enlarged in later years; both sections have been re-roofed several

95

much used from the outset, although some tender-first running was unavoidable when the service was extended to Borth in July 1863. The precise location of the first table is not known although a Minute of the Board, dated 31 July, 1868, provides a clue, whilst requesting the provision of an additional siding at Machynlleth;

> by making use of the old stone siding at the back of the station. This however would necessitate the removal of the turntable, which apart from the requirements of greater accommodation, might be placed in a better position in as much as at present goods trains are continually shunting over it causing it to get out of repair and as a necessary consequence the engines have to run tender-first.[12]

An official WR photograph taken to demonstrate the outward bowing of one of the main walls of the 1863 Goods shed at Machynlleth (top left), also records the old warehouse crane and goods in transit; bottled beer from Banks, barrels from Ind Coope and animal foodstuffs from Wm. Vernon's of Liverpool. 21.7.1949. *BR/WIMM*

times since construction but the main walls and window frames are original. The first request for an extension was tabled in 1871, but the small shed had to serve alone for a further twenty years, until 1891, when additional accommodation was again requested by the Engineer, 'to enable six more locomotives to be stabled there. The present building will only accommodate four engines'.[11] The slightly lower, triple-roofed, three road extension was constructed soon afterwards. Nine locomotives were then stationed at Machynlleth.

The first locomotive turntable at Machynlleth had been installed by September 1862 and was

Signalman David Evans, Machynlleth West Box. 22.4.1954 *GBJ*

96

This suggests that the original turntable was located somewhere in the area later occupied by the single-compound crossing. The Engineer's suggestion had been adopted by 1870,[13] and the First Edition O.S. Map (1887) confirms a new location beyond the Pump-house, on the eastern side of the shed and beyond the coal storage platform. The second table served until the turn of the century, when a new 50ft turntable was installed where the existing brick-built engine-men's mess room was later located. This third turntable was brought into use during December 1899. The introduction of larger locomotives by the Great Western some forty years later necessitated the installation of Machynlleth's fourth and final turntable. The initial intention was to transfer a table from Old Oak Common but construction of a reversing triangle at Aberystwyth released the GW's standard 55ft table at that location. This was then valued at £350; installation cost a further £1890, whilst the Aberystwyth triangle cost £3085. The work was carried out during autumn 1939 and the GW turntable at Machynlleth survived until the end of steam. It was scrapped on site in 1967.

The handling of coal at the depot was an extremely arduous task for the best part of a century. From 1862, engines were coaled the hard way without the benefit of any mechanical aid. Coal-men had the unenviable and exhausting task of heaving tons of coal over the sides of wagons into the tenders standing alongside. This process was carried out in the open, in all weathers, until a simple shelter was provided in 1934. Projected Great Western improvements of 1925 had featured a traditional Swindon-pattern coal stage set in a re-designed loco yard but the scheme was deferred because of the cost and site constraints. Virtually the last act bestowed on Machynlleth by the Great Western was the design and authorisation of an electric coal-hoist which was planned in 1946 and became operational during the spring, 1948. The other essential structure for servicing locomotives was the pump-house, so called because it housed two small steam pumps which drew water from the nearby well to feed the 16,132 gallon water tank. Legions of trainee engine-men first made their acquaintance with the basics of steam-raising here; the first rung for many *en route* to the foot-plate. The pump-house dated from the very earliest days and survived until May 1982. The location of a new and larger tank of 22,500 gallon capacity, alongside the electric hoist, was considered in 1950 but did not materialise.

The first rails at Machynlleth were probably laid during the autumn of 1861, in the vicinity of the pump-house, as ganger David Owen and his men blasted the Rock away and used the spoil to create the embankment eastward, toward Craig-y-bwch, where John Bennett's men were making rapid strides 'towards reducing this promontory to a level and to the will of the enterprising Contractor, Mr Davies.'[14] What later became the double-track section within the station confines would also have figured prominently in the early construction, as well as the ballast siding which would have been driven toward the Rock as excavation proceeded. Tracks into the engine and goods sheds would have been amongst the earliest laid. Construction of these two buildings utilised the rubblestone on site, although this was soft and slatey in character and markedly inferior for building purposes to the hard blocks quarried at Talerddig. The choice was expedient at the time, but the friable nature of the stone created problems for engineers in succeeding years. The engine-shed walls have survived reasonably well but those of the goods shed became cracked and deformed, although the structure somehow managed to stand until 1960, just three years short of its centenary. Ironically, it was replaced by a new building during the period of greatest decline in goods traffic since the line was built. When freight services were withdrawn in 1983, the building was leased to a private company, but since August 1984 is back in railway use and occupied by the Engineering Department, transferred from Caersws, now known as the Section Works Department.

Signal-boxes were non-existent at the outset: only small wooden huts, serving as shelters, were located near the levers. All have disappeared from the Cambrian scene, save one, which at the time of writing still survives, out of use, behind the ruins of Glandyfi station. As an indication of the importance of the points at the eastern approach to Machynlleth, the 'box' here was constructed of brick and later survived as a mess-room for the carriage-cleaners when the Machynlleth East signal box was opened in July, 1890. The station signal box, Machynlleth West, was located on the 'down' platform and also opened in 1890. In later years, the Great Western entertained several schemes to provide a single, central box but, as with the goods shed, it was left to British Railways to effect the improvement. Both East and West boxes survived until the new central box was commissioned in 1960. This is now the nerve-centre for the recently introduced radio signalling system and the only signal box in operation on the whole of the Cambrian, controlling movements as widespread as Hookagate Jc, Shrewsbury, Pwllheli and Aberystwyth.

No carriage shed was ever provided at Machynlleth, although the idea was mooted in 1870 when it was felt that the rolling-stock was suffering from exposure to the weather. The Engineer suggested:

> There is ample room in the yard for such a shed and it might be so constructed as to afford room for a compartment for Lord Vane's private saloon, and for which I am informed, his Lordship would be prepared to pay a rent . . .[15]

The shed was not built, nor is it known where Lord Vane's saloon was normally stored when in Machynlleth. Neither is it apparent which yard is referred to, for by 1870 a lower yard had been constructed to accommodate the slate traffic from the Corris Tramway. The cattle pens were located here until 1899 when dealers claimed that animals were difficult to control in the open spaces between the tracks, often suffering injuries amongst the timber and coal. In consequence, new pens were erected in the upper yard in 1900.

Without doubt the restrictions of the site at Machynlleth, bound on the one hand by the Rock and on the other by the flood-plain of the Dyfi, inhibited the full development of the station as the logical junction for the coast trains. The lack of bay platforms to handle the arrivals and departures of coast passenger traffic constituted the station's greatest operating weakness, but the Cambrian was well aware of this and prepared a scheme, sometime before the onset of World War I, for a departure bay on the 'down' side. A balancing 'up' arrival bay was not projected, presumably due to the enormous cost, but a departure bay on the 'up' side, for Oswestry or Shrewsbury bound trains, was considered at that time.

Sadly, none of these schemes were carried out; they would undoubtedly have improved the efficiency of the station and been much appreciated by staff and public in later years. Lack of adequate space at Machynlleth was also the prime reason for abandoning the scheme to double the line to Dovey Junction. Projected initially by the Cambrian as long ago as 1871, this plan was considered most seriously, perhaps, by the Great Western in the years immediately following the Grouping: its rejection was a considerable miscalculation, for Machynlleth-Dovey Junction constituted one of the busiest single-line sections on the Western and doubling the line would have been of greater benefit to Cambrian time-keeping than the Newtown-Moat Lane section, for example, where traffic was lighter and few services were timetabled to take advantage of the second set of rails.

The original sidings and facilities provided at the majority of the smaller stations proved adequate throughout their entire existence. The one possible exception was Moat Lane although, even here, changes were minimal despite several plans over the years; few were implemented as there were more pressing needs for capital investment elsewhere. A drawing of projected improvements to the locomotive department, by the GWR in 1923, represents a typical example.

BR Western Region later entertained two further schemes in the early 1950's, but again, no work took place until the old loco-shed was destroyed during a gale in 1955. It was replaced by a new structure two years later. Now in agricultural use, this is the only building to mark the site of Moat Lane Junction.

Apart from the opening of the Mawddwy and Van branch lines, and the doubling of the Moat Lane-Newtown section in 1912, only a few small changes occurred to the main-line in over 125 years: for example, a station was opened at Talerddig in 1896 and a passing loop was installed at Clatter in 1914. Tenants of Sir W.W.Wynn in the Talerddig area presented a petition to their landlord in 1862, which concluded,

> Trusting . . . that . . . you will exert your powerful influence to cause a station to be erected at the place, We are, Sir, most respectfully, Your obliged, obedient, humble Servants.

There followed forty-eight signatures, ten of the signatories from the Llanerfyl-Llangadfan area which was up to eight difficult, moorland miles away. Their plea was unsuccessful and nothing further came of the idea until 1893, when another request was advanced by the residents of Talerddig for a 'passenger station'. George Owen, still in office and still apparently reluctant to agree to anything which might impede the free passage of traffic, did not accede to this request either, 'seeing the locality and sparseness of the population . . .'[17] On this occasion, however, the people of Talerddig persevered; they formed a committee and in 1896 passed a cheque for £80 to the Company who then agreed to put the work in hand.

A loop-line was originally installed at Pontdolgoch, but this was used mainly for the storage of wagons. A report to the Board states that, 'during high winds, trucks were forced over the stop-block and have run away to Moat Lane Jc.'[18] To prevent a recurrence, and to save a turnout, it was proposed to remove these 'before the summer service'(1885).[19] When a passing place was necessary in the Caersws-Carno section in 1914, it was located at Clatter, where the grade was less severe. It remained open until c.1945 when the signal box was 'switched out' and the windows boarded up. The loop remained in situ until the mid-1950s. Passenger facilities at Talerddig were withdrawn on 14 June 1965, together with those at Pontdolgoch, Carno, Llanbrynmair, Commins Coch, (opened 1931) and Cemmes Road. Moat Lane had closed previously, on 31 December 1962: only Newtown and Machynlleth currently remain open. Scafell, the curious little station between Moat Lane and Newtown, was served only by 'up' services. When this section was doubled in 1912, no platform was provided on the 'down' side; Scafell closed in 1955.

. . . AND A FEW MISHAPS

The development of any new form of technology is rarely achieved without a series of unplanned occurrences, and our railways were certainly not built without a multitude of mishaps and disasters. Accidents on the Cambrian were legion and although, thankfully, no passengers are thought to have lost their lives on the N&M, the list of minor incidents in this sector alone appears almost endless. Only one or two of the more notable mishaps from the early days are recalled here.

The first serious accident involving a service train occurred near Caersws bridge on 1 February 1868, after severe flooding had destroyed the embankment at the eastern approach. The first 'up' train of the day, the 3.30 a.m. through goods and passenger train from Machynlleth, had managed to cross the river successfully that dark and stormy morning, but only after the driver had climbed down onto the spray-covered bridge, barely clear of the raging river, and signalled his fireman by hand-lamp to bring the train cautiously across. This was achieved, and after proceeding to Newtown the crew transferred to

Just a week before the Abermule disaster, Cambrian 0-6-0 No. 54 (GW No. 874) was derailed by a landslide in Talerddig Cutting. The driver narrowly missed being crushed, for he had been leaning out of the right-hand side of the engine, seconds before the incident. No. 54 seemed an ill-fated machine for, as GW No. 874, it ran into another landslide, on the Friog Cliff, on 4 March 1933, killing both enginemen; Driver John Humphreys, Machynlleth and Fireman John Kenny who, though stationed at Machynlleth, had changed duty with another fireman in order that he might visit his sick mother, in his native Pwllheli. 18.1.1921.

Ifor Higgon Coll.

the 'down' mail and goods train, which comprised of the 0-6-0 *Castell Deudraeth*,[20] four loaded trucks, six empty wagons, the goods brake van, two passenger coaches and the mail van.

The 'down' mail had begun to reduce speed as it approached Caersws, when it was suddenly and violently brought to an abrupt halt. The guard was thrown to the floor by the force of the impact, but after he had recovered from the shock, he climbed down and moved forward through the gloom of the storm in an attempt to discover the cause. On reaching the front of the train, he found the embankment had been breached just short of the bridge and the engine and the first wagons had almost disappeared into a chasm beneath the

track. The crew were trapped on the footplate and lost their lives.

George Owen was quickly summoned; he organised a special train at Oswestry and proceeded to the spot 'with such men and materials as he could gather at short notice', arriving about 11.20 a.m.[21] Driver Daniels was released about 3.45 p.m. but the body of John Davies, the fireman, was not recovered until nightfall. Removal of engine and wagons from the river commenced the following Monday but, owing to the depth of the hole and the continuously raging floods, this difficult task was not accomplished until 7.00 a.m. on Sunday, 9 February.

100

Owen concluded his graphic report to the Directors (dated 18 February) with the following tribute:

> I cannot pass from this part of my report without mentioning the able assistance afforded me by one of your Directors, Mr. David Davies. Not only had he before I could reach the spot on Monday morning sent me his best workmen, horses, baulks, pile engine, and tackle of every description, but he was there himself and remained during the whole week of fearful weather we had to contend with, giving me advice, encouraging the men and working himself as an ordinary navvie [sic] where necessity required: anything I might say would fail to describe his energy and perseverance, but I beg most earnestly to report that had it not been for him and the assistance he gave me, I should not, with the limited means at my disposal, have been able to complete the works even by this time.[22]

A second unusual incident occurred on the N&M some eighteen month later when the 'down' evening passenger train and a heavy, double-headed 'up' goods train collided at Carno, causing two of the carriages at the rear of the passenger train (one with Earl Vane on board), to break away and run unhindered for some five miles back down the incline. Somehow, the coaches managed to keep to the rails as they rattled through Pontdolgoch and Caersws, before finally coming to rest just short of the Llanidloes Road level-crossing. The solitary occupant of the second coach, a commercial traveller from Manchester, walked with Earl Vane to Moat Lane where a doctor was summoned to attend to the Earl's headwound. An engine arrived from Llanidloes around 4.30 a.m. and Earl Vane was able to proceed home, an adequate path through the wreckage at Carno having obviously been cleared by another engine which had arrived from Machynlleth about 3.00 a.m., with further carriages for removing the stranded passengers. Most were unharmed, although one William Griffiths, travelling from Oswestry to Aberystwyth in the compartment next to the engine, had a miraculous escape when the LNWR carriage in which he travelled was 'smashed into splinters by the collision'. On being asked to explain his escape, he could only reply that he found himself 'amongst the splinters of the carriage and the coals of the tender'.[23]

Derailments caused by malfunction or fracture of equipment were common occurrences during the early years. Locomotive No. 9 *Volunteer*, for example, was working the 'down' morning mail near Derwenlas in 1870, when the tyre of one of its wheels broke, causing the engine to leave the track and run alongside the rails for over 260 yds, fracturing 56 chairs in the process.[24]

Signalling and points failures were also commonplace and mishaps not attributed directly to worn or inadequate equipment were frequently caused by human error. Even to-day, mishaps can occur occasionally, although nowadays the majority are associated with the modern, ungated level-crossings where motorists, either through ignorance, carelessness or defiance, challenge the train on its 'home' territory. Few drivers of road vehicles have any notion of the braking distances required by trains and not all treat rail-crossings with caution and respect.

Chapter 6: Notes & References

[1] S&MT 3.1.1865.
[2] RAIL 92/18/ 21.2.1865.
[3] S&MT 4.4.1865.
[4] ibid. 21.2.1865.
[5] OA 25.11.1863.
[6] ibid.
[7] OA 2.12.1863.
[8] S&MT 27.11.1863.
[9] RAIL 517/1 p.196.
[10] SC 30.3.1865.
[11] RAIL 92/60. p.181.
[12] ibid. 92/19.
[13] CN 19.11.1870 and RAIL 92/52 p.27.
[14] OA 5.6.1861.
[15] RAIL 92/20. 12.5.1870.
[16] CCA (Ruthin).
[17] RAIL 92/62. p.17.
[18] ibid. 92/54. p. 235.
[19] ibid.
[20] Formerly *Countess Vane*. RAIL 92/19.
[21] RAIL 92/19.
[22] ibid.
[23] OA 11.1869.
[24] RAIL 92/26

Chapter 7

Locomotives & Rolling Stock

The Pioneers

The name of the first locomotive to venture on to the Machynlleth line at Moat Lane does not appear to have been recorded but when work commenced in February 1859, the only locomotives in the area belonged to the Llanidloes Company. Whilst these were never numerous, little is known of their history with the possible exception, perhaps, of *Dove*, the first railway locomotive to reach Montgomeryshire in December 1857, and *Milford*, the first brand-new engine, which arrived in 1859.

The only single-wheeler to operate in mid Wales, *Dove* was a 2-2-2 tender engine built in 1839 by Sharp, Roberts & Co. for the Birmingham & Derby Junction Railway, which later amalgamated with the North Midland and the Midland Counties to form the Midland Railway in 1844. *Dove* served the new company until replaced by a Kitson engine in 1852. Its whereabouts for the next five years are somewhat obscure but it worked awhile for Mr Sharpe, a railway contractor, before being purchased by Rice Hopkins the first engineer of the L&N, for the bargain price of £350. By that time *Dove* was obviously in need of repair for it was promptly sent to the Ukside Iron Company's Works at Newport for attention. On completion it was dispatched by rail to Oswestry and brought eventually by road to Llandinam, where its appearance on 23 December 1857 caused great excitement. *Dove*'s design represented a very early development of the steam locomotive and regardless of subsequent wear and repair, was badly suited for its new duties; it enjoyed only a brief and rather undistinguished career in mid Wales.

Dove's first trip on the L&N was to Dolwen on 31 December; on 1 January 1858 it reached Bontnewydd and it was last recorded at work on 31 May, 1859, when the recent opening of the cutting at Scafell enabled it to work 24 large trucks of goods from Newtown to Llanidloes with the help of *Enterprise*, believed to have been the L&N's second engine. Until the opening of the cutting, *Enterprise* had been confined east of Scafell so it is likely that *Dove* and *Milford* were the only engines available to assist with the earliest stages of N&M construction. In due course, no doubt, it was followed across the junction at Moat Lane, by *Enterprise* and probably the other Llanidloes engines but, sadly, although *Squirrel*, *Llewelyn*, and *Llanidloes* appear tantalisingly in various texts, very little is now known of them.[1] We have to await the arrival of the new engine on the L&N, Sharp Stewart 0-4-2T *Milford*, in April 1859, to provide us with the first authentic recording of an engine west of the Severn at Caersws. *Milford* was involved in an accident whilst working trains of spoil from the cutting at Scafell to Caersws; sufficient to bring its presence on the N&M to our attention.[2]

Completion of the O&N in June 1861 brought Oswestry engines to Moat Lane, resulting in further invasion of N&M territory, if only to work the Pontdolgoch 'services'. From October that year, the haulage of the construction trains along the upper reaches of the incomplete line to Talerddig became the province of David Davies's new ballast engine, *Llandinam*.[3] With its arrival, he was no longer dependant upon others for motive power and *Llandinam*, a Manning Wardle 'K' class tank engine costing £1200, was put to immediate use. Its polished metal and bright green paintwork must have presented a brave sight amongst the rocks and spoil of Talerddig.

Within six months, *Llandinam* had earned the distinction of being the first engine to steam into Machynlleth, albeit over the temporary bridges near Commins Coch. It was followed four months later by a sister locomotive named *Merion* which arrived at Machynlleth on Thursday, August 7th, where it was transferred to a horse-drawn road wagon. Intended for the A&WCR, *Merion* set off from Machynlleth for Aberdyfi by road on Saturday, 9th, but encountered considerable difficulty just beyond the station yard due to a collapsed culvert beneath the turnpike. Drawn by a team of twelve horses, it managed to reach Dyfi Bridge later that day, 'where it remained until Monday morning'.[4] The local papers reported its arrival at Aberdyfi, though none note the precise date nor its manner of transportation. The first account to emerge appeared in the *Advertiser* for Wednesday 13th which, allowing for conveyance of that report to Oswestry and the subsequent preparation of the presses, suggests that *Merion* completed its journey by road on Monday, 11th August, 1862. A further classmate of *Llandinam* and *Merion*, named *Cardigan*, operated on the A&WCR south of the Dyfi shortly afterwards. It was eventually transferred north of the river, probably by barge from Ynyslas. The only other engine recorded on the N&M during this early period was the Oswestry Company's 0-4-2 'Volunteer' Class, No.5 *Montgomery*, although it is likely that other visitors would have worked on this section at the time. *Montgomery* features in the N&M Accounts and it shared haulage of the noted Temperance Excursion to Commins Coch in 1862[5]. Between October 1864 and May 1865 it assisted with the construction of another of Davies's railway contracts, the M&M line, but later returned to the Cambrian fold and was shedded at Machynlleth for a period.

As the rails advanced toward Talerddig, it became essential that the N&M acquired its own locomotives and on 10 May 1861, Davies ordered

Originally ordered jointly for the O&N and N&M Rlys., the Davies-Savin split placed *Prince of Wales* briefly on O&N lists, before the formation of the Cambrian in 1864. *J. P. Richards Coll.*

two 0-6-0 tender engines from Messrs Sharp Stewart & Co. of Manchester, at a cost of £2445 each. Both were delivered within days of each other in December that year and carried the names *Talerddig* and *Countess Vane* in brass letters on a wrought iron plate. During the course of their careers both were re-named, *Talerddig* eventually becoming *Cader Idris* whilst *Countess Vane* became *Castell Deudraeth*.[6] They were unnumbered when delivered. The Sharp Stewart order books contain references to other locomotives ordered originally in the name of the N&M, but subsequently deleted after the Davies/Savin rift. The first order was entered on 3 July 1860 by Davies and Savin in the names of the Oswestry & Newtown and the Newtown & Machynlleth Railways, for two 0-6-0 goods engines to be named *Queen* and *Prince of Wales*; they were delivered in December 1861, just a few days before *Talerddig* and *Countess Vane*.

Order No 442, dated 10 January 1863 and headed 'Newtown & Machynlleth Railway', requested four further 0-6-0 Goods engines: Messrs Sharp, Stewart being instructed, 'The first three engines to be delivered as soon as possible and the fourth, eight months after Mr Davies's instructions to proceed with it.'[8] The first pair of this order, named *Sir Watkin* and *Cyfronydd*, were delivered in 1863 on July 6 and 8 respectively, and fitted with 4-wheel tenders similar to the original engines, each carrying 3 tons of coal and 1200 gallons of water. An amendment received by Sharp Stewart during April 1864, stipulated that the final pair of engines of this order were to have Krupps steel tyred wheels, at an additional cost per engine of £112, as opposed to the 'wrought iron wheels and Yorkshire tyres'[9] of the previous engines. The tenders of this final pair were to be of 1600 gallons capacity, carried on six wheels, and also fitted with the German steel tyres.

The Cambrian Regime

The last pair of N&M engines was completed during the summer of 1864 which meant that, almost within a fortnight of being formed, the newly constituted Cambrian Railways benefitted by the appearance on 8 August 1864, of *Rhiewport* and *Towyn*, duly delivered with the larger tenders and, one presumes, steel tyres from the Ruhr.

This versatile class, identical to the O&N 0-6-0s and known as the '*Queens*' after the first engine delivered, formed the backbone of the locomotive department for many years. As overall speeds were low, they were rostered for passenger as well as goods working although the elegant little '*Albion*' 2-4-0 class handled the more important passenger turns. The pioneer 0-4-2 '*Volunteer*' class was also available and performed mixed traffic duties.

The formation of the Cambrian Railways created a pooling of all the locomotives of the constituent companies and the RCTS publications, in particular, provide detailed histories of the various classes. Very little information specifically related to locomotive workings on the N&M section is available but, in 1885, the company conducted tests between hard and soft coal. These trials took place during the week of 1-7 July, when four locomotives crewed by the same enginemen and performing the same duties worked out of Machynlleth; they used hard and soft coal for two 3-day periods [*Table 1*].

It would appear the softer Rhymney coal offered a distinct advantage although such a brief trial made no reference to the general efficiency of each engine, the water consumption, or any long-term differences in maintenance and servicing costs.

No register of Machynlleth engines is available for the first decades but two interesting lists survive for the years 1894 and 1898 [*Tables 2, 3*]. The original names are included where applicable though these had been removed by this time.

No allocation for the Van Branch is available for 1894, but four years later No. 22, was rostered to work the meagre traffic from the Van mines.

Table 1

Locomotive	Plas Kynaston Tons consumed	Miles	Rhymney Tons consumed	Miles
Castell Deudraeth	11.4	495	10.2	495
Sir Watkin	11.12	636	9.11	636
Minerva	10.16	927	10.3	959
Mazeppa	10.0	937	9.12	959.[10]

Table 2

Machynlleth 8 August 1894 (Bank Holiday Monday)				
No.	Former name	Type	Remarks:	
28	*Mazeppa*	2-4-0	1st Cambrian loco across Barmouth Viaduct	
50		4-4-0	'Small Bogie' Class	
5	*Montgomery*	0-4-2		
27	*Cambria*	0-6-0		
39	*Sir Watkin*	0-6-0		
19	*Hercules*	0-6-0		
26	*Tubal Cain*	0-6-0		
1	*Victoria*	0-6-0		
35	*Castell Deudraeth*	0-6-0		
60		4-4-0	'Small Bogie' Class	[11]
52	*Harlech*	0-6-0		

The crew pose alongside No. 43 on the turntable at Machynlleth on 2 July 1909, with as much pride in their machine as some enginemen took in 'Castles' or 'Kings'.

Ken Nunn Coll.

105

Neilson-built 'Large Goods' Class, 0-6-0 No. 88, of 1899, was reboilered by Beyer Peacock in 1915 and sported a rather elegant chimney as a result. It stands in the lower yard at Machynlleth, c. 1923, in front of the large shed used by the Ratgoed Quarry Company. No. 88 was nearly scrapped in 1939, as GW No. 885, but was reprieved because of the War and survived until 1944. *J. P. Richards*

Cambrian 'Large Bogie' 4-4-0 No. 11 outside the shed at Machynlleth, c. 1923. *J. P. Richards*

106

Table 3

Machynlleth July 1898—(including Drivers' names where available)			
No.	Former name	Type	Driver/s
14	*Broneirion*	0-6-0	D. Parry
15	*Glansevern*	0-6-0	G. Humphries & T. Lloyd.
16	*Beaconsfield*	4-4-0	S. Ravenscroft: Evans & R. Williams
28	*Mazeppa*	2-4-0	T. Plumb
35	*Castell Deudraeth*	0-6-0	D. Thomas
40	*Cyfronydd*	0-6-0	W. Evans
45	*Rhiewport*	0-6-0	R. Jones
51	*Snowdon*	0-6-0	—
53	*Gladstone*	2-4-0	T. Plumb: S. Ravenscroft: R. Williams
56	*Whittington*	2-4-0	Michael Caffrey [12]

Table 4

Moat Lane 8 August 1894			
No.	Former name	Type	Remarks
65		4-4-0	'Large Bogie' Class
15	*Glansevern*	0-6-0	
49		0-6-0	ex-Mid Wales Railway [13]

Moat Lane July 1898			
No.	Former name	Type	Remarks
65		4-4-0	'Large Bogie' Class
10	*Marchioness*	0-6-0	[14]

25 Years in the Shadow of Swindon

After the 1922 Grouping, the Great Western designated the area the Central Wales Division and introduced some of their own locomotives to replace the most worn examples of Cambrian stock. Unfortunately, the replacements were not new engines, being frequently almost as ancient as the engines which they replaced. As early as 1922, for example, Machynlleth saw the appearance of 1875-built 0-4-2T No.846 to work the Mawddwy branch. Normally shedded at Dinas Mawddwy, it returned to Machynlleth for washing out and minor repairs. The Cambrian engines were quickly re-numbered, although not all survived long enough to carry the Swindon plates. A remarkable example of longevity, however, was provided by one of the Newtown & Machynlleth engines ordered in January 1863; No.45, (*Rhiewport*), survived to be withdrawn by the GW as their No.900 in September 1945, after a working life of 81 years. The allocation for the N&M depots in 1922 predictably shows a predominance of older types, before gradual replacement eroded Cambrian representation. Nonetheless, the last Cambrian 0-6-0 did not disappear from Machynlleth until the withdrawl of No.849 in October 1954. Nos.855 & 895 survived to the same date and were the final representatives of this class to operate from Moat Lane, although Nos.844 & 873, which also worked on the mid Wales line remained until the spring of that year.

Table 5

Machynlleth Allocation, 1922.					
GW No.	Cambrian No.	Builder	Type	Built	Withdrawn
19	8	Nasmyth, Wilson	0-4-4T	1899	1932
846*	—	GW Wolverhampton	0-4-2T	1875	1932
849	29	Beyer, Peacock	0-6-0	1918	1954
873	42	,,	,,	1919	1954
881	78	Vulcan Foundry	,,	1895	1932
892	93	Robert Stephenson	,,	1903	1953
1086+	47	,,	4-4-0	1897	1923
1112	60	Sharp, Stewart	,,	1891	1928
1115	16	,,	,,	1878	1925
1329**	1	GW Wolverhampton	2-4-0	1883	1927
2346	—	GW Swindon	0-6-0	1884	1936
3210	—	GW ,,	2-4-0	1889	1937
3521***	82	GW ,,	4-4-0	1887	1931
3546***	95	GW ,,	,,	1888	1927	15

+ GW number probably not carried.
* Sub-shedded at Dinas Mawddwy.
** Purchased from Bute Supply Co., 1921.
*** Both were much re-built during the course of their careers, being finally converted from 0-4-4T's No's 1095 & 1122, in 1899 & 1900 respectively. No 3546 had the more colourful history; constructed originally as a Broad-gauge Convertible 0-4-2 saddle tank, it was converted to an 0-4-4 side tank in 1890-1 and to the standard gauge in 1892. Both engines were purchased in 1921 to replace Cambrian No's 82 and 95, destroyed at Abermule. [RCTS p.G45/6 and K79.]

Table 6

Moat Lane Shed Allocation, 1922.					
GW No.	Cambrian No	Builder	Type	Built	Withdrawn
876	74	Neilson	0-6-0	1894	1946
1104	71	Sharp, Stewart	4-4-0	1894	1925	16

1922 witnessed the introduction of Great Western steam railmotors at Machynlleth, a fascinating development which has seemingly attracted only minimal attention. They proved most successful on the Dolgelley-Barmouth service, based at Penmaenpool, and also at various times worked some services between Barmouth and Criccieth, and Barmouth to Machynlleth, where routine servicing was normally carried out and a spare vehicle usually stabled. Machynlleth's August allocation included Nos.39, 40 & 58; all 70ft vehicles which were later prohibited from using the tunnels at Aberdyfi because of their length! Within the month, Nos.39 & 58 were re-allocated to Oswestry and Llanidloes respectively, suggesting, possibly, that they may have arrived at Machynlleth over Talerddig before the error was realised. 60ft No.74 was hurriedly drafted in by September, followed by No.75 in December.

108

After purchase from the Metropolitan Railway in 1905, No. 2 was shorn of its condensing gear at Oswestry, repainted in the Cambrian's black livery and embellished with its new owners' name, the Prince of Wales's feathers and a raised brass numeral before being sent with class-mate No. 34 to Machynlleth. Because they carried limited coal and water supplies they were not really suitable for main-line work and as they were heavy machines they were prohibited from branch-line duties. Consequently, No. 2 became the regular Machynlleth yard engine until scrapped at the Grouping in 1922.

Ken Nunn Coll.

Sharp Stewart 'Large Bogie' No. 67. as GW No. 1100 receiving attention outside the three-roof shed at Machynlleth during the 1920s. No. 1100 was withdrawn in July, 1930.

J. Burman

'Barnum' No. 3220, displaying 'A' class headlamps, stands at Machynlleth with a 'down' train; the carriage roof destination board indicates a through service. The bridge girder, featured in the ILN print of 1863, was still *in situ* at the time of this photograph (c. 1924); it survived until the bridge was rebuilt in 1927.
J. P. Richards

Recently re-boilered (1921), Cambrian 'Large Belpaire' Goods engine No. 89, later GW No. 887, stands on the turntable road at Machynlleth, c. 1923. The most intriguing aspect of this photograph, however, lies almost obscured in the *r/h* background, where a crimson-liveried Steam Rail Motor on the back road rests between turns at Penmaenpool.
J. P. Richards

No.40, the third of the initial 70ft vehicles, was based at Penmaenpool; it arrived and departed via Ruabon. All three left by July 1924, being replaced eventually by Nos.78, 30, 76 and 81.

Steam rail motors also worked a Moat Lane-Llanidloes service in 1922, with an additional trip to Builth and back. As there were no restrictions regarding vehicle length on this section, the Moat Lane/Llanidloes cars were all 70ft. vehicles; Nos.39,58,66,84 and 85. The experiment cannot have been successful, however, for the cars had departed by 1924. The Machynlleth allocation survived a further three years, but within five years of inception, all had gone. The final pair, Nos.30 & 81 left for Swindon in July 1927.[17]

The greatest need, however, was for larger, more powerful locomotives, but before these could be introduced, bridges had to be strengthened and the track itself re-laid with heavier material. The immediate remedy was an influx of small, light locomotives which, being mostly quite elderly machines, seemed to perpetuate the atmosphere of the old Cambrian system. Amongst the early newcomers were three GW 2-4-0 classes, the '*Barnums*', represented by ten of the class; the '*Stellas*', which had seven representatives and the large-wheeled '*3232*' class, of which there were four, Nos 3239/41 worked from Machynlleth whilst Nos 3232/51 assisted on Whitchurch-Oswestry—Brecon services. Most of the examples drafted into the area worked at some period from Machynlleth and some of the '*Stellas*' also worked for a time between Moat Lane and Brecon.

The Pannier which worked the Yard at Machynlleth during most of the 1930s was Wolverhampton-built No. 1924. It took over from the former Brecon & Merthyr 0-6-2ST No. 1677 c. 1928, until scrapped in 1938, when classmate No. 1965 arrived and 'held office' until, in turn, it also was withdrawn in January 1950. When No. 1965 was not available, No. 2151 assumed the duty. The last Panniers to work the Yard on a regular basis were Hawksworth's Nos. 1603 and 1636. Photograph 11.3.1933.

Ifor Higgon

Former Cambrian No. 98, as GW 1043, pilots 'Duke' Class No. 3287 *Mercury* from Machynlleth to Talerddig with an Aberystwyth-Manchester Express, 29.6.1932.

S. W. Baker

Larger locomotives took the form of further examples of the '*3521*' class, based at Aberystwyth and Machynlleth. All the foregoing, however, were virtually life-expired when drafted onto the Cambrian and were withdrawn by 1931 but the '*Dukes*', another class introduced during the early 20s, proved most useful and remained the mainstay of Central Wales Division motive power for over two decades until eventually superseded by newer, more powerful engines. Virtually the whole class visited the Cambrian, working between Oswestry and Aberystwyth and from Machynlleth to Pwllheli;[18] because of their weight, they did not work the Mid Wales line south of Llanidloes.

There is little doubt that the most versatile type introduced by the GW was William Dean's '23xx' class of 0-6-0 goods engines. Dating from 1883, Dean's design was one of the most success- ful to emerge from Swindon and the '23s' were introduced to the Cambrian at the first opportunity in 1922. They worked both goods and passenger turns all over the system and an impression of their usefulness is gained by the special train arrangements for 28 May 1932, when the Urdd National Eisteddfod was held at Machynlleth. The notes of return workings, by Ifor Higgon, reflect the dominance of rail travel at the time.

Only one double-framed example of this class was recorded on the Cambrian, but as with the 'Dukes', more may have slipped through unnoticed. After working a Chester-Pwllheli train in August 1936, No.2378, on the following day worked the 7.55a.m. Pwllheli-Machynlleth service and after visiting Barmouth again that day, arrived at Penmaenpool shed later in the evening.[19]

Table 7

Dep.(pm)	Train No.	Engine/s	Coaches	Destination
8.00	1	2484 & 2454	6	Merthyr Tydfil
8.15	3	2343 & 2546	6	Cardiff
8.30	2	3287 *Mercury*	no record	Swansea
8.45	4	2410	5	LMS Bangor
9.00	6	3283 *Comet*	no record	Llanelly and Fishguard
9.15	8	2555	6	Corwen
9.15	5	3255 *Excalibur*	no record	Newtown
9.30	10	2427	6	Bala
9.45	12	3257*	7	Pwllheli
10.00	14	2342	6	Barmouth

*Until May 1927, No. 3257 was known as *King Arthur*.
The name was withdrawn to avoid possible confusion
with the new 'King' Class introduced in July 1927.

Dean Goods 0-6-0 No. 2351 shunting at Moat Lane, 10.9.1947.   *S. W. Baker*

A representative of the Great Western's 'Small Prairie' tanks, No. 4528 arrived on trial in December 1924,[20] but further members of the class were not drafted into the area until 1936 when No. 5570 arrived in March at Machynlleth, to be joined by Nos.4549 and 4513 in May 1937.[21] Fifteen of the class bore the MCH stencil by 1947 and were to be seen at work mainly between Machynlleth and Pwllheli, although they frequently banked goods and passenger trains to Talerddig or more rarely, local services to Aberystwyth; No.5570 occasionally hauled evening locals down the old M&M to Lampeter. In 1937, some of C.B.Collett's new '2251' class 0-6-0s made their way onto the Cambrian and proved capable engines for a variety of duties. The first '22s' were visitors only, No.2279 (SRD) being an example, but by mid-1938 four carried the MCH code, Nos.2200, 2296/7/8 and a year later, Oswestry shed acquired Nos.2201/4/10.

Whilst the GW replacements were generally reliable engines, they were under-powered and

113

GW 'Stella' Class 2-4-0 No. 3519 at Machynlleth. c. 1923. *J. P. Richards*

GW 2-6-2T No. 5570 near Frongoch, on the deviation between Aberdyfi and Dovey Junction, August 1957.
GBJ

the motive power position was still critical in the mid 30s. The '45/55s' and the '22s', useful though they were, were not available in sufficient numbers and in any case were not the complete answer to the problem, particularly during the busy summer months when long, heavy trains were numerous. A new design was under preparation at Swindon but neither it nor the programme for the renewal of the permanent way was to be complete until later in the decade. The position was aggravated by increasing failures of the faithful old 'Dukes'; their main-frames were weakening and they were becoming increasingly expensive to repair. A short-term solution lay in re-building 'Duke' class boilers in the stronger frames of the slightly larger 'Bulldog' class, nominally too heavy an engine for the Central Wales line. The pioneer hybrid, No.3265 *Tre Pol and Pen*, whose name reflected its Cornish/Celtic lineage, had been produced in 1930, but there was then no need for further re-builds.

By 1936 the situation had changed so a programme was speedily arranged to convert a further 29 examples, known initially as the 'Earl' class. Names had been affixed to the first thirteen when these were suddenly transferred in 1937 to the more modern and larger engines of the prestigious 'Castle' class. The old 'Earl' class retained its numbers in the '32xx' series until 1946, when they were re-designated the '90xx' class (to vacate the '32xx' numbers for an extension of the '22xx' group). The first '90' to appear at Machynlleth, in July, was No.9004 sporting a traditional Great Western brass number plate but with a vermillion background to the numerals, as opposed to the normal black.

In their final years, unassisted engines of the former 'Earl' Class were only allowed 138 tons (4 bogie Coaches) between Machynlleth and Talerddig. On 10 June 1939, No. 3220 seemed in fine fettle as it tackled the final stages of the bank with the six-coach 1 p.m. Aberystwyth-Whitchurch express. *Ifor Higgon*

found themselves on shunting duties at Machynlleth, Moat Lane and elsewhere.

By 1938, the Engineer was almost ready to upgrade the Central Wales Division from a 'Yellow' to a 'Permitted Blue' route, allowing most of the larger engines in the 'Blue' category to work the old Cambrian main line to Aberystwyth and, eventually, the coast line to Pwllheli. 1938 thus saw the appearance from Swindon of the first of the new 'Manor' class, especially designed to provide extra power on secondary main lines such as the Cambrian. Initially, they worked Cheltenham—Banbury services and none is thought to have ventured on to Central Wales metals until No.7817 *Garsington Manor* (CNYD) had a trial run from Oswestry to Aberystwyth in December 1940.[22] A 'large engine' is known to have spent a week-end on shed at Machynlleth around this period, which could well have been No.7817 resting during protracted clearance tests.

Shortly afterwards, Churchward's versatile 'Moguls' began a long association with the Cambrian line, for early in 1941 No.6380 (BAN) appeared on an 'Evacuee Special' from Shrewsbury to Aberystwyth and during February and March that year, 'Moguls' appeared from time to time on the 2.40 a.m. Oswestry-Aberystwyth Goods and the 6.15 p.m. return.[23] Of all goods workings during the war, perhaps the most important along the Cambrian was the Llandeilo Jc.—Saltney freight. It left Aberystwyth at 6.55 p.m. and almost always boasted a different 'Blue' engine in charge; 'Moguls', 'Aberdares', 'Manors' and 'Bulldogs', all shared this duty, which included regular transhipments of High Explosives.

The larger engines were merely visitors at this time; sadly, the majority went unrecorded but amongst the few that were noted were Nos.4337 (OXY), 2673 (BAN), and 3455 *Starling* (LDR).[24] The Division was not able to boast 'Blue' engines of its own until the winter of 1942/3, when No.7807 *Compton Manor* and 7819 *Hinton Manor* arrived at Oswestry. Their most frequent duties were the 'down' Morning Mail returning with a

Trainloads of evacuees began to arrive in mid Wales within days of the declaration of war. Mr Mourby (white coated and bespectacled) and T. R. Bridgewater, Council Officials, form part of the Reception Committee at Newtown on 9.9.1939. Note Astons black on yellow enamel advertisement strips which were prominent at many of the Cambrian's larger stations during this period; truly a time of 'Astons for everything'.

Geoff Charles Collection, NLW

Most of the '32s/90s' worked on the Cambrian, but as with the 'Dukes', they were not authorised south of Llanidloes.

Small 0-4-2T and pannier tank engines were introduced to the area by the GW, the former for working the auto-trains which succeeded the steam rail-motors, whilst pannier tanks soon

Driver Ll. Roberts and Fireman A. B. Jones on 0-6-0 No. 3200, pose at Barmouth before working an evening passenger train to Machynlleth, in August, 1957. *GBJ*

mid-day Aberystwyth-Whitchurch working, and the 10.00 a.m. 'down' Whitchurch-Aberystwyth Passenger train, balanced by the 'up' evening Mail, leaving Aberystwyth at 6.00 p.m. Whilst on Whitchurch-Aberystwyth duties they had no cause to come on shed at Machynlleth, until one fine summer's evening in 1944 when both Compton Manor and Hinton Manor returned 'light-engine' after their normal day's work.

Turning an engine has always been a fascinating sight for onlookers and the double-summertime of the war years provided warm evening sunlight by which to witness the excitement, even of the more blase members of the shed staff, as 7807 and 7819 were turned at Machynlleth for the first time. Balancing the first engine proved more difficult initially than was expected until it was realised that, as it had come down from Oswestry very hurriedly after its previous duty, the water and coal levels were low. After re-fuelling the tender, the problem disappeared.

The 'Manors' were not at Machynlleth to test the turn-table, however; the reason for their unusual appearance was revealed as two lengthy and heavily laden troop trains appeared from Tonfannau, hauled by four of the smaller engines which were quickly replaced by the two 'Manors'. The destination of these trains, possibly somewhere on the South Coast, was not revealed at the time but, hopefully, the 'Special Notices' for this unique working could yet emerge, one day.

Exceptional war-time circumstances caused other unusual locomotive movements, notably the allocation of the first LMS locomotive to

Aerial view from the Rock. 4-4-0 No. 9013 is turned on the 55ft GW turntable at Machynlleth. The *Cordon,* used for storing gas for the older coaches and normally kept by the stop-block near the Foreman's Office (centre left), has been moved into the lower yard to make room for the S&T Department's clerestory Messing vehicle. 14.6.1954.

GBJ

Machynlleth. At least nine ex-Midland Railway Johnson 2F 0-6-0s appeared in the Central Wales Division as temporary replacements for 'Dean Goods' away on war-service. The newcomers were:— LMS Nos. 3038, 3039, 3047, 3085, 3126, 3196, 3536, 3689, 3739.

They worked between Oswestry, Machynlleth, Moat Lane and Llanidloes. When they left the section in November 1945, No. 3126 was allocated to Machynlleth; No. 3536 was a Moat Lane engine, and No. 3739 was based at Llanidloes. The remainder were all allocated to Oswestry and none is thought to have worked west of Machynlleth.[25]

Also during the war period, eight LNER 'J25' 0-6-0 engines were shared between Croes Newydd and Shrewsbury, although no visit to mid Wales appears to have been recorded. At least one LNER-type did, however, reach the coast when a J94 0-6-0 saddle-tank engine, destined for the military sidings at Harlech, was observed on-shed at Machynlleth c. 1945. It obtained water from the pump-house tank, and probably also received a fresh supply of coal and had its fire cleaned before making for the coast. Its brief visit lasted no more than a few hours. [A Manning Wardle 0-4-0T, No.1106 of 1888, had visited the Cambrian briefly in 1931, working on the Barmouth sea defence contract.][26]

Three additional 'Manors' appeared around 1946; No.7808 *Cookham Manor* arrived in Oswestry and No. 7802 *Bradley Manor* became the first of the class to carry the MCH shed-code, followed closely by No.7803 *Barcote Manor* which arrived from Neyland. Both MCH 'Manors' worked mainly from Aberystwyth as the coast was still barred to the larger engines.

During the final Great Western years very few of the locomotives passing through Machynlleth were able to boast any recognizable livery; the vast majority revealed an air of general neglect and bore the unmistakable signs of reduced maintenance. Engines normally returned from repair at Oswestry Works in an unpainted state but occasionally a coat of black paint might have been applied to smoke box or chimney. The first to receive paint after the war was No.9054 *Cornubia* which appeared in un-lined green c.1946 after a visit to Swindon, and No.7807 *Compton Manor* returned to service in October 1947 again in un-lined green livery but with the Coat-of-Arms flanked by 'G' and 'W' on its tender. The Great Western was endeavouring to recover from its war effort but the deficit was enormous and many saw the impending state ownership as its salvation.

Nationalisation, and a Golden October

The Great Western expired at midnight on 31 December 1947. No major changes were immediately apparent although, by the following spring, a few more engines emerged in green livery. No.2219 was an early example and the first to appear at Machynlleth with evidence of new ownership, carrying 'British Railways' on its tender, lettered in Swindon's own shaded version of Cheltenham Bold.

Two years after Nationalisation, there were still only 5 'Manors' in the Division and the shortage of adequate motive power remained

Signalman W. Roberts prepares to receive the Cemmes Road-Machynlleth token from the Fireman of 4-6-0 No. 7818 *Granville Manor*, on a Sunday Manchester-Aberystwyth Excursion, 18.8.1957. *GBJ*

Apart from the B&M's No. 1677, engines of the 0-6-2 wheel arrangement were distinctly rare in Mid Wales, but major repairs to the pumphouse at Moat Lane brought ex-Taff Vale 04 Class No. 205 to the area for temporary use as a stationary boiler. Withdrawn in July 1954, No. 205 arrived "dead", via Oswestry, as it was too heavy for the shorter, more convenient route through Mid Wales. Photographed at Moat Lane on 23.1.1955.

Ifor Higgon

acute. With the new BR Standard designs still on the drawing board, sanction was obtained to construct a further 10 'Manors' in 1950. These were entirely new engines, unlike the 1938 versions which incorporated some parts from withdrawn Churchward 2-6-0s. The arrival, at Oswestry, of Nos. 7820/21/22 in British Railways lined black livery released members of this class for goods duties on the Cambrian for the first time since the sporadic war time appearances on the Saltney Goods.

The arrival of the new engines during the 1950s unknowingly heralded the final flourish of steam operation in the Central Wales Division; a flourish which, on reflection, may be likened to the spluttering brilliance of a dying flame. The fifteen years from 1952-67 saw Cambrian steam thrive as never before, yet the same period saw its decline and eventual demise. Few who worked on or observed the variety of locomotives at this time foresaw such an abrupt end; fewer still then appreciated that the passing of steam would also eliminate a whole way of life.

The availability of larger engines in greater numbers finally heralded their regular appearance down the coast for, apart from the short section between Barmouth and Barmouth Junction which saw 'Blue' engines from Croes Newydd and Chester, the coast line did not see a 4-6-0 until November 1951, when No.7802 *Bradley Manor* undertook clearance tests through to Pwllheli. In February 1952, 2-6-0 No.7305 (CNYD) worked a permanent way train from Penmaenpool to Tonfannau and back,[27] and on 13 April 1952, 2-6-0 No.5395 worked a Troop Special from Machynlleth as far as Tywyn. These are believed to have been the earliest workings of Churchward 'Moguls' in this sector. The first

'Manor' to be pressed into service down the Coast was No.7823 *Hook Norton Manor*, on 2 June 1952.[28] It had worked the 3.05 a.m. 'down' train from Chester to Barmouth that day when an emergency arose as a result of the failure, at Barmouth, of the engine of the 5.35a.m. Pwllheli-Machynlleth. No.7823 was commandeered to worked the train forward to Dovey Junction; it returned light to Barmouth before leaving finally with the 10.30 a.m. to Ruabon. No.7806 *Cockington Manor* was amongst the earliest representatives of the class down the coast and No.7823 was also a regular performer in later years.

Another urgent requirement at this time was a modern replacement for the life-expired Dean and Cambrian 0-6-0s, particularly between Moat Lane and Brecon. No suitable Standard design was then available so a batch of LMS Ivatt 'Moguls' was constructed at Swindon in 1952, fitted with 'Western' right-hand drive. The British Railways version of the LMS design emerged from Doncaster soon afterwards, when Oswestry lost no time in conducting a brief

County Councillor H. R. Humphreys, J.P., prepares No 7806, a hurriedly cleaned eleventh-hour substitute, for the 'up' Cambrian Coast Express, at Aberystwyth. Driver Humphreys, in common with some of the more fastidious enginemen, wore an old jacket over his normal overalls when climbing amongst the grimy and oily parts of the motion. Regrettably, this obscures the characteristic copy of the *Financial Times* which protruded from the pocket: no *Daily Mirror* for H.R.H.! 13.4.1956. *GBJ*

BR Std. Cl.2 2-6-0, No. 78007, with an empty coach in tow to strengthen the set, runs 'wrong road' past the Coast portion of the Cambrian Coast Express, before setting back and working the train on to Pwllheli. 19.6.1957.

GBJ

comparative test between the two types. On 18 February 1953, BR Standard No.78001 and Ivatt No.46510 worked two Oswestry-Aberystwyth passenger turns normally rostered to 'Manors'. Apart from a brief 2-week period when 78xxx's worked the 'up' Cambrian Coast Express in June 1954, and a mid-day stopping train from Aberystwyth to Welshpool, they seldom worked regularly the length of the main line.

The first eight of the new 2MT Standard Class were allocated to Machynlleth, or 89C as it had become in BR lists. The newer engines had enclosed cabs which offered foot-plate crews much needed protection but were hardly any improvement in the essential matter of steam-raising. The seventy-year-old 'Dean Goods' was more than a match for them in this respect and, after controlled tests on the Swindon Test Plant involving a '23' and an Ivatt 2-6-0, the newer engines were improved and better able to stand comparison.

1953 saw yet another new class introduced to the Cambrian when, in November, Oswestry exchanged its six 'Manors' for the second Standard Class to appear, the 4MT '75XXX' 4-6-0 engines. If these were not universally welcome at the outset, they eventually earned the respect of many of the footplate crews and were the locomotive type to survive till the end of steam on the Cambrian. The first '75s' down the coast worked Troop Specials to the large army bases at Tywyn and Tonfannau. These generated a vast amount of extra traffic during World War II and created a resurgence of military 'specials' in the 1950s, with the introduction of the two-week 'Z'-training camps. Alternate weekends were extremely busy with as many as five 8-10 coach special trains being noted one Sunday morning in

122

1954. They arrived from all parts of the country and frequently brought green-liveried SR stock onto the Cambrian, one such set came complete with *London—Brussels, Dover—Ostend* roof-boards. No.75005 ran through to Towyn on one of these specials in May 1954.

GW 2-6-0s appeared in increasing numbers from the early 1950s, based first at Aberystwyth and later at Machynlleth, where they worked regularly to Pwllheli. Nos.6368/78 and 6392/5 were typical but by no means the only examples. Their ranks were further increased on summer weekends when the former '93' series was brought out of the restricted 'Red' category into the 'Blue' group by redistributing their weight. With their Collett cabs, they seemed more modern and appeared well-suited to the coast line but, rather surprisingly perhaps, were not drafted into the area in any numbers; Nos. 7325/8/9 and 7339 were typical examples.

One of the more interesting services operated by Machynlleth engines was the North Wales Land Cruise. Introduced in 1951 by the LM Region, the original Festival Land Cruise trains were hauled by Ivatt Class 2MT 2-6-0s from Rhyl shed, and completed a circular tour through former Davies & Savin territory to Corwen, then Barmouth, where there was a short break before returning via Afonwen and Bangor to Rhyl. This service proved immensely popular, and was extended the following year with a second train starting and finishing at Llandudno. The service was further increased in 1954 with the addition of a third train, this time from Conway, and the Western Region also decided to capitalise on the route's obvious attractions by operating its own stock, from Pwllheli. Both this train and the Conway service ran in the opposite direction to the Rhyl and Llandudno trains, the WR train carrying the further distinction of 'repeating' the

With a horse-box next to the tender, GW 2-6-0 No. 4377 pulls up the grade from Aberdyfi with the 10.25 a.m. Pwllheli-Dovey Junction service on 29.8.1957. Giving the impression of double-track at this point, the line nearest the camera was but the branch from the harbour.

Ifor Higgon

route from Afonwen to Barmouth, where it terminated. The fare on this train, which ran on Tuesdays and Thursdays only, was 20 shillings (£1.00) from all stations between Pwllheli and Bala. The LM trains ran on Tuesdays, Wednesdays and Thursdays.

The WR trains were worked initially by '22xx' 0-6-0s; No.3207 was a regular performer in 1954. Larger GW engines were prohibitted from the former LMS lines between Corwen and Afonwen because their outside cylinders were out of gauge.

Haulage of the 'Land Cruise' trains was later entrusted to BR Class 4MT 4-6-0s and from 9 July 1957 Nos.75006/24 were borrowed from Oswestry, to work the Pwllheli trains. In between these duties they worked on the coast as required. On Saturdays, one would double-head the Pwllheli-Paddington between Machynlleth and Welshpool, returning attached to the 'down' Cambrian Coast Express as far as Machynlleth before working the coast portion (usually made up to 8 coaches), forward to Pwllheli.

In August 1958, as all the Oswestry '75s' had been replaced by 'Manors', none was available for Land Cruise duty and haulage reverted to 22/32xx 0-6-0s which coped with five coaches single-handed, but had to be double-headed when the load was increased to seven. By June of the following year, Nos.75020/26 were transferred from Tyseley to Machynlleth to work the WR Land Cruises, then made up to seven vehicles, an occasion which heralded the first permanent allocation of the class to the coast line. Both WR & LMR Land Cruises ended in 1961, but the 75s remained to the end of steam.

A notable but short-lived experiment involved Ivatt Class 2MT 2-6-2T, No.41240, which was tried down the coast in March 1960 but, amongst other difficulties, lost 20 minutes re-starting its test train from Llangelynin Halt. Had the experience been a happier one there is little doubt that further members of the class would quickly have found their way onto the coast; a move foreseen but not relished by the Machynlleth men. The accompanying Footplate Inspector

From *Llandinam* to BR Standard Class 4.
Machynlleth depot closed officially for steam on 5.12.1966. In February 1967, however, charter work for BBCTV (at Glandyfi), brought No. 75033 down from Shrewsbury; it was serviced at Machynlleth but developed a faulty brick arch and was replaced for the final two days. Thus Driver D. Murray Evans prepared No. 75004, the last BR steam engine to operate from Machynlleth, on the penultimate day, 11.2.1967. No. 75033 regained the limelight three weeks later, on 3.3.1967, when it operated the final steam-hauled Cambrian Coast Express between Aberystwyth and Shrewsbury.

Steam returned briefly to Machynlleth when 4-6-0s No. 7819 *Hinton Manor,* BR Std., No. 75069 and Ivatt 2-6-0 No. 46443 worked a series of Cardigan Bay Expresses to Barmouth and Pwllheli during the summer of 1987.

GBJ

Destined to work the last 'Cambrian Coast Express' between Aberystwyth and Shrewsbury in 1967, BR 4MT 4-6-0 No. 75033, then a Rhyl engine, heads a returning 'Cambrian Radio Cruise' at Aberdovey, on 3.9.1957.
GBJ

Some measure of the achievements of Ganger David Owen in 1861/2, is apparent in this 1957 photograph of Class 4 4-6-0 No. 75020 in the top yard at Machynlleth. The locomotives are, *l/r:* Nos. 4560, 2285, 4575, 75020, 78007 and 78006.
GBJ

may well have been aware of the crew's complicity but their 'performance' must have been convincing and well up to the mark, even if the steam was not! No further 2MT tanks appeared.

The alternative to the little Class 2 was the marginally larger exLMS Class 3. A number of these, in the '40XXX' series, had appeared during 1960 from the recently closed Rhosddu Shed at Wrexham and, perhaps because they were in a worn and neglected condition, proved to be the least popular engines to work along the coast in recent times. They were removed at the first opportunity, bring superseded by the BR Standard 3MT 2-6-2T '82XXX' version. If the '82s' again were not everyone's favourite, they at least received a warmer welcome that the LMS engines and 10 examples were on the coast by 1962.

The largest and in many ways the most popular tank-engines to work the Cambrian were the Standard BR 4MT 2-6-4T '80XXX', which arrived in the area in the summer of 1962. They were the only tank engines to work the main line on a regular basis, but were appreciated most of all between Machynlleth and Pwllheli. Here they were confined to passenger workings as a rule, due to concern over water supplies between Portmadoc and Barmouth, but the comfort and power they offered footplate crews could not have been imagined by the stalwarts who drove the primitive open-cabbed 0-6-0s through gale-whipped spray at Tonfannau or Llanaber in the 1860s.

The final class of Standard engine to appear on a regular basis was the Class 4MT '76XXX' 2-6-0s which initially worked into the area from Shrewsbury before three examples, Nos.

BR Class 4 2-6-4T No. 80132 storms towards Carno with a 10-coach Manchester to Aberystwyth and Barmouth express on 27 July 1963.
Ifor Higgon

Newtown & Machynlleth Railway

To the Landowners, Tenants, and Residents in the Counties of Montgomery, Cardigan and Merioneth.

MY LORDS AND GENTLEMEN,

For some time past an almost universal cry has been raised among you, to this effect:—
"Are we never to have a Railroad? Are we to be eternally shut up within our Valleys, with only the old Stage Coach to help us out of them, with only the Old Waggon to carry out our produce, with our Cattle from a thousand hills, slowly trailing along the old Highways---and losing half their weight before they reach the Great Central Markets?--A manifest loss to the Farmer and the Community."

Well! The cry has been responded to—Aroused by it, a few leading influential Men of the Country, have nobly set their shoulders to the wheel, have raised monies among themselves and their friends, have paid into the Bank of England the heavy deposits required by the Standing Orders of Parliament—and the Bill, authorizing the making the road, now awaits the decision of the House and of yourselves.—I say, of *yourselves*; for the matter now rests with you to say—whether you are content to linger for another 50 years behind the rest of the Kingdom, or that the Bill shall be carried through, vigorously and at once. Many of you, I apprehend, have not yet joined in this our Undertaking, from the fear that it will fall to the ground like the previous ones—Be not alarmed! The Promoters are decided with your help to bring it to a successful issue. But you must remember that Railroads will not drop down from Heaven, simply because you want them—you yourselves must help to make the one you want. And remember too, that the true spirit of enterprize is fairly up through the length and breadth of our Country. Let not the Steam go off, for lack of fuel—if you do, you will never get it up again.

Therefore, Friends and Countrymen—be up and stirring! Committees will be formed in every Town, Village, and Hamlet to receive subscriptions for shares. Those Shares too, depend upon my words, will, in the course of a twelvemonth be at a premium.

Once more, I urge you not to lose this golden opportunity of conferring a lasting benefit on yourselves and on your Country.

Very faithfully yours,

A SHAREHOLDER.

January, 1857.

Shrewsbury, 3, 47, 59, 62, 64, 68, 98, 116, 124, 134, 136
Shropshire Union Canal, 20
Signal Boxes, 73, 85-9, 98
Spades, 16, 17, 55
Specification of Works (N&M Rly.), 22-8
Staff (plates), 32, 44, 54, 56, 61, 63, 96, 117, 121, 124, 127
Steamer (*Elizabeth*), 80, 81
Steam Rail Motors, 108

Talerddig, 2, 16, 18, 23, 25, 26, 28, 29, 31, 33-6, 40, 43, 44, 46, 53, 55, 66, 68, 94, 97, 99, 100, 102, 108, 113, 136
Talerddig, tunnel, 16
Thruston, Charles T., 5, 8, 9, 12, 15
Tre'rddol, 2, 40
Tyler, Capt., 46-8

Vale of Clwyd Rly., 19
Van Rly., 90
Vane, Earl, 5, 7, 9, 10, 12-5, 22, 42, 44, 50, 54, 55, 63, 98, 101, 129-30
Vane, Countess, 16, 44, 50, 55; see also Marchioness of Londonderry
Vignoles, 1

Ward, John, 33, 93
Webb, Thomas, 48, 56
Whalley, G.H., 83, 84
Williams, Sir Hugh, 13, 14
Wynn, Charles, 5, 54
Wynn, Sir Watkin Williams, 5, 12-4, 42, 52, 55, 99
Wynne, Watkin William Edward, 5, 7, 11-4

Ynys Edwin, 74, 75
Ynyslas, 1, 31, 40, 74-6, 78, 80, 83-6, 103

Llanbrynmair, 5, 27, 29, 33, 38, 42, 44, 46, 47, 48, 53, 55, 57, 63, 76, 99, 136
Llandinam, 4, 5, 22, 34, 44, 46
Llanidloes, 3, 8, 44, 45, 59, 101, 108, 111, 116, 118, 134
L&N Rly., 4, 10, 11, 16, 19-23, 26, 29, 33, 42, 48, 50, 57, 73, 84, 93, 102, 130
Londonderry, Marquis; see Vane
Londonderry, Marchioness, 91, 130
LNWR, 3, 42, 59, 62, 64, 101
Locomotives
    Contractors, 19, 37, 38, 102-4, 118
    N&M Rly., 43, 45, 53, 100, 104
    O&N Rly., 21, 29, 45, 57, 102-4
    Cambrian Rly., 104-7, 121
    GW Rly., 107-8, 110-7, 119-24, 128
    B&M Rly., 111
    LMS, 117-8, 121, 123-4, 126, 128
    LNER, 118
    TVR, 120
    BR, 122, 124-6, 128
    HST, 128
    Sprinters, 87

Machynlleth, 1-4, 8, 15, 26, 29, 32, 35, 37, 38, 40, 43-8, 50, 53, 54, 55, 57, 59, 60-9, 71-3, 80-2, 87-9, 93-9, 103-7, 111-30, 135-6
Machynlleth U.D.C., 55
MA&T Rly., 31, 72, 75
M&M Rly., 2, 8, 42, 79, 113
Mawddwy Rly., 39, 40, 66, 89, 91, 99
Mindovey Rly., 79
Moat Lane, 7, 17, 21, 28, 44, 45, 48, 53, 59, 60, 62, 64, 73, 98, 99, 101, 107, 111, 118, 120-1, 128, 134
Morben, 1, 38, 71, 74, 79, 87
Morgan, Catherine, 42
Morgan, John, 93, 94
Morgan, T.O., 5, 8
Morris, John Carnac, 5

Newtown, 2-4, 20, 21, 43-5, 50, 53, 54, 59, 62, 93, 98, 99, 116, 136
N&M Rly., 4-8, 14, 19, 21, 22, 27-9, 31-3, 41-3, 46, 47, 50, 51, 53, 56-60, 62, 66, 68, 69, 72, 73, 82, 84, 93-5, 99, 101-4, 107, 130, 134
N&MR Common Seal, i, 14, 15
N&MR Prospectus, 8, 9

Oswestry, 19, 44, 59, 60, 64, 100-1, 108, 111-2, 116-20, 122, 128, 130
O&N Rly., 4, 8, 20, 21, 31, 33, 42, 48, 50, 57, 58, 84, 102, 130

Overend & Gurney, 84
Owen, David, 38, 97
Owen, George, 34, 48, 75, 84-6, 91, 93, 99-101, 136

Parry, 19
Parry & Pritchard, 35
Penhelig, 74, 77-9, 82, 83, 85
Pennal, 67, 87, 88
Penson, T.M., 93, 94
Penstrowed, 19, 27
P&T Rly., 42
Piercy, Benjamin, 5, 7, 8, 15, 28, 34, 78, 82, 84, 136
Piercy, Robert, 22, 84
Pontdolgoch, 27-9, 48, 57, 99, 101, 102, 136
Porth Dinllaen, 1-3, 66, 67
Postal Services, 62-4, 136
Poundley, Mr., 50
Pritchard, David, 5, 8, 9, 11-3
Projected schemes,
    A&WCR (1861), 31, 66, 72
    CMA&TR, 67
    CM&RDT Extn., 68
    Gt. North & South Wales Rly., 2
    Gt. Welch Junction Rly., 3
    MA&TR, 31, 72
    M&M (1845), 2
    Montgomeryshire Rlys., 3
    Shrewsbury & Chester Extn., 4
    Vignoles C.B., 1, 2
    West Midland Rly., etc., 66
    Worcester & Porthdinlleyn Rly., 2
Pryce, Robert Davies, 5, 9, 42, 48, 55

Radio signalling, 89
Ruck, Laurence, 5, 8, 10-4
Robertson, Henry, 5
Royal Assent
    A&WCR, 73
    CM&RDT, 68
    L&NR, 4
    Maw.R, 89
    N&MR, 4, 14
    O&NR, 4
    Van R, 90,

Sarn, 60; see also Carno
Saunders, Charles A., 42, 46
Savin, Thomas, 11, 19, 22, 31-3, 73, 75, 76, 80-4, 93, 94
Savin, John, 33
Scafell, 99

Index

Aberdyfi, 1, 31, 38, 40, 41, 67, 72, 73, 76-85, 103, 108,128
   ferry, 9, 79-81
   viaduct, 76-9
Aberystwyth, 2, 4, 8, 9, 31, 40, 59, 63, 64, 66-8, 73, 76, 77, 80, 90, 97, 98, 101, 112-3, 116-7, 119, 122-4, 128, 134.
A&WC Rly., 11, 31, 32, 33, 59, 60, 68, 71-82, 84, 103
Accidents, 99-101

BR Midland, 134
BR Western, 99, 134
Borth, 59, 60, 62, 64, 71-6, 80-2, 96
Barmouth, 2, 40, 60, 67, 89, 108, 118, 120-1, 124, 134
   viaduct, 78
Barry Rly., 78
Bell, George, 35
Bell's Bridge, 35, 36, 136
Big Culvert, 36
Blandford, Marquis of, 53
Board of Trade, 28, 42, 44, 46, 60, 73, 77, 80, 82, 85
B&M Rly., 84
Brunel, I.K., 1-3
Brunlees, 77, 82, 85

Caersws, 8, 16, 23, 24, 28, 34, 42, 43, 48, 53, 57, 68, 90, 91, 97, 99, 100, 101, 136
Caersws Junction, 22, 47, 48
Cambrian, 4, 11, 24, 25, 27, 64, 76, 84, 87, 88, 90, 91, 93, 98, 99, 104, 111, 112-3, 116, 120, 129, 136
Cambrian Coast Express, 122, 124, 125, 133, 134, 136
Carno, 23, 25, 28, 30, 31, 42, 43, 46, 48, 57, 99, 101, 136; see also Sarn
Carriages; railway, 33, 43, 44, 52-4, 129-31
Cemmes Road, 35, 39, 40, 42, 48, 57, 60, 94, 95, 99, 136
Churchill/Duke of Marlborough, 64; see also Blandford
Cerrig-y-Penrhyn, 74, 80
Clatter(gate), 99
Clough, Henry, 37
CMA&T Rly., 82
CM&RD Tramroad, 67, 68, 71, 74, 90, 98
Coach services, 59, 60
Coal merchants, 41
Commins Coch, 27, 35, 37, 40, 42-4, 45, 47, 99, 136
Conybeare, H., 84
Cubitt, J., 15

Davies & Savin, 11, 15, 19, 20, 29, 31, 33, 104
Davies, David, 4, 5, 11, 13, 15, 19, 20, 22, 27, 28, 31-5, 37, 38, 40, 42, 44, 46, 48, 50, 54-9, 79, 83-5, 97, 101-3, 129, 134, 136
Davies, Lord, 90
Derwenlas, 1, 2, 38, 40, 69, 71, 74, 82, 87, 88, 101
Dinas Mawddwy, 2, 3, 89, 90, 107
Dolgellau, 7, 8, 31, 60, 67, 108
Dovey Junction, 75, 87, 89, 98, 121; see also Glandovey Junction
Dovey Reclamation 72, 74
Dyfi estuary, 3, 74, 79, 83
Dyfi valley, 1, 4, 5, 34, 35, 38, 55, 66, 67, 71, 73, 89, 98

Eleri, River, 74, 75, 80
Evans, David, 34
Evans, John, Y Morben, 1, 79, 83, 88
Excursions
   Llandinamites, 44
   London, 62
   Temperance, 44
   Yeomanry, 44
   Land/Radio Cruise, 123-5

Foulkes, John, 5, 8, 13, 14, 42, 55
Friog, 84

Garreg, 73, 74; see also Glandyfi
Glandovey bridge, 1, 85
Glandovey Junction, 71, 85, 86, 88, 89; see also Dovey Junction
Glandyfi, 98, 135
Glyntwymyn bridge, 37, 43, 45, 48
Gradient profile, 27
Great Western Rly., 42, 43, 46, 50, 54, 56-8, 64, 68, 88, 90, 97, 98
Grierson, James, 43, 44, 46,

Howell, Abraham, 5, 31
Howell, David, 4, 5, 7-15, 22, 31, 33, 37, 42, 48, 56, 136
Hughes, David, 34
Hughes, J. Ceiriog, 91

Jones, Robert Davies, 5, 8, 9
Jones, William, 11, 12,

Kinsey, David, 46

Bibliography

ARCHER, Michael S. *Welsh Post towns before 1840.* (1970). Phillimore.
BAUGHAN, Peter E. *North and Mid Wales.* Regional history series. (1980). David & Charles.
BEHREND, George *Gone with Regret.* (1967). Jersey Artists.
BOYD, James I.C. *Narrow Gauge Rails in Mid Wales.* (1986). Oakwood.
CHRISTIANSEN, R. & MILLER, R.W. *The Cambrian Railways, Vols I&II,* (1967). David & Charles.
CORRIS SOCIETY, *Return to Corris.* (1988). Avon Anglia.
COZENS, Lewis *The Corris Railway.* (1949). Cozens. *The Van & Kerry Railways.* (1953). *Mawddwy Railway.* (1954).
DALTON, T.Patrick. *Cambrian Companionship.* (1985). Oxford Pub.Co.
GASQUOINE, C.P. *The Story of the Cambrian,* (1922). Woodall, Minshall, Thomas & Co.
GREEN, C.C. *Cambrian Railways Album, Vols.I&II,* (1977/81). Ian Allan. *North Wales Branch Line Album,* (1983). Ian Allan.
HARRIS, Michael *GW Coaches from 1890.* (1985). David & Charles.
HARRISON, Ian *GWR Locomotive Allocations 1921.* (1948). Wild Swan.
HOLDEN, J.S. *The Manchester & Milford Railway,* (1979). Oakwood.
HOSEGOOD, John G. *GWR Travelling Post Offices.* (1983). Wild Swan.
JOHNSON, Peter *The Cambrian Lines.* (1984). Ian Allan.
JONES, Elwyn V. *Mishaps on the Cambrian Railways,* (1972). Severn Press.
KIDNER, Roger W. *The Cambrian Railways.* (1954). Oakwood.

LEWIS, Huw *Pages of Time.* (1989). Lewis, Aberdovey.
MORGAN, D.W. *Brief Glory.* (1948). Brython Press.
MOUNTFORD, Eric R. *Register of GWR Absorbed Coaching Stock.* (1978). Oakwood.
OWEN-JONES, Dr Stuart *Railways of Wales.* (1981). National Museum of Wales.
POCOCK, Nigel & HARRISON, Ian *GWR Locomotive Allocations for 1934.* (1987). Wild Swan.
PRICE, M.R.C. *Pembroke & Tenby Railway.* (1986). Oakwood.
R.C.T.S. *Locomotives of the GWR,* Pt 10. (1966). RCTS.
ROBERTS, Askew *Gossiping Guide to Wales.* (1879). Hodder & Stoughton, and Woodall & Venables.
ROWLEDGE, J.W.P. *GWR Locomotive Allocations; First & Last Sheds, 1922-1967.* (1986). David & Charles.
THOMAS, Ivor *Top Sawyer.* (1938). Longmans.

Journals:
The Engineer: Saloon carriage for Earl Vane. 29.4.1870. p.258. *British Railway Journal*: A Cambrian Collection. Spring 1985.p236-9. *British Railway Journal*: A Cambrian Journey. Autumn 1987. p.376-82. Issues of *The Railway Magazine, Trains Illustrated, Railway World.*

Newspapers:
Aberystwyth Observer, Montgomeryshire Express, Baner ac Amserau Cymru, Newtown & Welshpool Express, Cambrian News, Oswestry & Border Counties Advertiser, Eddowe's Shrewsbury Journal, Shrewsbury Chronicle, Merionethshire Herald, Shropshire & Montgomeryshire Times, Merionethshire Standard, Western Mail, Montgomeryshire County Times, Y Cymro

'The train was about an hour earlier than in previous months and we were about 5 minutes late . . . '—Miles Cheeseman, driver of a luggage train involved in an accident on a private crossing near Caersws, 3 July 1869. [N&WE 13.7.1869].

'As there is no cover on the 'up' platform, I cannot see that the mere fact of crossing the bridge in the dry would have any useful effect . . . '—Engineer's reply to a Machynlleth Urban District Council request for a covered footbridge between the platforms, 1914.

Mrs Pugh, who ran Robert Pugh's coal business at Machynlleth until the mid 1950s had, as a young girl, worked as a porter on the Cambrian during WWI. After the war, the Cambrian started to sack its lady porters but she spoke with Earl Vane and was retained. She was on the platform at Machynlleth on the morning of the Abermule disaster and exchanged greetings with the Earl and his valet. Before they boarded the train the Earl was heard to remark; *'. . . It will be spring when I return to Machynlleth'.* [Related to M.M.Lloyd].

HERBERT John	Coal	27.10.60
HUMPHRIES ED. Carno	Cartage	2.7.59
INGRAM Ed. Oerffrwd	Horse-work & stabling	26.2.61
JONES & GRIFFITHS	for Powder etc.	7.7.60
JONES Ishmael	Saddler's bill @ Cock	21.5.61
JONES Thomas	Raising stones, Penstrowed	8.3.61
JONES Thomas	Straw	24.1.62
LEWIS Edward	Fencing	8.3.61
LEWIS William	Putting up Newtown Station	25.6.61
LEWIS Henry	Oats and beans	4.8.60
MANUEL David	to fetch carriages	10.6.59*
MANUEL Edward	Horse work	9.3.61
MARTINDALE	Hire of coaches	15.8.60
MORGANS Huw	Powder bill	29.8.60
NEWELL Thomas	at the ballast	30.6.60
NICHOLSON Inspector		12.3.60—2.8.60
OLD MAN AT THE POINTS	[Moat Lane Junction?]	2.7.59
PARRY & PRITCHARD	River diversion, Talerddig	23.2.60
PROCTOR General	Timber	5.5.59
POWELL	Hire of coaches	29.8.60
SAVAGE Mrs	Oil for the engine	18.5.61
SUDELEY Lord	Timber	31.7.60
WATKINS John	Repairing Big Culvert	15.6.61**
WILSON	Pumping water for engines	2.7.61
WILLIAMS Thomas	Stone to turntable	10.6.59*

* The early date indicates work for the Llanidloes line, but entered on the N&M Accounts.

** These entries may possibly be related although, hitherto, no details have emerged of any collapse of the Big Culvert during construction.

*** Could this refer to the incident related in *Top Sawyer,* (p.64), when David Davies rushed from London to Talerddig after dreaming that the works there were about to be flooded?

Appendix III

RANDOM CAMBRIAN QUOTES

The Newtown & Machynlleth Railway was given, '... *freely, the enormous advantage of 5 miles of our line, without the slightest reciprocity granted or asked for.*'—George H. Whalley, Chairman of the L&N. [SC 13.6.1862]

Thomas Savin, regarding a Petition against proposals for developments at Aberdovey; '*That petition is in very general terms. It contains nothing specific, and only says that the proposed works will be ruination to everybody in Aberdovey*'. A Voice: '*If it will be ruination to everybody, that is specific enough!*' [ESJ 1.2.1865]

'*Mr Savin is only a half Welshman, I am a whole one . . .* '—David Davies, before Parliamentary Committee, (A&WCR General Act of 5 July 1865). [OA 10.5.1865.]

'*Two engines were unable to draw the long line of carriages with sufficient expedition to ensure punctuality*'.—Newtown Notes. [S&MT 1.8.1865.]

MWYAR'S	—Cutting	John Pryce	18.5.61 —1.6.61
DYRN	—Ballast Hole		
COMMINS COCH	—Cutting —Lower cutting	David Hughes Thomas Davies	9.3.61 —1.6.61 23.4.61
GLYNTWYMYN	—Cutting	Thomas Davies	30.5.61—26.7.61
TY'N-Y-RHOS	—Cutting	Thomas Gibbins	30.5.61—26.7.61
GWASTADGOED	—Cutting —Building	Daniel Pryce Thomas Jones	20.5.61 20.5.61
ABERGWYDOL	—Cutting	Joseph Roberts	30.5.61—26.7.61
PENYBONT	—Cutting	Joseph Roberts	14.6.61
DOLGUOG	—Cutting	John Downing	30.5.61—26.7.61
CRAIG-Y-BWCH	—Cutting	John Bennett	30.5.61—28.6.61
MACHYNLLETH	—Station site	David Owen	28.6.61—26.7.61

Appendix II

Newtown & Machynlleth Railway Construction (II)

MISCELLANEOUS ENTRIES

BEBB, Talerddig	Sheep killed	24.1.62
BECKINGHAM	Hire of coaches	15.8.60
BENBOW, Abermule	Horse-work	13.8.60
BREESE Maurice	Saddler's bill @ Cock	21.5.61
DAVIES Edward	Hire of coaches	9.3.61
DAVIES Ino.	Pay Gates to fetch engine	25.7.59*
DAVIES R.	Stabling	23.3.61
DAVIES Thomas Smith	Smith-work	26.2.61
EDWARDS Dr.	Medical attention	17.6.61**
EVANS Evan	Candles	26.2.61
	Stopping water	30.5.61***
FARMER George	Timber	27.7.60
GORNALL Philip	Painting, plumbing etc,	28.6.60
GRAVENOR	Cartage	25.6.59—24.1.62
GRIFFITHS Dr.	Medical attention	15.6.61**
GRIFFITHS Mrs	Corn and drugs	9.3.61
GROVES Mr	Bullock killed by railway	16.4.60
HAMER William	Fencing	25.7.59

Appendix I

Newtown & Machynlleth Railway
Construction (I)

The main construction sites are listed below with the names, where available, of the gangers responsible. Work at each site obviously extended beyond the dates quoted, when other personnel may well have been involved. Regrettably, no details have yet been traced of the size of the workforce/s at the various sites.

LOCATIONS		GANGERS	Sample Dates
CAERSWS	—Bridge	John Jones, Piling	26.2.59 —14.3.59
	—River	John Elkington, Diversion	19.3.59
	—Fencing	John Holt	26.2.59 —4.6.59
PONTDOLGOCH		J.Jones	5.4.59
		J.Elkington	4.6.59
	—Mill	Wm.Morris	9.3.61
CLATTERGATE—			
OERFFRWD—			
CARNO	—Sarn, approach.	Thos. Gibbins	5.4.61
		H. P. Gibbins	23.3.61
		John Jones, Piling	4.5.61
	—R. bridge nr Sarn	John Watkins, Masonry	16.7.61
TALERDDIG	—Rock/Big Cutting	David Hughes	4.6.59 —26.2.61
	—Big Cutting	David Evans	26.2.61 —1.6.61
	—Buildings	John Jones	27.5.61
BIG CULVERT		John Watkins	20.5.61 —15.6.61
BELL'S BRIDGE		George Bell	27.7.61 —6.8.61
LLAWRYCOED	—Cutting	William Edwards	4.5.61
	—Dingle	William Edwards	15.6.61
PLASBACH	—Cutting	William Edwards	1.6.61
CAETWPA	—Cutting	Thomas Davies	8.4.61
LLANBRYNMAIR	—Cock(Station)	Joseph Roberts	4.5.61
	—Cutting	Thomas Brown	21.5.61 —14.6.61
TRIPP GATE	—Cutting (by Pont Lloyd George)	David Davies	17.6.61

had failed when its brick-arch collapsed. Both engines at this time were based in Shrewsbury, from whence they also worked the final steam turns into mid Wales (morning and evening Mail trains and the 'up' and 'down' Cambrian Coast Express). Other passenger services were the responsibility of the DMU's. The 'CCE' was withdrawn on March 3rd; No. 75033, a one-time Rhyl engine which used to visit the Cambrian Coast on 'Land Cruise' duties, operating the last steam-hauled train from Aberystwyth, and No. 7502 worked the final 'down' train from Shrewsbury.

The most evocative sounds, sights and smells of the old railway have all disappeared for ever; yet, despite our losses, we realise we are fortunate that so much remains. Rails of polished steel still thread through the narrow defile at Talerddig, over the big culvert and Bell's Bridge and on down the Dyrn; the line through the cutting at Commins Coch still delivers a little 'kick' when one travels at anything above a modest speed and Davies's imposing viaduct 'of best Ruabon brick', at Ty'n-y-rhos, continues to carry the line faithfully over the Twymyn, 70ft below. Trains and rolling stock are not as numerous as formerly, but the line now sees a limited amount of air-conditioned coaches and there are promises of more and better to come. Time will tell, but there is a gradual re-building of Cambrian optimism and the line and infrastructure are probably in better order now than at any time since the dark days of the 1960s and '70s. The station buildings at Caersws, Pontdolgoch, Carno, Llanbrynmair and Cemmes Road still survive, albeit in private hands, and although Moat Lane has been demolished, the station at Newtown continues to offer a service and the former headquarters of the N&M at Machynlleth is now the undisputed fulcrum of the present-day Cambrian system.

There are encouraging indications of a new resolve and cohesion between the parties who now share some of the responsiblities with British Rail but, nonetheless, our debt to the early entrepreneurs and to the legions of Cambrian men, of all eras, remains as great today as ever. It is, in truth, a debt which can no longer be fully discharged although we are, perhaps, finally learning to re-appraise and more fully appreciate their priceless legacy. The vision and tenacity of Howell, the planning of Piercy & Owen and the enduring construction of David Davies and his men provided a line which realised most of the expectations of the early promoters. Hopefully, this rich heritage is now being cherished and developed anew, for if the 'whistle of the engine' is no longer heard in our valleys, may its successor flourish and be adapted to serve succeeding generations in mid Wales and along the Cambrian Coast.

Steam power was seen by those in authority to epitomise all that was out-moded and decaying. Yet, although the steam engine was certainly an anachronism by the 1960s, other factors such as the perpetuation of nineteenth century practices and prejudices made equal, if not greater, contributions to the inefficiency of the railways.

Corporate bodies became image-conscious in the 1960s, and BR saw electric traction as a long-term motive power solution, suitable for intensely used major routes, whilst diesel power, with its greater flexibility, lower capital costs and short-term availability seemed to encapsulate all that was necessary for service on secondary lines.

The first diesel to venture into mid Wales had been a GW single-car unit, DRC No.4, in 1953. GW Railcars appeared again on Talyllyn Railway Preservation Society excursions to Tywyn in 1954 and the first BR DMU visited Cambrian metals on 8 September 1957 when an 8-car excursion ran from Llandudno to Aberystwyth. The water-shed, however, occurred in 1967, with the final demise of steam and the emergence of the new power. English Electric Type 3 locomotives, at that time in the 'D68xx' series, were the first to visit on summer Saturday passenger workings; the first was noted on 25 June 1966, on a Manchester to Aberystwyth train. By early October, the first Small Sulzer locomotives ('D5xxx' series) had arrived at Machynlleth for crew-training and steam ceased to operate from that depot from 5 December 1966. The last steam locomotive on shed at Machynlleth, however, was BR 4MT No.75004 which was stabled there over the week-end of 11/12 February, 1967, working as far as Glandyfi for the purposes of filming for a BBC TV production. It replaced No.75033 which had performed that duty earlier in the week but

The first BR DMU visited the N&M when an 8-car set appeared on a Llandudno-Aberystwyth excursion on 8 September, 1957.

GBJ

three of Mr Hawksworth's comfortable and modern coaches destined for Pwllheli and another three bound for Aberystwyth; the complete chocolate and cream ensemble being well within the capabilities of one of Aberystwyth's often immaculate 'Manors'. The restaurant cars worked through to Aberystwyth, with the exception of the summer of 1958 when they were diverted to Pwllheli, the only regular working of restaurant cars down the coast on service trains. The weekday restaurant car service survived until 1961, after which the car was removed at Shrewsbury and replaced by a special carriage containing one compartment converted into an automatic mini-buffet. This vehicle worked only to Aberystwyth and consequently spent time in the sidings when it might easily have earned extra revenue attached to the coast portion, *en route* to Pwllheli. Shorn of its restaurant car and distinctive Western Region livery, so reminiscent of the Great Western's yet not quite the same, and hauled by a 'common-user' BR '75', the 'Cambrian' became a pale shadow of its former self. It still offered a through service, of course, but was no longer as attractive a train and soon fell victim of the economic stringencies of the 1960's; it was withdrawn in 1967.

In addition to the introduction of modern rolling-stock during the 1950s, track maintenance reached its zenith and stations and other structures were in good order, being painted in shades of chocolate and cream or green and cream, so reminiscent of the old companies. Many goods trains still required 'banking', despite the increased use of 'Manors', and passenger trains, particularly on Summer weekends, were longer and heavier than ever, being frequently loaded to fourteen bogie vehicles. Yet, a decade which started with considerable activity and optimism was to end with a dramatic change which arrested the progress of the railways of Britain, in real terms, by some twenty or thirty years. Instead of rising to meet the growing challenge of the motor-car and lorry, by adaptation and innovation, the easier options of

British Rail rarity. A Cambrian Coast Express luggage label. *GBJ Collection*

regression, entrenchment and cut-back were chosen. The deficiencies in the service were thus exposed and emphasised by new and constantly improving road vehicles; the consequent loss of revenue was inevitable and as a result of cold, commercial strategy, contraction of the network became inevitable.

The Mid Wales line was the first to succumb, on 30 December 1962; with it disappeared the passenger services of the N&M's oldest ally, the line from Moat Lane to Llanidloes. The goods services as far as Llanidloes were retained until 1967.

The events of 1 January 1963 would not have been appreciated by David Davies for, almost precisely a century after the official opening, control of the Cambrian passed from Paddington to Euston as a result of regional boundary changes. Within two years, the Cambrian lost further important link lines, the Ruabon-Barmouth and Aberystwyth-Carmarthen routes; both were closed hurriedly and untidily at the end of 1964. Many felt that the transfer of the area from the Western to the Midland Region had adversely affected the eventual outcome and the new regime did not inspire confidence at the outset; the general decline in morale was inevitable and the gloomy atmosphere of redundancies and cut-backs intensified with news of the closure of most of the intermediate stations between Shrewsbury and Aberystwyth, 'on and from' Monday 14 June 1965.

Chapter 8

All Change

The increasing challenge of the internal-combustion engine during the 1920s and '30s was arrested briefly by the frantic activities of the war years, and the immediate post-war period witnessed valiant attempts by the railways to return to the 'normality' of 1939. Deficiencies of maintenance were slowly made good and the early 1950s saw something of an Indian Summer on the Cambrian. New locomotives and carriages were more numerous than at any time since the opening of the railway and the introduction of a daily restaurant car service to Paddington, the prestigious Cambrian Coast Express, helped to restore some lost 'pride in the job'. The Cambrian Coast Express title was first used in 1921, and applied to various summer express trains between Paddington and the Cambrian Coast. It was not until 14 June 1954 that the Western Region introduced a through restaurant car train destined, for the first time, to serve Montgomeryshire and the resorts along Cardigan Bay throughout the year.

The most glamorous version of the train operated during the 1950s when the regular weekday load consisted of seven bogie vehicles; a GW restaurant car was 'sandwiched' between

The long shunting 'neck' at Llanbrynmair creates the illusion of double-track as 4-4-0 No. 9017 and 4-6-0 No. 7818 *Granville Manor* attack the final miles of the daunting climb to Talerddig with an 11-coach Cambrian Coast Express on 12.8.1958.

Ifor Higgon

it is more accurate to state that all bar *Meteor* were noted on the Cambrian by Ifor Higgon.

[19] ibid.
[20] Christiansen, R. & Miller, R.W. (1967) *The Cambrian Railways, Vol.II.* p.157. David & Charles, Newton Abbot.
[21] Higgon, I.A.
[22] ibid.
[23] ibid.
[24] ibid.
[25] Rowledge, J.W.P.
[26] Higgon, I.A.
[27] ibid.
[28] ibid.
[29] *Monmouthshire Railway Society Journal*; 8/1966.
[30] Dalton, T.P. (1985) *Cambrian Companionship,* pp93-4. Oxford Publishing Company.
[31] WIMM.
[32] RAIL 517/1. p.150.
[33] LDMP: NLW.
[34] GWS/WIMM.
[35] The Engineer; 29.4.1870.
[36] ibid.
[37] N&WE. 26.4.1870.
[38] RAIL 92/57. p.41.
[39] ibid. 92/61. p. 8.
[40] GWS/WIMM.
[41] LDMP: NLW.
[42] RAIL 92/1. p.39.

Observation in repose. As GW No. 4072, one of the six-wheel observation cars introduced by the Cambrian in 1894 to take advantage of the scenic splendours of the coast route, rests between turns behind the station at Machynlleth. The date is not recorded but the vehicle was scrapped in 1936.　　　　　　　　　　　　　　　　　　　　　*LGRP*

The Engineer handed in a Register of the Rolling Stock now in the possession of the Company.[42]

Without the help of such a document, our knowledge of the early companies will remain incomplete. Happily, later developments are well documented elsewhere and any reader seeking further data is referred to the Bibliography.

Chapter 7: Notes & References

[1] Thomas, I. and Gasquoine, C.P., for example.
[2] Higgon, I.A. Private Notes & Papers.
[3] After completion of the N&M contract, Davies took *Llandinam* to help construction of the P&TR. It was first given a mechanical repair and re-paint in the Moat Lane/Llandinam area, during the spring of 1863, and probably left for the P&T in April around the time that Richard Metcalf, Davies's loco driver, was also transferred south. *Llandinam* eventually ended its career with David Davies in the South Wales coalfield; it went initially to the Aberdare area in 1867. LDMP: NLW.
[4] OA 13.8.1863.
[5] LDMP: NLW.
[6] From 1875, the name *Talerddig* was carried by a new 0-6-0T, based at that time at Machynlleth on yard and banking duties. The name *Countess Vane* was carried by No.41, a 2-4-0 passenger engine, from the mid-1860s until names for this class were abandoned between 1886-1891. RCTS p.K63 & K58.
[7] SM.Lib: SK.
[8] ibid.
[9] ibid.
[10] RAIL 92/54. p.285.
[11] Higgon, I.A.
[12] ibid.
[13] ibid.
[14] ibid.
[15] Rowledge, J.W.P. (1986) *GWR Locomotive Allocations*, David & Charles, Newton Abbot.
[16] ibid.
[17] Higgon, I.A.; Tutton, R. and RAIL 254/80.
[18] Several publications state that, with the exception of No. 3286 *Meteor*, all the 'Duke' class visited the Cambrian. As these references stem from the observations and notes of one person,

131

measured 27ft-6ins on the inside and was divided into three main compartments; the principal saloon was situated centrally with, at one end, a ladies saloon separated from the chief saloon by a small toilet compartment, whilst a servants' compartment was located at the other end, and separated from the main saloon by the entrance vestibule. There was only one door on each side. The vehicle emerged from Oswestry Works with the lower external panels painted in ultramarine, relieved with orange and white lining on the ironwork; the upper panels were white. Every effort was made to create a luxurious interior; polished hardwoods were used generously, maple with walnut mouldings or polished mahogany with mirrors were employed for the panelling, the long drop-leaf table in the central saloon was of polished mahogany, the sliding communicating doors had amber-coloured handles and plates, and all the windows were fitted with silk blinds. Above each plate glass window was a smaller window of stained glass depicting, in the main saloon, the four seasons, whilst Welsh inscriptions and a rose, shamrock and thistle scroll supporting an earl's coronet featured in the other saloons. The ceilings were 'beautifully stencilled' in blue and gold.[35]

Sound-proofing, using a lamination of indiarubber and board, together with a further 1/4 inch of rubber underlay beneath the carpet, was attempted in construction of the floor. The wheels were Mansell's patent fitted with Bessemer steel tyres. The central saloon was upholstered in an embossed crimson velvet; the ladies' saloon had drab-coloured upholstery whilst the attendants' compartment boasted morocco leather. Beneath the seats were 'Capacious lockers . . . a wine cellaret, and a refrigerator'.[36]

The carriage left Oswestry for York on Monday, 18 April, en route for Earl Vane's seat in Northumberland and made its maiden visit to Machynlleth the following Thursday, 21 April, when Earl Vane and family . . .

> . . . were conveyed in his lordship's new saloon carriage, which was highly admired for its beauty and the excellence of the accommodation afforded.[37]

It was much used until 1885 when, as a result of Earl Vane's death, it was offered to the Cambrian. The Engineer reported in 1888 that the wood generally was in fair condition but the upholstery showed 'considerable wear, not having been renewed since the coach was made'.[38] The cost when new was £731 and its probate value in 1885 was put at £250. The Engineer concluded that £250 would be about its value to the Company, but no further development took place until 1892 when the Secretary reported to the Board that, 'The Marchioness of Londonderry is agreeable to accept the price offered (£80) at the last Board meeting'.[39]

Earl Vane's special saloon ended its days as Cambrian saloon No. 228 and spent many of its later years working out of Oswestry on the Tanat Valley line. It did not survive the Grouping and was condemned at Swindon on 25.2.23.[40] Although the GW commendably photographed many pre-grouping veterans before committing them to the torch they appear, sadly, to have missed the significance of the Earl's saloon; no photograph of it is known to exist.

Information on Newtown & Machynlleth goods stock is even more obscure than that available on the ordinary carriage stock; indeed, it could well be that any wagons at the outset were hired either direct from wagon manufacturers, (as did the Cambrian later on), or from the neighbouring Oswestry and Llanidloes Companies. Gornall's lists feature only one reference to wagons;

> 24 September, 1863, 2lbs of red paint for marking waggons.[sic][41]

Whether this refers to N&M vehicles, or to the preparation of Davies's own ballast wagons before transfer to the P&T and M&M contracts is not revealed.

Amongst the more tantalising Minutes now deposited at Kew is the following reference to an 1864 list, which may no longer exist;

Rolling Stock

Scant information is currently available on the original N&M rolling stock, listed in the N&M/GWR Agreement of 8 August 1861 as:
2 new locomotives, 4 new composite carriages, and 1 new Break Van, [sic].

It is questionable whether these items were actually on the line at that date.

Hitherto, only two sources of information have emerged which shed any light on the earliest purchases. The first reference occurs in the Minutes of the Board when, at a meeting on 6 February 1862, payment was approved by cheque of £336 to Messrs Ashbury's of Manchester for one carriage with 2nd & 3rd Class accommodation. The following meeting of 26 February 1862 approved the payment of a further £1070 to Messrs Ashbury's, being the 'remainder of Bill for Rolling stock'.[32] The carriages were probably built in December 1861/January 1862.

The second reference appears in a fascinating and detailed list of work carried out by Philip Gornall, a plumber, painter, glazier and general handy-man employed by David Davies. In one of two itemised bills submitted by Gornall to Davies,[33] he lists repairs, (mainly replacement windows), to N&M 3rd Class Carriage No. 1 on 24 July 1862, N&M Carriage No. 2 on 19 December 1862, and N&M 1st Class Carriage No. 3 on 23 July 1862.

These early coaches were 25ft-6in long and weighed around eight tons apiece; no reference has been traced of the original N&M livery. Renumbering would certainly have taken place on formation of the Cambrian in 1864, possibly earlier, but no list has emerged which reveals the Cambrian numbers or the eventual fate of the N&M vehicles, which do not appear to have survived long enough to be entered in the Cambrian Register of 1902-22.[34]

Apart from the original stock, one of the most fascinating vehicles to have graced the yard at Machynlleth would have been the private saloon owned by Lord Londonderry. This colourful 6-wheel carriage was built at Oswestry under the direction of Alexander Walker, the Locomotive Superintendent, in 1870 and was used by the Earl's family principally between Machynlleth and Northumberland but probably also between either seat and London (Euston). The coach

Private Carriage built for Earl Vane in 1870, at Oswestry Works. The dark, vertical panels are thought to represent densely coloured glass. Tasselled silk blinds were fitted to the larger windows which, from *l-r* indicate the servants' compartment, the entrance door (one either side), leading to the vestibule, the main saloon (two windows), toilet compartment (with false external door), and the Ladies Saloon. *The Engineer*

76038/43/86, boosted the much depleted Machynlleth allocation for the last summer of steam operation in 1966.[29]

At least three very unusual, possibly unique, engine workings noted by T.P.Dalton are worth recalling.[30] The first involves the use in 1966 of a BR Class 5 '73XXX' on the 6.20 p.m. 'up' ('Last') Goods; it was brought off the shed at Aberystwyth by the late Jim Everson; sadly, the date and balancing 'down' working were not recorded.

The date of the second incident is also lacking but the engine is believed to have been GW 'Large Prairie', No.8103, which worked empty carriage stock from Aberystwyth to Aberdyfi. That particular day, Driver E.G.Kenny was in charge of the '81', which was held at Ynyslas to cross the 8.10 a.m. 'down' passenger train from Machynlleth, causing Driver Kenny some concern owing to limited supplies of water on this section. The '81s' worked occasionally to Aberystwyth from Carmarthen in later years, but visits from Oswestry were much rarer although No.8103 was no stranger to this section, having been observed at Machynlleth in 1947/8 and 1960, on both through-passenger and ballast workings. The visit of an '81' to Aberdovey, however, probably occurred only once.

The third observation was of an LMS 8F 2-8-0 at Moat Lane in 1965. The only previous occasion 8Fs had found themselves on Cambrian metals in west Wales was in 1955, when Nos.48309 & 48707 worked the Royal Train from Aberystwyth to Carmarthen. Apart from these rare visits, 2-8-0s were not seen west of Welshpool although they would have been more than useful over Talerddig. GW '28XX', '38XX' and '30XX' ex R.O.D. engines worked from Ruabon to Barmouth Junction, particularly during the war years, but none ventured as far as Machynlleth.

Cambrian HST. Leading unit No. 235 035 passes the sites of the East Box (l) and Pump-house (r), at Machynlleth, 19.6.1983.

Neville Pritchard

Driver A. Fleming prepares a grimy '75' during the final months of steam. September 1966. *GBJ*

Informal group 'on shed' at Machynlleth, 1967. *l-r:* D. Hughes; W. E. Hughes; E. Jones; D. O. Bowyer; J. Morgan; D. M. Evans; D. Ridge. *GBJ*